T0329967

INVESTING IN FINANCIAL RESEARCH

Additional praise for *Investing in Financial Research*

"*Investing in Financial Research* is a very thorough, thoughtful and well-organized book and a must-read for any serious investment professional. Cheryl's deeply researched content, real world case studies, and tearsheets provide both a practical framework and applicable toolkit for readers to use in their own investment research process. This book is now a staple on my bookshelf. Thank you, Cheryl, for this contribution to the investment community."
—**Albert Luk, Portfolio Manager, Cayre Family Office**

"*Investing in Financial Research* is the most pragmatic, in-depth, and comprehensive hands-on guide for conducting investment research available. Einhorn's process will deliver insightful, unbiased, and perceptive investment decisions. The book is a straight forward and systematic guide to clarity."
—**Paul Johnson, Adjunct Professor of Finance, Columbia Business School, Columbia University, and co-author of *Pitch the Perfect Investment***

"Why wasn't there a book like this when I started out as a stock market sleuth?"
—**Bill Alpert, Investigative Reporter, *Barron's***

"Cheryl Einhorn, step by step, takes us through how to apply her highly acclaimed AREA Method to financial research. *Investing in Financial Research* is exceptional, easy to read, and complete with examples of the method's applications. While the book's natural audience is investigative journalists, it will undoubtedly benefit securities analysts and business school students and should be an essential part of a reference library for accounting, valuation, and finance professionals."
—**Vladimir V. Korobov, Partner, Marcum LL**

INVESTING IN FINANCIAL RESEARCH

A Decision-Making System for Better Results

CHERYL STRAUSS EINHORN

Foreword by Tony Blair

An AREA Method Book

Published in Association with Cornell University Press
Ithaca and London

Copyright © 2019 by CSE Publishing

All rights reserved. Except for brief quotations in a review, this book, or parts thereof, must not be reproduced in any form without permission in writing from the publisher. For information, address Cornell Publishing Services, Sage House, 512 East State Street, Ithaca, New York 14850.

First published 2019 in association with Cornell University Press

Library of Congress Cataloging-in-Publication Data

Names: Einhorn, Cheryl Strauss, author.
Title: Investing in financial research : a decision-making system for Better
    results : an AREA method book / Cheryl Strauss Einhorn.
Description: Ithaca [New York] : Cornell University Press, 2019. | Includes
    bibliographical references and index.
Identifiers: LCCN 2018029024 (print) | LCCN 2018030152 (ebook) |
    ISBN 9781501730955 (pdf) | ISBN 9781501730962 (epub/mobi) |
    ISBN 9781501730948 | ISBN 9781501730948 (cloth) |
    ISBN 9781501732751 (pbk.)
Subjects: LCSH: Finance—Research—Methodology. | Finance—Decision
    making—Methodology. | Research—Methodology—Problems, exercises, etc. |
    Decision making—Methodology—Problems, exercises, etc.
Classification: LCC HG152 (ebook) | LCC HG152 .E55 2018 (print) |
    DDC 332.63/2042—dc23
LC record available at https://lccn.loc.gov/2018029024

Disclaimer: All of the research in this book represents a snapshot in time. Websites and documents are routinely updated and information changes so what any of my students, or even I, found may not be indicative of anyone else's experience now. All of the research and decisions were made at a moment in time by one person with one set of personal Critical Concepts. You, your Critical Concepts, and the information you will find with them will be different. Names in this book have been changed to protect the individuals' privacy.

This book is dedicated to Rachel, Naomi, and Mitchell, who always teach me old and new things.

One night I was reading bedtime stories from a children's version of the Bible to my middle child, who was then about seven years old. We'd read the stories of Abraham, Isaac, and Jacob. My daughter interrupted my reading to ask, "Mommy, why do you always tell me to be kind when God is not?" The question stopped me. I thought I was reading stories of heroism and commitment, but they were also filled with terrible tests, sadness and tragedy. In our family, we stressed leading with kindness but in these stories God was not kind. Several questions ran through my mind: why didn't any of these stories end happily? What did I want my daughter to take from them? But then I focused on her question. What an astute observation, an interesting and terribly complex question. How shall I answer? Will my response impact how she sees God? Will it impact how she thinks about kindness? This moment showed me something that I've come to realize more and more often in my adult life: that the experience I was having was fundamentally different from that of the person I was experiencing it with. We were reading the same story, together, but we didn't share the same perspective. I thought I was reading a bedtime story and sharing a nice moment, while my daughter thought I was reading a contradiction to our family's core principle of leading with kindness. She showed me that we should not assume that we know what another person is thinking. There are many difficult questions in life—some come from seven-year-olds—and to solve them we need to step into other perspectives, gather data, ask questions, listen to the answers, and update our understanding of reality.

"What we find changes who we become."
—Peter Morville

Contents

Foreword   *Tony Blair*   xiii

Acknowledgments   xv

Introduction: Blue Skies   1

1. The Origins of the AREA Method   6

2. Research Like a Cheetah   10

3. How to Use This Book: The AREA Journal, Cheetah Sheets, and Thesis Statements   16

   Cheetah Sheet 1. A Thesis Statement Recipe   19

4. Cognitive Biases and the AREA Method   21

5. AREA at Work and Critical Concepts   30

6. AREA = A: Absolute   34

   Cheetah Sheet 2. Absolute: Getting to Know Your Target   36

   Cheetah Sheet 3. Absolute: Just the Numbers   37

   Cheetah Sheet 4. Absolute: Your Target's Business Model   41

   Cheetah Sheet 5. Absolute: Your Target's Story   46

   Cheetah Sheet 6. Absolute: Reconciling the Data and the Narrative   46

   Cheetah Sheet 7. Absolute: Your Target's Website   48

   Cheetah Sheet 8. Absolute: Your Target's History   51

   Cheetah Sheet 9. Absolute: Your Target's Leadership   54

   Cheetah Sheet 10. Absolute: Your Target's Governance Structure   55

   Cheetah Sheet 11. Absolute: Your Target's Research Reports   56

   Cheetah Sheet 12. Absolute: Your Target's Press Releases   57

Cheetah Sheet 13. Absolute: Your Target's Share Price Performance 58

Cheetah Sheet 14. Absolute: Your Target's Stock Price–Press Release Relationship 59

Cheetah Sheet 15. Absolute: A Last Look 63

7. AREA = R: Relative 64

Cheetah Sheet 16. Relative: Planning Ahead for Exploration 66

Cheetah Sheet 17. Relative: Industry Mapping 67

Cheetah Sheet 18. Relative: Literature Review Sources and Search Techniques 73

Cheetah Sheet 19. Relative: Literature Review Analysis 75

Cheetah Sheet 20. Relative: Literature Review Summary 76

Cheetah Sheet 21. Relative: Synthesizing Your Literature Review 77

Cheetah Sheet 22. Relative: Earnings Calls 80

Cheetah Sheet 23. Relative: Earnings Call Q & A 82

Cheetah Sheet 24. Relative: Analyst Research Reports 85

Cheetah Sheet 25. Relative: Shareholder Base 89

Cheetah Sheet 26. Relative: Activist Investor Communications 93

8. AREA = E: Exploration 95

Cheetah Sheet 27. Exploration: Finding Good Prospects 101

Cheetah Sheet 28. Exploration: Finding More Good Prospects 102

Cheetah Sheet 29. Exploration: Getting Help with Your Search 104

Cheetah Sheet 30. Exploration: Great Questions Roadmap 105

Cheetah Sheet 31. Exploration: Types of Great Questions 105

Cheetah Sheet 32. Exploration: Great Questions: Direct, Broad, and Theoretical 106

Cheetah Sheet 33. Exploration: Great Clarification Questions and Feedback 108

Cheetah Sheet 34. Exploration: Techniques for Staying on Track 109

Cheetah Sheet 35. Exploration: Great Closing Questions 110

Cheetah Sheet 36. Exploration: Vetting Your Great Questions 114

Cheetah Sheet 37. Exploration: Storyboarding Your Great Questions 116

Cheetah Sheet 38. Exploration: Taking Great Notes 126

9. AREA = E: Exploitation   129

    Cheetah Sheet 39. Exploitation: Pro/Con Analysis   134

    Cheetah Sheet 40. Exploitation: CAH Exercise Directions   141

    Cheetah Sheet 41. Exploitation: Visual Mapping   148

    Cheetah Sheet 42. Exploitation: Developing a Scenario Analysis   152

    Cheetah Sheet 43. Exploitation: Scenario Analysis Assessment   153

    Cheetah Sheet 44. Exploitation: Plots and Ploys Hidden Value   156

    Cheetah Sheet 45. Exploitation: Plots and Ploys That Pad Value   160

    Cheetah Sheet 46. Exploitation: Plots and Ploys Warning Signals   162

    Cheetah Sheet 47. Exploitation: Plots and Ploys Corporate
    Deception Warning Signs   164

10. AREA = A: Analysis   168

    Cheetah Sheet 48. Analysis: Getting the Data Right   172

    Cheetah Sheet 49. Analysis: Pre-Mortem   174

    Cheetah Sheet 50. Analysis: A Fundamental Investment Checklist   177

    Cheetah Sheet 51. Analysis: Appraising Your Thesis Statements   179

11. Warren Buffett and Untangling Your Plate of Spaghetti   184

Appendix   189

Notes   215

Index   221

Foreword

The essence of the AREA Method of decision-making is to control the rhythm and texture of how we make an important decision. How do we calibrate speed with accuracy of knowledge; how do we iron out thinking that may derive from how we want the world to be rather than how it is; and how do we ensure that the incentives of those who may participate in the decision-making with us are well motivated and aligned with our core objectives?

Nowhere is this more crucial than in the financial decisions we may take. This could range from the personal—what home to buy or what mortgage to take out—to business and investment decisions. In each case the wrong process of decision-making may likely lead to the wrong decision. The right process doesn't guarantee the right outcome but it increases the odds of getting it right.

Investing in Financial Research leads on from Cheryl's first book on the AREA Method, called *Problem Solved*, but applies the reasoning specifically to financial decisions.

In doing so it has the great advantage of reducing the process of decision-making to clear practical steps that can broadly apply to any type of decision.

The AREA Method breaks down the process of making a decision, teaching you how to avoid bias and preconception—which may be misconception—allowing you to define accurately the Critical Concepts at the core of the decision and enabling you to assess what is really the objective you seek to achieve and how.

It draws an analogy with the way a cheetah hunts. The key is the animal's ability to decelerate and pause, giving it the opportunity to turn and change direction where necessary to pursue its prey. In the same way, when taking a critical decision, Cheryl shows how at crucial moments it pays to slow down, to reassess, and sometimes to switch course.

Many of us today need to make decisions about investing our savings, choices often hard to make but big in impact on our lives. We also face everyday business decisions, from which project to move forward to how and whether to expand overseas. Those in executive positions have to go through rigorous analysis of the facts, combined usually with a gut feel about what seems sensible. The AREA Method helps make the process as rational as possible, pausing to reflect at the right moment and striking fast where necessary.

There is no substitute for painstaking research and hard work but there is a way of utilizing the effort to the maximum effect. This is the purpose and the pleasure of this book.

Tony Blair, former Prime Minister of the United Kingdom

Acknowledgments

In 2007, Columbia University invited me to create and teach a course in business, economic, and financial journalism at the Graduate School of Journalism. I had spent about a hundred hours developing my curriculum and lesson plans, but as I began the spring 2008 semester, the financial crisis shook the world. Bear Stearns collapsed, Lehman Brothers went bust, and the stock market lost 30 percent of its value, among the worst performance in US financial history. It was a frightening time for the economy but a fascinating time to be back on a college campus and in the classroom. That year I did what I had always hoped my teachers would do when big news broke: I chucked much of my syllabus in favor of lessons for my journalism students about how to research and understand what was going on financially and how to cover the evolving disaster. What was the research process? Who would they talk to? How would they listen to them? What would they want a reader to learn? And how could they know they were being mindful of their own mental shortcomings? And: what's a CDO?

I remember the students furiously taking notes in class. It reminded me of my own college days, walking home from lectures with fingers that were cramped from note-taking. Sometimes my notes were illegible from trying to write too fast. I'm sure the same was true for my students that semester: I went too fast and covered too much material.

Over the years, I slowed down and made sure my students understood the material before I moved on. But I also began to feel that students shouldn't have to get all the material the first time, in the few hours of our class time together. If I wanted them to be thoughtful in their work and mindful of their process, their thinking and analysis, they should also have the opportunity to absorb my material thoughtfully and mindfully, to have time to sit with it and to reread it. Otherwise, each year, as my students graduated, all the knowledge I'd shared walked out the door. That's when and why I decided to write this book.

I did not write this book alone; I benefitted from many conversations and thoughtful feedback from numerous people who were instrumental in discussing it and working on it with me. Peter Lawrence, a former student, later a coteacher at Columbia Business School and friend, was all-important in our conversations and work together. I would not have enjoyed this project nearly as much if I did not have the thoughtful friendship and advice of Cathleen Barnhart, who once taught my kids and now has taught me not only about storytelling and writing but also about friendship. To my parents, who were close readers and cheerleaders, and to Dean Smith, the director of Cornell University Press, who believed in me, my AREA Method, and this book: thank you for your guidance and your friendship.

Many other friends and colleagues read the manuscript and shared their thoughtful, useful feedback—Tony Blair, Kevin Carmody, Jesse Eisinger, Vlad Korobov, Albert Luk, David McCombie, and Joe Platt—as did too many students to name, but these in my 2018 course shared reflections week in and out all semester long. Murillo Horta, Dheeraj Devata, Ryan Kelly, Haoyuan Li, Arturo Melo, and Chris Waller: thank you.

For readers who would like to stay in touch, I look forward to hearing from you about how the AREA Method works for you. Please contact me through my website, areamethod.com.

INVESTING IN FINANCIAL RESEARCH

The AREA Method   CHEETAH SHEET

Turning Good Ideas into Great Solutions

	IDEA	THINKING
A	**Absolute** Understand your target	1. Look at the numbers 2. Explore the website 3. Learn about leadership
R	**Relative** Research related sources	1. Map the industry 2. Review the literature 3. Reconcile narratives
E	**Exploration** Broaden your perspective	1. Identify good prospects 2. Craft great questions 3. Conduct interviews
E	**Exploitation** Challenge assumptions	1. Consider the rival hypotheses 2. Conduct pro/con exercise 3. Analyze future scenarios
A	**Analysis** Reduce uncertainty Make your decision	1. Think about mistakes 2. Conduct a pre-mortem **3. Come to conviction**

Introduction: Blue Skies

Reality is merely an illusion, albeit a very persistent one.
—Albert Einstein

Several years ago, my then twelve-year old son and I went to New York City to see the Henri Magritte exhibit at the Museum of Modern Art. The exhibit, titled "The Mystery of the Ordinary," was organized around the concept that we are unable to really see what is before us in part because we cannot easily escape our past experiences; they effectively "fill in" our present and taint our future.

Magritte consistently deals with the relationship between language, thought, and reality and although his style is highly realistic it is meant to undermine what we think we know both of ourselves internally and of our experience of the world. His paintings do what our mind inadvertently does: they displace, transform, misname, and misrepresent images and information. Magritte reminds us that we go about in half-waking states.

In his painting *The Palace of Curtains*, Magritte presents us with two frames containing respectively the word *ciel* ("sky" in French) and a pictorial representation of a blue sky. Oddly enough, both the word and image represent the "real thing"- -one works by resemblance, the other by an intellectual but subjective association. In other words, Magritte says, there are many ways to experience the "real thing."

The fact that there are few absolutes—and many "real things"—is one of the reasons why I put together my research and decision-making

Figure 0.2. *The Palace of Curtains* by Rene Magritte. Reproduced by permission from the Museum of Modern Art/Licensed by SCALA/Art Resource.

system, the AREA Method: to provide a way to navigate our gray areas by managing for our cognitive shortcomings.

But even heightening our awareness of mental distortions and shortcuts and inoculating our research against them is not enough to aid in making complex research decisions, and so the AREA Method does much more: it makes your work *work* for you, to make the process of collecting and analyzing data more effective, efficient, manageable, measured, relevant, reliable, and, most important, reusable.

For while research is about ideas, ideas aren't enough; there is an important gap between having ideas and making good decisions about what to do with them. It's easy to invest in ideas, but to make sound decisions you have to vet them, weed out the lemons, and have a way to develop conviction and maintain faith when it takes time to really see the impact of the decision.

History is littered with stories of good ideas botched by poor process. Take the story of Xerox's Palo Alto Research Center (PARC), which was the most successful corporate research lab in the 1970s. The engineers at PARC had brilliant, innovative ideas that laid the foundation for many of the transformative technologies that we use today, including laser printing, the ethernet, the modern personal computer, and operating systems that fueled the rise of Microsoft and Apple. The problem: Xerox never commercialized these technologies; it was too slow to realize PARC's value.

Xerox hadn't determined the purpose of PARC and didn't have a clear vision of what constituted a successful outcome for its research arm. Xerox failed to see PARC as an integral part of the company.

Xerox viewed PARC as being engaged in open-ended research and it viewed itself as a copier company. The company's outlook was short term, while PARC's, by the very nature of pure research, was long-term. It was a classic case of misaligned incentives. And yet, that might not have been fatal if the company had had a clear focus on what to do about PARC's discoveries, namely to resolve that PARC could drive Xerox's success by providing it with innovative commercial products.

PARC's discoveries could have been life changing for the company, but at the end of the day, Xerox lacked the right process to capitalize on PARC's brilliant and innovative ideas. As Steve Jobs said in a speech in 1996, "Xerox could have owned the entire computer industry . . . could have been the IBM of the nineties . . . could have been the Microsoft of the nineties."

But it wasn't.

PARC is a great example of a bad process. But a good process, if you follow it well, not only leads to logical thinking, creative insights, and, yes, an edge that gives you the confidence to act on your ideas, but also, and importantly, it limits mistakes. I believe the AREA Method is a process that enables you to take advantage of your ideas. With the right framework, the right approach to decision-making—*the right process*—you can turn good ideas into great decisions.

I've taught the AREA Method in my graduate courses at both the Columbia Business School and the Columbia University Graduate School of Journalism. At the Graduate School of Journalism, I created and taught courses in business, economic, and financial journalism. At the Business School, I created and taught a course in persuasion that educated students in aspects of behavioral finance to better understand our own and others' incentives and decision-making. Advanced Investment Research, a class I've cotaught first with Ken Shubin Stein and later with Peter Lawrence, combines aspects of my other classes to train students in how to conduct financial sleuthing.

Despite the diversity of my students' backgrounds and abilities—my journalism students often had little or no finance experience, and many of my business school students had never conducted an interview—I taught all of my classes from one main vantage point: a good research process makes all the difference.

The AREA Method guides you to see past your biases and your tendency to rush to judgment. It allows you to live your life mindfully and to increase your self-awareness, empathy, and understanding. It does not discriminate. It is an equitable tool that levels the playing field. Good, responsible research makes the world a better, fairer, more honest place.

How does it do so? Anyone can follow it. The AREA Method provides you with a system that has

1. Defined tasks that guide and focus your research on your vision of success;
2. A structure that isolates your sources, giving you insight into their perspectives, biases, and incentives;
3. Investigative resources, tips, and techniques to upgrade your research and analysis beyond document-based sources;
4. Exercises to foster creativity and originality in your thinking; and
5. A sequence and framework that bring your disparate pieces of research together to build your confidence and conviction in your financial decision.

No matter what you are researching, the context matters. Data doesn't exist in a vacuum. AREA addresses both the data—the many facts and figures that you collect and analyze—and the context—how the data is interpreted by the people who work with it. It addresses incentives, assumptions, and judgments, which, whether they are yours or someone else's, are significant: they color our understanding and interpretation of the world and, as Magritte observed, they may or may not reflect reality at any one time.

But AREA can be more than a process that you apply. It's a muscle that you build and it can become second nature; it can be part of the frame you bring to the world.

While this book is about mastering and applying a straightforward process to conduct investigative research, it also aspires to help us do in our work something both logical and, at its heart, very grand. Perhaps, as Magritte implies, it's impractical to try to master anything. But if there is anything that we *can* master, it's our decisions, and so the AREA Method strives to do something that many of us want to do with our lives: to make sense of the world, to work with—and through—ambiguity, and to move forward with conviction.

A Good Process + Good Information = A Great Decision

Chapter One

The Origins of the AREA Method

There's an alternative. There's always a third way, and it's not a
combination of the other two ways. It's a different way.
—David Carradine

Every day, people around the world make financial decisions. They choose to invest in a stock, sell their holdings in a mutual fund, or buy a condominium. These decisions are complex and financially tricky—even for financial professionals. But the literature available on financial research is dated and either focuses narrowly on only one aspect of financial sleuthing, such as earnings quality, or provides a bird's-eye view without any real practical application. Until now there's been a gap in the literature: a book that shows you *how* to conduct a step-by-step comprehensive financial investigation that ends in a decision.

This book gives you that *how*.

Investing in Financial Research: A Decision-Making System for Better Results is a guidebook for conducting financial investigations. The book lays out my AREA Method—a research and decision-making system that uniquely controls for bias, focuses on the incentives of others, and expands knowledge while improving judgment—and applies it to investigating financial situations. AREA is applicable to all sorts of financial sleuthing, whether for investment analysis or investigative journalism.

I first laid out my AREA Method in a general interest book about how to make complex personal and professional decisions. That book is titled *Problem Solved: A Powerful System for Making Complex Decisions With Confidence and Conviction.* For my *Problem Solved* readers the basic

AREA roadmap is largely the same. However, this book uses financial case studies, drills down deeper into company financials, has an in-depth discussion of fraud and deception, and includes many more financially focused Cheetah Sheets.

If you are new to the AREA Method: Welcome aboard! The AREA Method helps you make smarter, better decisions by improving upon classic research and decision-making pedagogy.

How does it do that? First, AREA recognizes that research is a fundamental part of decision-making. Second, AREA organizes your research process based on the perspective of the source of your information. Third, it addresses the critical component of timing head-on, incorporating calculated and directed reflections that promote insight, slowing down to speed up the efficacy of your work. And fourth, AREA provides a clear, concise, and repeatable process that works as a feedback loop in part or in its entirety. Result: AREA is the first decision-making system to control for bias, focus on the incentives of others, and expand knowledge while improving judgment

My research process is called the AREA Method because of the different perspectives it addresses. AREA is an acronym for these perspectives: Absolute, Relative, Exploration and Exploitation, and Analysis.

The first "A," or "Absolute," refers to primary, uninfluenced information from the source or sources at the center of your financial research. "R," or "Relative," refers to the perspectives of outsiders around your research subject. It is secondary information, or information that has been filtered through sources connected to your subject. "E," or "Exploration" and "Exploitation," represents the twin engines of creativity, one being about expanding your research breadth and the other about depth. Exploration moves your research beyond written documents to teach you to listen to other peoples' perspectives by developing sources and interviewing. Exploitation asks you to focus inward, on you as the decision-maker, to examine how you process information, exploring and challenging your own assumptions and judgment. The second "A," "Analysis," synthesizes all of these perspectives, processing and interpreting the information you've collected. Each of these steps will be explained in detail in the chapters that follow.

Together the "A" and the "R" provide you with the tools necessary to create a framework for gathering and evaluating information. The latter part of the AREA process, the "E" and the "A," provide detailed

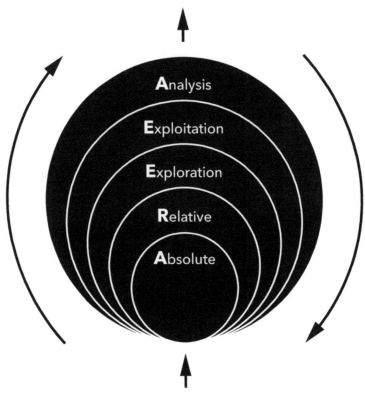

Figure 1.1. Cycling through the AREA Method. AREA is a step-by-step decision-making process focused on mining the insights and incentives of others to help you manage for mental short-cuts. The steps build on one another, radiating out from the center but also serving as a feed-back loop. The views and insights of other stakeholders are separated until you, the decision maker, fit them all together.

examination tools gleaned from experts in other fields such as investiga-tive journalism, intelligence gathering, psychology, and medicine. They help you make some of your mistakes *before* you make them.

The AREA Method's ability to address perspectives makes the process and this book unique. It teaches you to isolate and categorize information based upon its source. By inhabiting one perspective at a time you can attempt to control for and counteract some of your cognitive shortcuts while also building empathy and understanding with the other stakehold-ers involved in your research decision.

The idea for AREA initially came to me during the decade when I worked as a columnist and editor at *Barron's*, the business magazine. There I ended up specializing in what was called the "bearish" company story, one that takes a skeptical look at a company's financials or strategy.

When my stories were published, there was often a large share-price reaction. At times, an exchange might halt trading in the stock or regulators might get involved. In a few cases, the companies I investigated and wrote about went out of business. In one case, the chief executive was sentenced to ten years in jail.

I became concerned about the human toll of my stories. They were not only affecting people's investment portfolios or retirement accounts; they were also impacting the employees of the companies I investigated, as well as the customers. When I wrote a series of investigative stories about a company called PolyMedica, then one of the largest diabetic test-kit makers, I recounted how the company was raided by the FBI, a story that ended up adversely affecting both customers and employees. At the same time, customers who had bought used car batteries thinking they were new from Exide—the subject of another series of investigative pieces—received important information from my stories.

I wanted to write these important stories but I also wanted to ensure that I was conducting sound research, that I was taking into account the incentives and motives of my sources, that I was thinking about having evidence to back all my assertions, and that I was considering where I might be biased and judgmental in how I looked at and interpreted the data. In essence, I needed a way to control for and catch some of my thinking errors and, given my background in research, I wondered if I could set up a construct to do that, something that would push me out of my mindset, focus me on others, and give me distance to critically assess the validity of my viewpoint. That's how I came to the idea of the perspective-taking that frames my AREA Method.

I also recognized that I needed my perspective-taking research steps to sit inside a broader operating system, so that I could clear my mind before settling in to work. That mental preparation is what follows in the next four chapters, which cover Cheetah Pauses, the AREA journal, thesis statements, cognitive biases, edges and pitfalls, and Critical Concepts.

These chapters are important spadework. Anyone can do research, and many of us do dive right in without thinking about the outcome, but that's like building a house without a plan. To effectively build a sturdy house, or conduct meaningful research, you need to have a blueprint: a clear picture of a successful outcome. And the plan alone isn't enough; you need the right tools—the hammers, nails, drills, etc.—to get it done. Once you have that blueprint, you'll have the mental map for the problem solving you're about to do and be better able to effectively use the A, R, E&E, and A tools of the AREA Method.

Let's start by meeting the cheetah.

Chapter Two

Research Like a Cheetah

Do research. Feed your talent. Research not only wins the war on cliché, it's the key to victory over fear and its cousin, depression.
—Robert McKee

A few years ago I stumbled upon an article in the *New York Times* that analyzed the cheetah's hunting success. Contrary to what many people think, speed is not the secret to the cheetah's prodigious hunting skills. Although cheetahs habitually run down their prey at speeds approaching sixty miles per hour, it is the cheetah's agility, and in particular its ability to *decelerate,* that makes it such a fearsome hunter. Cheetahs are able to cut their speed by nine miles per hour in a single stride, an advantage in hunting greater than being able to accelerate like a racecar. This allows cheetahs to make sharp turns, sideways jumps, and direction changes.

As Alan M. Wilson, a wildlife researcher, explained in the article, stability and maneuverability at high speeds are a real problem. "The hunt is much more about maneuvering, about acceleration, about ducking and diving to capture the prey."[1]

What do cheetahs have to do with research and decision-making? Quite a bit, I think. A quality research process does not move consistently forward. Instead, it benefits from calculated pauses and periods of thoughtful deceleration that enable researchers not only to consolidate knowledge but also to decide whether to pivot and move in a new direction or stay the course before accelerating again.

AREA's cheetah pauses improve the hunt by dovetailing with AREA's perspective-taking: together they work against our mental shortcomings and prevent us from making poor decisions out of a poor decision-making process. As you inhabit the perspectives of each of your decisions' stakeholders, the cheetah pauses give you time for thoughtful reflection about what you've learned and how to continue the hunt.

Research and decision-making is fraught with landmines—the researcher's own biases, the differing incentives of a company's or entity's storytellers, the overwhelming amount of information that is not critical, and the opacity and obscurity of information that is critical. By researching like a cheetah—using an agile system that inserts strategic stops at critical junctures in your work—you can not only make a daunting task more manageable, but also improve the hunt itself.

Perspective-Taking to Counteract Bias

The AREA framework of perspective-taking offers a way around bias by making it easier to see insights and understand an experience that someone else is having. By imagining others faced with the same questions you would ask yourself, the AREA process helps you check your ego, enabling you to better judge the incentives of others and explore a situation more objectively.

Perspective-taking also forces you to see what is actually in front of you rather than what you believe you should see and filters the noise coming from too many inputs at once. By starting with a narrow lens limited to communication from your research target, you avoid having your views prejudiced by other stakeholders such as the media or broader industry, analyst, or academic communities.

Uncovering the essence of anything is hard. By identifying and isolating essential sources of information, the AREA process attempts to break down the morass and present a more accessible way to conduct research. It may show us things we already know, but it may also expose the otherwise invisible essence of the situation.

How does it do that? Perspective-taking gives us a two-for-one. It creates a mirroring effect: by inhabiting someone else's position, we push ourselves out of our own thinking and assumptions momentarily. This distance helps us move from bias to objectivity, enabling us to look critically at our own assumptions, judgments, and biases. We gain better self-awareness of our own thinking even as we gain an appreciation for the vantage point of the other people and organizations we want to better understand in order to solve our research puzzle holistically.

Critical Concepts to Focus Your Research

When a cheetah begins her hunt, she scans her environment until she identifies a target: her prey. Then she keeps her eye on the prize, literally. For the cheetah, success means only one thing: catching the prey. For humans, the research hunt—and the vision of success—aren't always so clear, especially at the beginning of the process. But AREA pushes you to be more cheetah-like by determining what constitutes success for you personally in your investigative hunt. AREA doesn't guide you to assess all options, but rather helps you to identify the few variables that you determine will define the success or failure of your research process.

Those variables, which I call your Critical Concepts, become the few factors that you will want to deeply and creatively investigate to get you to *your* picture of success, whether it is determining an investment outcome or finding the real story about an organization beyond the headlines. It's a fundamentally different—inverted—way to approach research and decision-making.

Why invert? Because open-ended research is not terribly productive. It's not only time consuming but can feel overwhelming and ultimately counterproductive. The AREA process recognizes this and asks you something that you likely can answer even without knowing exactly how you'll solve your research puzzle: *What do you need to see happen in the outcome of your research decision to know that the decision has succeeded for you personally?* From there, from that vision of success, you can determine your Critical Concepts.

Critical Concepts (CCs) are the one, two, or three things that solve for your vision of what you determine to be a successful outcome. They answer the question, "What am I really solving for?" There's no one right answer. Critical Concepts vary from person to person. Different decision-makers will have different time horizons in which to conduct their research, different personalities, and different goals. Two people looking at the same data may well have different CCs and may make entirely different decisions.

In addition, like the cheetah's hunt, which requires constant recalibration as prey moves and the environment changes, your Critical Concepts won't always stay the same—and often they shouldn't. As you move through the steps of your AREA research hunt, you will incorporate new information and analysis, often revising and refining your Critical Concepts.

Using Critical Concepts to shape and frame your research process will make the difference between a frustrating, unhelpful process and a life changing affirmation that comes from a decision well made.

More on this fundamental principle can be found in chapter 5, "AREA at Work and Critical Concepts."

Advantages of the AREA Method

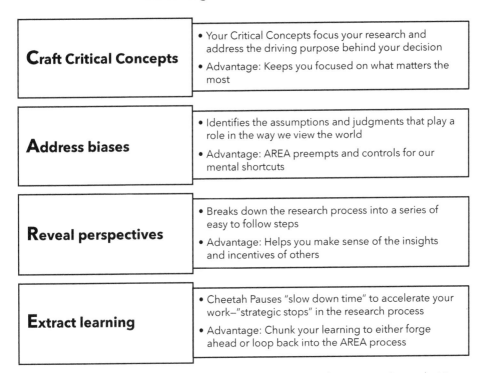

Craft Critical Concepts	• Your Critical Concepts focus your research and address the driving purpose behind your decision • Advantage: Keeps you focused on what matters the most
Address biases	• Identifies the assumptions and judgments that play a role in the way we view the world • Advantage: AREA preempts and controls for our mental shortcuts
Reveal perspectives	• Breaks down the research process into a series of easy to follow steps • Advantage: Helps you make sense of the insights and incentives of others
Extract learning	• Cheetah Pauses "slow down time" to accelerate your work–"strategic stops" in the research process • Advantage: Chunk your learning to either forge ahead or loop back into the AREA process

Figure 2.1. The AREA Method helps you bring greater CARE to making smarter, better decisions

Being Flexible and Agile in Your Hunt

Like the cheetah's hunt, a quality research process is about depth, flexibility, and creativity. The AREA Method's cheetah pauses work as strategic stops during and after each part of your research. They enable you to chunk your learning, prevent you from going off course, and provide a clear record of your work at each stage. But most important, they will help you hone in on and refine your Critical Concepts.

While every hunt a cheetah undertakes is different, at the same time there are patterns. The same is true for financial research investigations: a solid research process should be explicit, improvable, flexible, and, above all, repeatable so that although each research idea that you investigate will be new, the process you use to investigate your ideas doesn't need to be recreated each time. Instead a good research process is one that can be repeated, so that each hunt builds on the previous one, your knowledge compounds, and you become a more experienced hunter.

For example, in 2010, in the Advanced Investment Research class that I cotaught, one of our students researched GameStop, a video game retailer whose shares had fallen from $60 to $20 as investors became concerned about mounting competition and the possibility of digital disintermediation. The student, Max, was able to refer back to work on Blockbuster, a movie rental business that had gone bankrupt earlier that year under increased competitive pressure from Netflix, a digital alternative, and Redbox, a kiosk-based rental business. By having a sound and flexible process and a comprehensive AREA journal where he recorded his work, Max had a useful template for analyzing GameStop.

His work on Blockbuster revealed that at the time preceding Blockbuster's terminal decline, the company faced heavy discounting from larger merchants like Walmart, its management generally ignored competitive threats, and Blockbuster was rated favorably by sell-side analysts, with over 60 percent of analysts rating Blockbuster a buy. These data points sensitized Max to the significance of video game price cuts at Walmart and Best Buy, shaped his interpretation of GameStop's resistance to developing its own digital download business, and moderated his concerns about GameStop's popularity among analysts, more than 60 percent of whom rated GameStop a buy.

Furthermore, Max's work on Blockbuster revealed that Blockbuster's decline was nonlinear—it would fall off rapidly at times and appear to stabilize at others. This armed him with signposts for how to interpret GameStop's results going forward. A stable quarter wasn't a sign the business wouldn't become obsolete, and conversely, a negative quarter wouldn't necessarily be succeeded by another negative quarter. His ability to refer back to Blockbuster provided a valuable and unique information source that improved his analysis and understanding of GameStop.

In the three years after Max's research, GameStop played out almost exactly as his analysis concluded: its shares chugged along, trading well north of $20 per share, and, importantly, its dips have not been terminal (yet). It's still in business (and my son still shops there, even though he could buy his games online at any time).

Like Max, you will gain experience as you apply AREA to your research and build mental muscles that will enable you to discover new information and insight while also capitalizing on previous experience. AREA pushes you, however, to avoid well-worn pathways of thought simply because they are what you know. Like the cheetah, you maintain flexibility and maneuverability and you get to determine your hunt.

Chapter Three

How to Use This Book: The AREA Journal, Cheetah Sheets, and Thesis Statements

Research is formalized curiosity. It is poking
and prying with a purpose.
–Zora Neale Hurston

Research—even focused, limited research—is messy. There's a wealth of information and details to keep track of. I suggest keeping all of your research organized in an AREA journal. Record the data, your impressions about the information, and the date of each entry. By cataloguing your work and thoughts you will not only have a record that you can refer back to as you move through the AREA process, but you will also prevent thesis creep, those pesky evolving hypotheses that make us feel that we have a rational reason to do something despite a change in circumstances or a lack of data. Your written records will also provide you with a roadmap for your research. You can find an example of part of an AREA Journal in the appendix.

What does your roadmap look like? Every AREA journey will follow the same itinerary:

1. Your decision problem
2. Your vision of success. If the decision is successful what has happened?
3. Your Critical Concepts, derived from your vision of success
4. Your A, R, E&E, and A research, analysis, and thesis statements
5. Your decision

You'll see AREA applied to actual research cases throughout the book. I've used a variety of examples, some from my work as an investigative journalist and some from the work my students have done in my Advanced Investment Research class at Columbia Business School. I follow the research process and AREA Journals of two students in particular. Patricia researched whether the telecommunications company Sprint would make a good investment opportunity as the company was going through a merger with Nextel. I had chosen Sprint as a research target for Patricia's class because the situation was complex, the future ambiguous, and the outcome was going to have a big impact on the company's prospects. Although Patricia was in Columbia's MBA program, she had no background in the complex telecommunications industry. She was a former college lacrosse player with a quick mind and a keen curiosity.

The other student we will follow is Matthew, who arrived at Columbia from a traditional finance background, having worked as a research analyst at a few different financial firms. He was assigned to evaluate Delta Airlines, which had a stellar reputation as one of the most reliable carriers. Industry consolidation had left the four major carriers with 70 percent of the market share domestically, and Delta's share price had been steadily rising. However, fuel prices were unnaturally low and low-cost carriers were growing rapidly and taking market share. Again, the situation was complex, the future ambiguous, and the outcome unclear.

At the points in this book where I recommend a Cheetah Pause, a strategic stop in your work, I include a Cheetah Sheet—a graphic organizer that will help you build and hone the skills that you need to carry out the AREA Method. The Cheetah Sheets highlight sources of information, provide you with key questions to ask of the data you collect, and offer interpretation and analysis guidelines. They also provide you with checklists and exercises to help you effectively and efficiently conduct your research and hone your Critical Concepts. A full list of the Cheetah Sheets, which also serves as an overview of the chapters, can be found in the table of contents. You can download an AREA Journal template that includes digitized Cheetah Sheets from my website, **areamethod.com**.

As you document in your AREA Journal the material you collect and analyze through the Cheetah Sheets, I encourage you to record both the questions that arise during the process and the answers you find. By keeping the journal, you'll be writing the story of your research and decision-making process. You'll sum up each "chapter" of your work—A, R, E&E, and A—by consolidating your learning with one or more thesis statements. These statements sum up your research, your findings, your interpretation of your findings, and your judgment about what it all means.

By summing up these four facets of the process you will also answer the "So What?" of your research, pointing to the path forward or the path back into the process.

Pausing to construct thesis statements asks you to chunk your learning. The task requires you to be specific, to express a main idea, *and* to take a stand. It may feel artificial, and even frustrating, to pause at various prescribed points in your research process, but remember the cheetah: the pause will make your hunt more effective. Strategic deceleration builds agility and flexibility.

It's difficult to write a good thesis statement. However, I believe it is critically important to do so, and when done well, a thesis can provide you with "Aha" moments. A compelling thesis statement is an upfront time investment that will save you time later on making your work *work* for you.

By pushing yourself to reach conclusions about discrete sections of research, you are not just collecting information, but also synthesizing and analyzing your work as you progress. Focusing on the meaning of the information helps you hone and refine your Critical Concepts, which in turn makes your research process continually more effective and efficient.

Writing *is* thinking. Having to write the thesis out—putting your research and its significance into the language of a cause and effect—often also points out the holes in your understanding. As Albert Einstein said, "If you can't explain it simply, you don't understand it well enough." I find this true time and again: when I am struggling to make a clear argument—when I can't define what I've done or why—there's a reason, and it's generally that I need to do more work.

At its best, a clear, concise, and cogent thesis statement will be no longer than a paragraph, just a few sentences that can be supported and explained by means of examples and evidence. Here is an example of a thesis written by an Associated Press reporter after Abraham Lincoln was shot in Ford's Theatre in 1865. Although this is the lede of a news article, in its brevity and clarity it illustrates some of the best components of a thesis:

> *The President was shot in a theatre tonight and perhaps mortally wounded.*

In this example, the first half of the thesis statement demonstrates that its author has gathered and compiled evidence. The second half of the thesis statement shows the analysis of that evidence leading to an insight. Note that the news lede is clear, concise, and cogent. It makes an argument for what *will happen* based upon all the evidence present at the time. It gives the reader the news *and* its implication. Of course, "perhaps mortally wounded" is a judgment call, and is based upon the perspective of the reporter's sources. All thesis statements make a judgment call, and that call is only as good as the data that informs it. Finally, the thesis statement gives a clear recommendation for what the reporter might want to investigate next: *Is Lincoln mortally wounded?*

That's everything your thesis statements should accomplish as well: the information you've collected, the perspective it comes from, and what it all means. Based upon what you know at this point, what is your judgment call?

To guide you as you think about thesis statements, here's the first Cheetah Sheet, which, like all Cheetah Sheets in this book, is meant to be a checklist, a guide for where and how to conduct your research, and/or a list of what questions to ask of the data you collect. This will enable your work to stay focused and productive. Feel free to personalize them, changing and adding information and questions as they pertain to your specific research decision. To help you locate the Cheetah Sheets, each page containing one has a cheetah pattern bookmark.

CHEETAH SHEET 1
A Thesis Statement Recipe

The ingredients of a good thesis statement:

1. Findings: the facts of the case, the data and empirical results
2. Interpretations: explanations and inferences that can be drawn from the findings
3. Judgments: your opinions about the findings and interpretations
4. Recommendations: your plan for moving forward

Recording your evidence, thoughts, and convictions in thesis statements points you to what you need to research next and exposes gaps in your work that need to be addressed before moving forward. At each point, consider what your thesis statement is directing you to investigate next. Follow the signposts. They can teach you about not just the decisions that work out well but also those that won't turn out as planned.

We will revisit thesis statements and how and why to construct them throughout the book as you follow Patricia and Matthew on their research journey—and begin your own. Beginning in chapter 6, on Absolute research, you will take Cheetah Pauses to craft thesis statements for discrete sections of research and put together the first part of your AREA puzzle.

By the end of the AREA process, you will have a series of thesis statements to compare, contrast, and knit together. With a concrete record of your thinking, you won't have to recreate your ideas and won't as easily fall prey to hindsight bias, where we fool ourselves into thinking something that might not have been so. And you will have created an audit trail of your work that you or someone else can follow and replicate.

As you proceed with your research, further questions will come out of the thesis statements you develop. I suggest that you write down every question that arises from the research process and answer the questions as you go along. But most important, never erase the questions themselves, so that you retain the trail of your thinking as you map out your AREA of investigation.

Being a good researcher is not only about the quality of your decisions but also about the results that come from those decisions. Your research may not be efficient early on, and that's fine. The AREA system is meant to make you—and your work—more effective over time. The goal is to streamline your decision-making by bringing structure, focus and awareness to the process.

To see one user's personalized and condensed AREA hunt, please see the end of the appendix.

Chapter Four

Cognitive Biases and the AREA Method

The element of chance in basic research is overrated.
Chance is a lady who smiles only upon those
few who know how to make her smile.
–Hans Selye

Mental shortcuts are critical for our well-being. They help us process information quickly and allow us to move through our day without being continually overwhelmed by the decisions we have to make. Imagine if we were in the cereal aisle at the supermarket and *didn't* know which type and brand of cereal we prefer: we'd have choice fatigue. Thank goodness we can get in and out of the store easily by letting these shortcuts—our cognitive biases—guide us to what we know.

But making decisions quickly, without continuous mental effort, necessarily involves relying upon cognitive biases—snap judgments. As a result, these same shortcuts or biases that we need for our everyday lives also limit us as objective thinkers and observers and are antithetical to quality research, which is fundamentally about gaining *new* information and insight. That's why we need to not only control for, but also counteract cognitive bias. It's insufficient to just heighten our awareness of when and how we commit common thinking flaws. We also need to pry open cognitive space to become more expansive in our thinking and open new channels to exercise true objectivity and creativity.

An extreme example of the dangers of cognitive biases is explored in detail in chapter 9, on Exploitation, in the subsection titled "Spotting Fraud." That section presents a case study I developed for a course at Columbia Business School. The case study, "Spotting Signs of Deception and Fraud," outlines what to look for when you suspect fraud, and lays out some of the eerie commonalities between three very famous frauds: the energy company Enron, the gold mining outfit Bre-X, and the investment manager Bernie Madoff. What's clear is that the warning signs were there, but assumption, judgment, and bias kept too many people from spotting them.

There are many good articles and books on the topic of cognitive biases and flawed thinking. Two of my favorites are a 1995 speech given at Harvard University by Charlie Munger, the vice-chairman of Berkshire Hathaway, entitled "The Psychology of Human Misjudgment," and Robert Cialdini's excellent book *Influence*.[1]

Table 4.1 presents a list of common cognitive biases that can impede good decision-making but that the AREA Method can help you overcome. The list is organized into two columns. The name of the bias, along with its significance and an example of how it may impede clear thinking, appears in the left column. In the right column, you will find information about how the AREA Method tackles this bias and where in the book you can find steps to counteract it.

These biases are all difficult to counter on their own, but are even more powerful when they are combined. If one bias is present you might be able to recognize it, but if several biases are at work at the same time, it is much harder. Berkshire Hathaway's Charlie Munger calls this the "Lollapalooza effect."

Table 4.1. Common cognitive biases and AREA Method remedies

Cognitive biases	AREA Method remedies
Planning fallacy The planning fallacy is our tendency to underestimate the time, costs, and risks of completing a task, even though we've previously experienced similar tasks. Time management is a significant issue in the research process. We may miss out on an opportunity because we've underestimated how long it takes us to conduct our research.	The AREA Method is designed to counteract the planning fallacy in two ways: 1. The **Cheetah Sheets** let you know how much to wring out of each part of the research process, which aids you in assessing the time that it will take to complete each section. 2. By repeating a consistent process, you will also reduce the likelihood of poorly planning your time.
Confirmation bias Confirmation bias refers to a form of selective thinking in which we seek out and overvalue information that confirms our existing beliefs, while neglecting or undervaluing information that is contradictory to our existing	The AREA Method was created specifically to counteract our disposition to make assumptions and pass judgment while enabling us to better assess the incentives of others. The AREA Method is designed to reduce confirmation bias in the following ways:

beliefs. It is related to commitment and consistency bias where we behave in a way that validates our prior actions. It is also related to the incentive bias where we adapt our views to what benefits us. A confirmation bias may lead us to interpret information falsely because it conflicts with our prior views and beliefs. Confirmation biases can lead to overconfidence in personal beliefs, even in the face of contrary evidence. In collecting and evaluating data, be mindful that this bias may lead you astray.

Optimism bias

This is a bias in which someone's subjective confidence in their judgments, or in the judgments of others, is reliably greater than their objective accuracy. For example, we are only correct about 80 percent of the time when we say we are "99 percent sure."*

Projection bias

Without meaning to, we tend to project our thoughts and opinions onto others, assuming that they think and act as we do. This can lead to "false consensus bias," in which we assume that other people reach the same conclusions that we have reached. Projection bias also leads us to believe that what we do and think now will be what we do and think in the future. In short, this bias creates a false sense of confidence. For example, when planning how much money we should save each month we might underappreciate that consumption tends to rise over time, which may lead to poor future planning.

Social proof

We tend to think and believe what the people around us think and believe. We see ourselves as individuals but we actually run in herds—large or small, bullish or bearish. Institutions move in herds even more than individuals: investments chosen by one institution

1. Perspective taking separates information sources.
2. Thesis statements discourage you from cherry-picking information.
3. In the **Exploration** chapter (chap. 8), you will learn to craft objective questions.
4. In the **Exploitation** chapter (chap. 9), both the **Competing Alternative Hypotheses** exercise and the **Pro/Con** exercise will help to prevent this bias.
5. In the **Analysis** chapter (chap. 10), the discussion about the **Rule of Three** and the **Pre Mortem** exercise both tackle confirmation bias.

The AREA Method is designed to reduce optimism bias in the following ways:
1. In the **Absolute** chapter (chap. 6), the guidance to read numbers before narrative will counter this bias.
2. In the **Exploitation** chapter, the **Pro/Con** and **Scenario Analysis** exercises address it as well.
3. In the **Analysis** chapter, the **Pre-Mortem** exercise will help you to counter this bias.

By following the AREA Method you will be using a perspective-taking system that is structured to heighten your awareness of your own thinking while focusing clearly on other people's viewpoints.

The AREA Method is designed to reduce projection bias in the following ways:
1. In the **Exploitation** chapter, the **Competing Alternative Hypotheses**, **Pro/Con,** and **Scenario Analysis** exercises control for this bias.
2. In the **Analysis** chapter, the **Pre Mortem** exercise addresses it as well.

The AREA Method provides a natural defense against this bias because it is a structured process and it encourages you to do your own original work, broken down into discrete and manageable research pieces. With AREA, you are always aware of the sources of your information and focused on their incentives as well as your own.

(Continued)

Table 4.1. (Continued)

Cognitive biases	AREA Method remedies
predict the investment choices of other institutions to a remarkable degree. Investors also often track each other's investment strategies. For example, the 13D filings of famous investors often lead other investors to buy the same stocks.	The AREA Method is designed to reduce social proof by: 1. In the **Exploration** chapter, you will develop new sources of information and learn how to ask objective questions. 2. In the **Exploitation** chapter, the **Competing Alternative Hypotheses** exercise structures how we analyze assumptions against data to avoid bias. The **Pro/Con** exercise will also battle this bias. 3. In the **Analysis** chapter, the **Checklists** discussion will help you think about crafting lists to check and challenge your thinking and information.
Salience bias Salience bias refers to the tendency to overweight evidence that is recent or vivid. For example, people greatly overestimate murder as a cause of death. In fact, murder isn't even among the top fifteen causes of death in the United States There are more than ten times as many deaths from heart disease (the leading cause of death) as from murder. In the housing market leading up to the 2008 financial crisis, investors paid attention to the fact that housing prices were going up and started to believe that they would always go up rather than looking at the bigger picture. Housing prices went up until they didn't.	By using the AREA Method you will be focused on your cognitive shortcuts so less susceptible to salience bias. The AREA Method is also designed to reduce salience bias in the following ways: 1. In the **Exploitation** chapter, exercises like **Competing Alternative Hypotheses** systematically ensure you consider all of your information equally. **Visual Mapping** and **Scenario Analysis** will also address this bias by putting your evidence into context. 2. In the **Analysis** chapter, the section on **Thinking about Mistakes** as well as the **Checklist** exercise will challenge you to focus on significant issues, as opposed to salient ones.
Narrative bias We prefer stories–narratives–to data. Narratives are crucial to how we make sense of reality. They help us to explain, understand, and interpret the world around us. They also give us a frame of reference we can use to remember the concepts we take them to represent. However, our inherent preference for narrative over data often limits our understanding of complicated situations. A good story can sell almost anything–as you'll see in the "Plots and Ploys" section on detecting fraud and misrepresentation.	The AREA Method is designed to reduce narrative bias by: 1. Beginning with numbers and data in the **Absolute** chapter; 2. Distilling and analyzing information with the **Cheetah Pauses**; 3. Summing up discrete pieces of research through crafting thesis statements; 4. Conducting **Visual Mapping** and **Scenario Analysis** in the Exploitation chapter. These exercises allow you to both pictorially display your data and create multiple narratives for your research target's **Critical Concepts.** They enable you to use different versions of storytelling as a strength instead of a weakness.

Cognitive biases	AREA Method remedies
Loss aversion Empirical estimates find that losses are felt almost two and a half times as strongly as gains. For instance, if we have recently lost money in an investment, we might be unlikely to make similar investments in the future.	The AREA Method is designed to reduce loss aversion in the following ways: 1. In the **Exploitation** chapter, exercises like **Competing Alternative Hypotheses** ask you to withhold judgment and consider scenarios that at first might not appear likely. **Pro/Con** and **Scenario Analysis** also ask you to project possible outcomes. 2. In the **Analysis** chapter, the **Pre Mortem** exercise will guide you to consider failure *before* you make your decision to further battle this bias. You'll develop a plan to counteract failure and boost your confidence that your decision is set up to succeed.
Relativity bias The relativity bias is about how we rely too heavily on comparisons. For example, if a company is in an overvalued part of the market, we might be susceptible to overvaluing it based upon its comparisons.	The AREA Method is designed to reduce relativity bias in the following ways: 1. In the **Exploitation** chapter, the **Pro/Con** exercise counters this bias as well as the **Competing Alternative Hypotheses** exercise. 2. In the **Analysis** chapter, the **Pre-Mortem** exercise will focus on what could go wrong with comparisons so that it won't.
Authority bias This bias refers to our natural inclination to follow and to believe in authority figures. For example, Nike pays the professional golfer Rory McIlroy millions of dollars to wear the company's logo, betting that consumers will follow his lead.	The AREA Method is designed to reduce authority bias in the following way: 1. The AREA Method uses perspective-taking to separate sources of information so you can suss out the incentives and motives of others and question your own assumptions. If the information you receive from an authority figure conflicts with information you have received from another source, you will know to identify the dissonance.
Liking bias If you like someone or something, you will interpret data in their favor. We tend to like people who are like us, or have qualities that we admire. For example, you might be inclined to favor a candidate who went to your alma mater. This bias is closely related to the reciprocity bias in which we tend to want to reciprocate a favor that someone has done for us.	The AREA Method is designed to reduce liking bias by: 1. Separating **Absolute** information from information that you receive from other people, such as those encountered in the **Relative** and **Exploration** phases. 2. In the **Exploitation** chapter, the **Competing Alternative Hypotheses, Pro/Con,** and **Scenario Analysis** exercises will help you separate and objectively analyze your data and your hypotheses.

(Continued)

Table 4.1. (Continued)

Cognitive biases	AREA Method remedies
Scarcity We tend to covet things we believe are scarce, sometimes irrationally. For example, during the real estate bubble, investors became concerned that only a limited amount of land was available to be developed with no real evidence that this was the case.	The AREA Method is designed to reduce scarcity bias in the following ways: 1. AREA asks you to constantly vet your thinking by finding data to check it and guides you to bring data to bear upon situations even where you think data might be scarce. 2. In the **Exploitation** chapter, the **Competing Alternative Hypotheses, Visual Map,** and **Scenario Analysis** exercises address how we approach and evaluate discrete data points in context. 3. In the **Analysis** chapter, the section on **Thinking about Mistakes** counters our adaptive ignorance and mental shortcuts.

Edges and Pitfalls

In addition to controlling for bias, AREA's perspective-taking also helps you to be mindful of the edges and pitfalls in your research world. Some research is easy to do: the information is accessible, plentiful, and clear. Other research is cumbersome and tricky: the information may be opaque or insufficient. Recognizing where things may be working for you—where you have an edge—and where you may be at a disadvantage—facing a potential pitfall—can make the research process more effective and efficient for you, even before you begin.

Edges and pitfalls are two sides of the same coin; they are assumptions about advantages and disadvantages that researchers bring to the research process, and by recognizing them researchers can better capitalize on or control for them.

There are four categories of edges and pitfalls. The four categories are: Behavioral, Informational, Analytical, and Structural. Together they spell out BIAS, a reminder that even as you're identifying where you might have an edge in the research process, or where you might face a pitfall, you're making assumptions about how the process will go.

- *Behavioral:* A behavioral edge means having a better and different reaction to new information or events. It's about paying attention to your biases and behavioral patterns and how they can influence you in a way that may not be constructive. By being mindful, you may spot your biases and patterns, and can sidestep or change them. For example, a friend and her husband were walking in New York City when they heard the sound of a car crash. They turned to see a bicyclist pinned beneath a car. My friend froze, a natural behavioral response. Her husband, a physician, ran out into the street, towards the victim. His medical training gave him a behavioral edge in responding quickly in the face of this disaster. One more example: time and again pieces of bad news about a company may become salient and sensational and get reinforced by consistent declines in the stock price. That persistent wave of negative feedback can be a hard fog to see through. A seasoned investor can use her behavioral edge to take a Cheetah Pause and hold, or even add to, her position.

- *Informational:* An informational edge means that you have better information than other researchers. Maybe you've done more thorough work than others. Or maybe you've tapped unique sources that others are unaware of. In any case, an informational edge isn't magic. It's achievable, but it can be time- and labor-intensive. For example, Tom, a student from my Advanced Investment Research class, was assigned to evaluate the Mexican food chain Chipotle after it suffered from a series of foodborne illness outbreaks. One of the keys to Chipotle's success had been the high productivity of its stores due in part to an assembly line–like food preparation process. Specifically, sales per square foot far exceeded those of the competition. But Chipotle had instituted new food handling safety procedures in response to the outbreaks and Tom was concerned that these new procedures would come at the cost of efficiency, and therefore customer satisfaction. He faced an informational pitfall: there seemed to be no data on how the new procedures were affecting food prep and customer wait times. However, he decided to do the legwork himself. He conducted interviews with store managers and an anecdotal observational study, visiting several different Chipotle

restaurants all at the same busy weekday lunchtime to see how
fast the lines moved (slowly), whether customers got frustrated
and left (some did), and if the food tasted any different (not
really). Tom also asked friends in other states to do the same for
him. What looked like a pitfall became an edge.

- *Analytical:* This frame is about your ability to synthesize
  your data well. To avoid an analytical pitfall requires tools to
  make sense of the information you gather so you can distill
  key insights. An analytical edge means that you have a better
  understanding than the general public. You may have better
  insight into an organization or a financial issue, or a clearer
  picture of market trends or competitive dynamics. You may have
  asked better questions or better understood the answers. For
  example, Saba, another student of mine, was assigned to research
  AutoNation. At the time, car sales were at an all-time high and
  there was analyst concern that sales would cool off and hurt the
  company's share price. The margins were low to begin with, so
  AutoNation looked like a real risk. However, Saba looked more
  deeply at the company's revenues and spotted something others
  had missed: although the bulk of AutoNation's revenues came
  from low margin car sales, an important chunk also came from
  the company's repair business, which had much higher margins—
  and wouldn't be affected by a slowdown in sales. Saba realized
  that the repair part was almost as meaningful to the company's
  earnings as the much larger car sale component, something the
  market was missing. An analytical edge is achievable, but may
  take time to develop.
- *Structural:* This frame is about the limitations and opportunities
  of your environment. It gets at flexibility and timing. Some
  decisions are constrained, for example, by a short time horizon
  while others may be made under less pressure. A structural
  edge is not always within your control, and you need to be
  opportunistic to spot it. One consulting client of mine, John
  Christopher, the founder of a Nepal-based basic healthcare
  charity called the Oda Foundation, had been thinking about
  how to expand his organization. When a devastating earthquake
  struck Nepal, John discovered that he had a giant structural
  edge because Oda was already on the ground in Nepal. Charities

that weren't already there needed local partners. "We were able to meet Operation USA when they landed in Katmandu," says John. It gave his tiny charity a spotlight "and that made a huge difference."

By encouraging you to think about your edges and pitfalls before you begin—for example, where you think you may run into trouble gathering data, or where you think you might incur time pressure—AREA gives you a chance to confront your biases and look for evidence to shore up or tear down assertions and judgments. It can also point toward where you might need to direct deeper areas of research as you identify your Critical Concepts, those factors that make or break your research decision.

Chapter Five

AREA at Work and Critical Concepts

Research is to see what everybody else has seen,
and to think what no one else has thought
–Albert Szent-Gyorgyi

Critical Concepts are fundamental to the AREA Method. They are the few factors that really matter to you and answer: *So what? What am I really solving for?* In my experience, although there are typically numerous relevant and material data points that you may collect, only a few factors are critical to the success of your research investigation.

For instance, a few years ago, a friend who is a jeweler considered selling a new line of jewelry made by a Danish company called Pandora. The company sold charm bracelets that had become popular, but when he took a closer look at Pandora, he noticed that growth had flattened.

He noted that, in response to missed growth projections, Pandora's stock price dropped by 80 percent as analysts worried the bracelets might be a fad and the company could shrink as quickly as it had grown. At this point, there was a wealth of information about the company, but almost all the information—such as the rate of inventory turnover, trends in input pricing, and prospects for expanding its store base—was irrelevant to identifying greater certainty about its future sales success. All that really mattered was whether or not the business was a fad.

The jeweler's research focused on determining whether charm bracelets were a fad. He called third party retailers to understand the context of slowing customer purchases and the level of ongoing customer interest, analyzed resale channels to determine the extent to which bracelet owners were dumping previously purchased jewelry, measured Pandora-related Internet activity to gauge ongoing consumer engagement patterns, and interviewed industry veterans to understand the composition of historical fads.

Ultimately, his AREA research concluded that the slowdown in sales was concentrated in a few noncore items, and that consumer interest was still robust: Pandora's success wasn't a short-term fad. The jeweler developed an informational edge by identifying the one Critical Concept that truly mattered and the result was a successful and profitable decision to sell Pandora's bracelets and charms.

My jeweler friend knew he didn't need to focus on the overall business; he needed to understand this one particular piece of the picture.

Like the jeweler, you will want to invert your research process by focusing on the outcome. Your Critical Concepts ask you: What do you need to see happen for your research to succeed?

Thus the goal of the AREA research process is not to be the most knowledgeable researcher about everything related to your research target. In my experience, focusing on the tenth, eleventh and twelfth most important data point is often more of a distraction than a help. Your goal is to correctly identify and creatively and intensely research the one, two, or three Critical Concepts that will determine the success or failure of your research so that you become a knowledgeable researcher about what really matters to your hunt. To me, that's the foundation of practical and actionable research.

One more brief example: imagine that you're thinking about researching Netflix as an investment opportunity. You love it as a consumer, but if you're thinking about whether or not to buy its shares, there are real questions as to whether Netflix's business model of developing its own proprietary content is sustainable. Creating successful content is costly and hit-or-miss, and the market has become very crowded. A Critical Concept for Netflix might be whether the expense of creating content will continue to outpace revenue. However, Netflix has shown itself time and again to be a nimble and flexible company: it moved from providing mail order entertainment to streaming, and then when others entered the streaming market, Netflix began creating its own original content. Its show, *House of Cards*, became a blockbuster, and once again, the naysayers were proven wrong. This is a perfect example of how different researchers with different time horizons may have different Critical Concepts for the same research target, or may even have the very same one but interpret the data differently. If you're a short-term investor, Netflix's nimble management may not be salient for you. If you are a long-term investor it may well be.[1]

AREA recognizes that quality research is much more akin to playing a poker hand than it is to either your everyday decisions or your long-ago school research assignments. You're in the game to win, but so is everyone else at the table. How do you increase your odds of winning—of choosing the best path forward? You've got incomplete information, and the future will change in some ways you can predict and in many you can't. But as the pros at the poker table will tell you (unless they're playing against you), there's information you can gather to give you better odds—and even an edge—in playing the hand you're dealt. The pros know they don't have to know *everything* because they only have to focus on what hands their cards can beat.

What are the outcomes that matter for you in this game? By crafting your Critical Concepts you won't have to think about all possible hands. In fact, that would be distracting and counterproductive. Now you, like the poker pro, can focus on those hands—those outcomes—that will win this game for you. Every poker player has a set of skills, but starts each hand fresh, figuring out what's critical for that hand. As they say in poker, that's where you're "pot-committed." You've got chips on the table and a vested interest. The game is highly personal, subjective, and specific to your situation.

We all know that, at times, even a good process may have a poor outcome. You might have bad luck or dumb luck; sometimes you get your just desserts and sometimes your just rewards. I believe that in applying the AREA Method, you will gain the processes, tools, and confidence necessary to improve and enhance your research process.

Value-added research, as this process applies it, is a step to developing a comprehensive, objective analysis of a problem that focuses not just on prudent information collection, but on analyzing the information in a rigorous, unbiased manner. The goal: to feel that in completing the AREA Method you have both the comfort and the conviction to make a well-informed, thoughtful decision.

At the end of this process you will have mindfully conducted research that will allow you to move forward with an analytically supported decision. And, as you'll see in the following chapters, it's an extraordinary experience to conduct a quality research process. For John at Oda, following the AREA Method meant more than growing his charity, it meant saving lives. For Patricia and Matthew, it meant making a successful investment that the market hadn't recognized at the time. For you, it could mean confidence in the job you choose to take or a fresh angle on an investigative journalism piece.

There is no one right way to conduct research, just as there is no one right way to eat an ice cream cone. While I lay out a clear order of operations and many research steps, the AREA process does not always have to be applied as a whole. I encourage you to read through the book and understand all of the steps and how they work together. These steps aren't interchangeable; each scaffolds onto the previous one. However, once you understand how the process works, you may want to choose the steps that resonate with you and that are most relevant to the research project you're undertaking. If, for example, you're trying to capitalize on a short-term trading opportunity, you may well want to truncate your research process to fit a tight timeline. Remember the cheetah: the process is meant to be agile and flexible for you.

The book can be used like a guidebook long after an initial read. Flip back to the table of contents to find a list of the Cheetah Sheets, each of which will take you to sections of the AREA Method that you might like to use. There you will have at your ready useful lists of suggested sources of information and questions to consider as you collect, analyze, and synthesize the data related to your research decision.

Look at the different tools and methods I describe as suggestions and feel free to refine your research process however it feels best to you. But keep in mind: by pushing yourself to do research and analysis out of your comfort zone you will push your thinking in constructive ways.

To dig deeper and share your own thoughts, join the AREA community by checking out my website, **areamethod.com**. In addition to the downloadable AREA Journal and Cheetah Sheets, there you will find further discussion about the method and related research and articles, as well as how to post your own questions and research and decision-making experiences.

At its core, there are two kinds of learning: knowledge and skills. The AREA Method is a skill. I can explain it and teach it to you, and by simply using it you may get better at it, improve upon it, and make it your own.

We can't control our luck, but we can control our process.

Chapter Six

AREA = A: Absolute

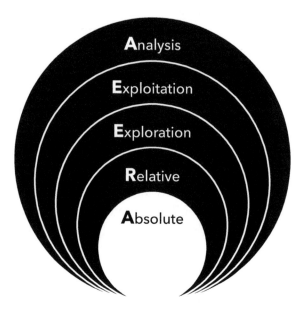

Somewhere, something incredible is waiting to be known.
–Dr. Carl Sagan

The first "A" in AREA stands for what I call Absolute information because it is information that represents your research target's perspective as it sees and presents itself (which does not mean that it is unbiased). The information collected in this phase is primary-source information from the target, unfiltered by outside sources. By looking narrowly at the target's perspective, you allow it to represent itself and to put its best story forward.

By letting the target speak first, you will also begin to understand how the target would like its stakeholders—including its investors, customers, and employees—to see and interpret its results and prospects. You won't taint your impression of the entity with outside or Relative-source information. The experience gained from this preliminary reading will provide a foundation for comparison of the target's version of events versus those of other sources of information, making it easier to spot the red flags later on.

Getting Started

Some of you may be investigating a single target such as a company you are considering investing in or a government entity that is the focus of an investigative story. This was the case for my former students Patricia, who evaluated Sprint, and Matthew, who studied Delta Airlines, both as potential investment opportunities.

However, some of you may have several "targets." You may be researching a number of companies to identify the best internship opportunity, or you may be exploring an industry sector or even deciding between different growth opportunities for your business. In that case you'll want to conduct an AREA investigation for each target.

Where should you begin your research on your target? For almost all of us, research now begins on the computer, and you may be tempted to type your target's name into Google and look at the first five hits that come up—but don't. Your goal is to control for and counteract cognitive bias while also building your internal compass to collect, understand, and analyze information. The results of search engines are biased by the algorithms that sort how they present the results to you. Don't let a search engine filter your information and your sources; *you* are in charge with AREA by isolating the sources of information so you can determine the incentives and motives of each information provider and gain distance on your own assumptions and judgments.

Similarly, at times professionals will use shortcuts to find financial data, relying upon companies that provide investment analytics tools like FactSet or Bloomberg. While these data searches save time, if you rely solely upon them they may also inhibit your ability to have unfiltered access to both data and your target's ecosystem, which may impact how you understand the numbers and your ability to ask the right questions about them. When you allow a search engine or a financial analytics firm to do your work for you, you're layering in bias and separating yourself from primary source information.

If you are researching a public company, the best place to start will be with the research target's financial filings. You can find these either on the Securities and Exchange Commission's website, or on your target's website. Be aware that regulated company filings such as 10-K forms require companies to disclose their numerical data according to Generally Accepted Accounting Principles. Management may prefer other metrics and choose to present a different numerical story when it has greater leeway, such as in investor and other presentations.

From reading the SEC filings there are several basic pieces of information that you can gather. You can figure out what the business does, how it operates, its assets and liabilities, and the key markets that it operates in. You also get a glimpse into management's behavior and a representation of the profitability of the company. More on that later.

If you're researching a nonprofit you also have a few choices for where to look for information: a charity database like GuideStar or Charity Navigator or, again, the target's website. For a privately held company you'll likely need to start with the company's website, although a site like D&B Hoovers maintains a database of private company information. For government entities, start with the target's website as well.

It may seem enticing to browse the whole website or filing, but stay focused on following the path laid out by the Cheetah Sheets. It will guide you through AREA's order of operations for how to collect your data and analyze it.

Below is the second Cheetah Sheet. As you begin to ask and answer questions, be sure to write out your questions and answers in your AREA journal. You will also want to compose a list of unanswered questions for further study and make a list of sources of information for where you may go for answers.

CHEETAH SHEET 2
Absolute: Getting to Know Your Target

1. What are your critical entities and your Absolute targets? Why?
2. Who are the critical people at those targets? What is their involvement and impact?
3. What does it mean as it relates to your research puzzle?

Numerical Data

After you've decided on your targets, begin with the numerical data that they provide. The reason: all research decisions have numbers involved. The purpose of limiting your initial focus to the numbers is multifold.

First, it enables you to see them as objectively and as uninfluenced by other perspectives as possible. This helps to control for and counteract narrative bias, our preference for a story over data. Second, it forces you to think seriously about the nature of the data presented and to become familiar with the information used and the analyses undertaken. Third, having perused the data at the start, you may then approach the narrative with specific questions that you've gleaned from the data. Moreover, reading the data first makes the reading of the narrative more focused and often more interesting. Fourth, you are more likely to be able to better examine the company's conclusions and interpretations having already arrived at your own. Finally, it may make the reading of the rest of the material faster: most organizations present data on what they consider to be their main issues and thus reading the numbers first may quickly highlight what the target considers most critical beyond what it is obligated to disclose.

CHEETAH SHEET 3
Absolute: Just the Numbers

1. What kind of numerical data is available?
2. Does the numerical data make sense?
   a. Does it seem reasonable?
   b. Is there a connection between, or among, the data?
   c. How does the data pertain to your Critical Concepts? Are some more relevant to your CCs than others? Which should you focus on?
3. Are the numbers complete? Are they readable without a narrative?
4. Are they labeled and explained? If they are hard to understand, you've already exposed an inadequacy. If the numbers don't make sense, the story might not either.
5. What is the story that the numbers' charts and tables tell about your target?
6. Consider whether there are calculations you may want to make that help you derive value. For example, if you're evaluating compensation for CEOs at two different companies, you'll want to factor in cash and noncash compensation.
7. What is the significance of the numerical data for the target and for you?

Thus beginning with the numbers before you read anything else enables you to start building your own internal compass about the target. You'll strip away the noise of whatever hype there might be around your target or any emotional impression the target wants you to have. Over time, as you strengthen your internal compass, you will also be building your confidence as a researcher.

Reading and analyzing the numbers first also keeps you from having to assume that whatever the research target says can be backed up by the data presented in the tables, charts, or financial documentation the target divulges. This is often a misleading assumption. I have found that a careful reading of the data opens up interpretations not included in the research target's analysis.

Spend the time to figure out the numbers on your own and then write down the key data and what you think it means, as well as any questions it raises in your AREA journal.

Matthew, studying Delta's numbers in its SEC filings, realized that operating expenses were relatively fixed and therefore the number of passengers per plane was critical. For example, if a flight went from 90 to 100 percent capacity, there were few incremental costs in the form of fuel, salaries, and other expenses, allowing the company to recognize significant profits on incremental seats being filled.

He noted that all fixed costs were not equal: fuel alone made up close to 35 percent of Delta's fixed operating expenses. For Matthew, this seemed like a Critical Concept for his research. Delta already had some of the industry's highest ticket prices. If fuel prices increased, would Delta be able to pass that on, or would it eat into margins?

At this point, many researchers might have turned to the experts to understand what they thought about the future of fuel prices, but Matthew postponed that and stayed with Delta's perspective to give the company a chance to explain its behavior. He noted that in preparing for his Relative work he'd want to follow up with industry experts. Matthew took a Cheetah Pause and asked himself: what was the story the numbers told? He answered this question by crafting his first thesis statement.

Here is Matthew's thesis statement from "Absolute: Just the Numbers":

For Delta, whose operating expenses are relatively fixed, incremental passenger growth is critical, but the macro trends appear to be good for now: revenue passenger miles are increasing, as are available seat miles, passenger mile yield, and load factor. Fuel prices are 35% of Delta's operating expenses, and prices are currently low, but the number of gallons consumed is increasing. Future fuel trends for both usage and cost will be critical to Delta's profitability.

Matthew's experience shows that reading the tables is a good test of how well your target communicates numerically. If you're looking at a chart that shows a correlation between two things, consider whether the correlation is meaningful or not. For example, look at the chart presented in figure 6.1 below.

Clearly, the chart shows a very high correlation between the number of people drowning by falling into a pool and the release of Nicolas Cage films, but logically we know that this is spurious. We tend to assume that data is accurate and meaningful. But it isn't always. As you conduct your research, remember not to watch *National Treasure* while sitting by the pool, and question all data.

There are many ways that data may be flawed. We'll touch on this again in chapter 10, on Analysis, so for now, one more point to consider when reviewing data sets: always make sure you understand how a study was designed and conducted. A scientific study, widely publicized in the *New York Times* and other media outlets, warned that sterilizing kitchen sponges in the microwave or dishwasher was counterproductive, possibly dangerous. However, astute home sponge sterilizers noted that the

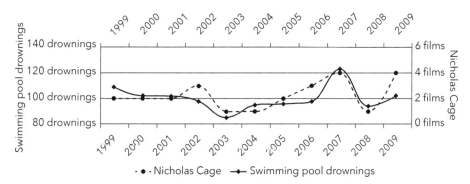

Figure 6.1. Number of people who drowned by falling into a pool (solid line) correlates with films Nicholas Cage appeared in (dotted line).
Source: http://www.tylervigen.com/spurious-correlations.

study was suspect on two fronts: the sample size was very small (only fourteen sponges), and the germs that survived home sterilization efforts were mostly harmless. In fact, one of the bacteria found on the sterilized sponges lives on our skin. There was nothing dangerous or flawed about home sterilization. The danger lay in not understanding how the study was conducted and what kind of conclusions could be drawn. Even the *New York Times* reporter took at face value the researcher's comment that the density of bacteria on the sponges was "the same density of bacteria you can find in human stool samples," implying that the sponges were dangerous.[1]

You may collect data from your target that is unreliable. Given the influence of authority bias—our tendency to defer to authority figures such as scientists and government officials—it can be easy to take data as gospel, but don't. For example, the government collects inflation statistics. We all think of the government as a reliable, unbiased reporter. But the government uses those statistics to calculate increases in entitlement payments, so it has an incentive to keep a lid on these numbers. Might your target have an incentive to show one result or another that might make its information unreliable? The bottom line: question everything.

Putting the Numbers in Context

Your initial look at the numbers educates you about what data your targets provide and how they represent that data. For some of you, this may be enough.

Putting your numbers in context asks you to think about the meaning of the data provided. The idea is to think conceptually about the target's business and its operating model. How and why does it do what it does? And does it do it well? The goal is to more fully understand how the target represents itself, its market position and its products or services. This level of research assumes some comfort with accounting principles, and if you're researching an investment opportunity you'll want to follow this fourth Cheetah Sheet. If you're not conducting this type of research, you may want to simply skim the questions in Cheetah Sheet 4 and Cheetah Sheet 5 or skip them altogether.

CHEETAH SHEET 4
Absolute: Your Target's Business Model

1. What is your target's market size and is the market growing?
2. What has happened to margins and profitability recently? Historically?
3. What drives margins?
4. What does market share look like now and what direction is the trend?
5. Break down the company's working capital, fixed assets, and other investments.
6. What's the return on capital? How much capital is needed for each dollar of new sales?
7. Have there been any mergers or acquisitions? How have they worked out and how can you tell?
8. Are there regulatory, legal, or patent issues that you need to be aware of? Are there any new regulations that may affect the company?
9. Consider the company's finances and accounting:
   a. How is the company financed?
   b. Understand the company's accounting approach: Assess earnings quality, including earnings versus cash flow from operating activities and revenue recognition policies and changes.
   c. Is there any evidence of moving expenses to different periods or underestimating liabilities?
   d. Is there evidence of any possible manipulation of cash flow?
   e. Is there evidence of any possible failure to disclose liabilities?
   f. Is there evidence of irregular movement of inventories or possible channel stuffing?
   g. Look at Generally Accepted Accounting Principles compared to cash taxes paid.

How does your target's accounting compare to the economic reality of the company's assets and operations? At times the economic substance of a company's assets diverges from the accounting for them, either favorably or unfavorably. If a company has a high ratio of fixed costs to variable costs, a small percentage change in sales will lead to increased profit margins. If the company possesses a high degree of operating leverage, the degree of success or failure often depends upon volume of sales.

The point of understanding your target's business is not only to get to know it, but also to be able to identify key points of leverage where changes in the target's performance in a few areas may have an outsized impact on the entire entity. For example, investors have found hidden value and profited by realizing that, although real estate gets depreciated and written down under Generally Accepted Accounting Principles (GAAP), it may actually increase in value over time. I suggest making notes and writing questions as they arise in your AREA journal.

Drilling Down on Your Target's Financials

If you are researching a company as an investment, the questions in Cheetah Sheet 4 will give you a good grounding in your target's numbers. However, you may want to dig deeper into the filings. What stones might you turn over and why? Below I have highlighted "touchy" areas where management and accounting rules and presentation may unduly influence financial performance. Note that over time the reporting standards and the data that you look for may change. Know, too, that if you'd like assistance with your financial sleuthing at any time, when you get into the Relative and Exploration parts of the book you'll find Cheetah Sheets that provide lists of industry and other sources as well great questions to ask them so that they may guide you as to how to evaluate your target's challenges and opportunities.

Read the Risk Factors

Be aware that lawyers concerned about preempting lawsuits write these factors, not management, and they have different goals. While lawyers are usually concerned about risk and liability, management is usually more concerned with operations and financial performance. Given that management is not often able to put their spin on the risk factors write-up, new additions can be important red flags.

Look at Your Target's
Credit Situation and Capital Structure

What kind of future debt commitments might the company have? Is there land that's been held for a long period of time? Are there other items material to understanding the company's financial results that may be improperly valued in the company's filings?

Watch Out for Vague Categories

Categories that might raise issues include "prepaid expenses and other current assets," "noncash revenue," or "unbilled receivables." They may allow companies to fudge the numbers. For example, if prepaid expenses or other soft assets suddenly rise, you might consider whether the company might be manipulating expenses. Might it be capitalizing normal operating expenses in an effort to delay the recognition of expenses or to look like a more profitable company?

Look for Unusual Transactions

Are there any unusual transactions that may pose potential conflicts of interest, or may be related-party transactions? Is there is a business deal or arrangement between two parties who are joined by a special relationship?

For instance, if you had been studying natural gas giant Chesapeake Energy and considering these questions a few years ago, you might have uncovered that then-CEO Aubrey McClendon borrowed over $1 billion from several major Wall Street banks that later received lucrative work as public-offering underwriters or financial advisers to Chesapeake. The loans were made through three companies controlled by McClendon that list Chesapeake's headquarters as their address. The money was used to help finance a lucrative perk of the CEO's job: the opportunity to buy a stake in the very same oil wells that he was using as collateral for the borrowings. Such insider dealings should raise a red flag as to whether the company is being run for the insiders or the shareholders and how well incentives are aligned.

Look for Large Write-Offs

These can be legitimate reflections of a plant closure or other changes in a company's assets, or an excuse to lower the value of assets so future performance looks even better. Hidden reserves can also provide a nice secret fund to tap when times turn bad, giving a misleading boost to the bottom line. In short, have a healthy sense of skepticism about anything that has the potential to hide a company's true earnings picture. That means questioning accounting shifts that stem from so-called changes in strategy, as well as understanding what make up the different categories on a company's financial statement.

I will delve deeper into forensic accounting in chapter 9, on Exploitation.

Financial Footnotes

I highly recommend reading the notes to financial statements, frequently referred to as "footnotes" or "financial notes," as you read the SEC filings. They contain some of the most important information in corporate financial reporting. It is not possible for companies to provide all the necessary details in their financials. The notes, therefore, are used to provide critically important additional disclosures and are considered to be an integral part of financial statements.

Reading financial notes is as much an art as a science. **Not all disclosures are created equal.** Disclosures in corporate annual reports, called 10-K filings, are much more informative than corporate quarterly reports, or 10-Qs. This difference is a holdover from the predigital age, when companies argued that it was too costly to provide full disclosure every quarter. Even though everything is now digital, regulators still haven't yet made quarterly updates a requirement, so some important information on key areas such as pension data is not updated each quarter.

Moreover, to find warning signs, you have to know where to focus your reading. To do this, you need to be aware of the possible areas where trouble could first develop. This varies from industry to industry and from company to company, which is why it's beneficial to read not just one SEC filing or corporate report but several years' worth of a company's financial reporting from cover to cover.

For example, the auto industry (and any heavily unionized industry) more frequently has underfunded pension plans than the high-tech industry so you'll likely want to spend more time analyzing the pension note for an auto company than you would the pension note for a high-tech company.

Generally, the red flags are buried in long paragraphs filled with legal language that may be difficult to read and understand. But the hard work it takes to do some digging does pay off with an insight that is often overlooked.

For instance, Enron, despite its many flaws, provided disclosure in its financial notes that made a few careful investors worried about its off–balance sheet partnerships and conflicts of interest. Read and think about the questions that the footnote disclosures raise and you too may find that you've identified an important topic to investigate.

Keep in mind that disclosures may change from filing to filing as assumptions or events change a company's results. This means that you can't read just one disclosure and expect to have the whole story or gain insight into the quality or credibility of management thinking.

For instance, assumptions about healthcare costs have changed markedly over the years. Has the company you are studying adjusted its healthcare cost assumptions appropriately, or is it keeping estimates low to minimize the adverse impact on earnings? The company that assumes health care cost increases in the double-digit range will have more credibility than the company assuming single-digit cost growth.

Absolute Numbers: Reconciling the Data and the Narrative

My student Patricia, researching Sprint, needed to think about whether her Absolute target had an incentive to portray the data in a particular light. For Patricia to begin with the numbers meant she needed to look at the company's financial filings with the Securities and Exchange Commission. She went to the annual reports and the most recent quarterly filings but kept focused on the numbers alone, skipping all the carefully crafted management narrative until she'd had a chance to think about the company's numerical data and whether or not it made sense to her.

After she studied the company's numbers alone and then considered its business model, Patricia followed the next step of the AREA Method

to assess whether the company's story—its management discussion and narrative of the numbers—corresponded with the story the data told her. If you are looking at a publicly traded company, this would be your next step as well, to understand how the company wants to represent the data it is disclosing in its charts and tables.

CHEETAH SHEET 5
Absolute: Your Target's Story

1. What does management say about its plan to create economic value? What are the components of the plan? Does this fit with your understanding of the business model?
2. How sensitive does management say sales are to macro developments or to internal factors?
3. How sensitive does it say profitability is to changes in sales?
4. What does management say the company's growth potential is?

Once you've finished exploring the data and the narrative that your target tells about its data, you are ready to craft your next thesis statement.

CHEETAH SHEET 6
Absolute: Reconciling the Data and the Narrative

1. What is the company's story from the numbers alone?
2. What is the company's story from its narrative, its management discussion?
3. Do the two stories confirm each other or conflict with one another?
4. Why might there be discrepancies between the company's narrative and the numbers' story alone? For example: might management be cherry-picking non-GAAP metrics to create a narrative?
5. How has the story changed over time, and why?

Write out your answers in your AREA journal, composing a list of unanswered questions for further study and making a list of places where you may go for answers.

At the time Patricia began her research, Sprint's shares were changing hands for about $6 per share. Reading the Ks and Qs for Sprint, she noticed that Sprint's legacy wire line segment, which provides customers with voice, video, data, and network communication services, was declining in the mid-teens. She also noticed that Sprint's older network, known as an Integrated Digitally Enhanced Network, or iDEN for short, was losing subscribers rapidly while the newer network, known as a Code Division Multiple Access, or CDMA, which had historically lost subscribers, had recently begun to add subscribers. Due to the relatively strong performance of the CDMA network, her research led her to believe that it would become a bigger part of Sprint's business over time. Her Absolute thesis statement from the company's numbers and narrative read:

> *While Sprint's aggregate results are unimpressive, the company is losing subscribers, and profits are declining, the more technologically advanced CDMA network is a bright spot and is becoming a larger part of the business.*

This clear, concise, and cogent thesis showed not only what Patricia read and understood from her Absolute research on Sprint, but also what she believed the information meant. She focused on the data points that she found compelling and what was changing in the business. The thesis statement was forward-looking and thus clearly pointed her where to look next—namely to investigate CDMA as a Critical Concept for making the decision to buy, sell, or hold off on the investment.

Absolute: Your Target's Website

Once you've explored the numbers and management narrative, it's time to look more broadly at your research target by diving into its website. The website is where your target makes its most public case and has the most latitude to describe what it does, why it does it, and how well it's succeeding.

Websites are flexible. They're not regulated, so they are valuable real estate where the target can choose what it wants to say about itself with limited outside interference. Different entities will prioritize different information, but almost all will try to convey their value and their message to their identified audience. How clear is that message? Your goal here is to scour your target's website for data related to your research topic.

And don't just look at the website today; look back at how the company's website has changed. One cool tool for a historical look at a website is the Wayback Machine (http://archive.org/web/web.php). This allows you to look at the previous versions of your target's website to assess changes.

CHEETAH SHEET 7
Absolute: Your Target's Website

1. Who is the website targeting? How do you know?
   a. What does the target's homepage convey?
   b. How is the website set up and oriented? What tabs does it have? To whom are they directed: Customers? Investors? Of what age, and background?
2. What kind of content and language does the entity use on its site? Is it forward- or backward-looking? Is it updated frequently? What does it advertise as its key accomplishments?
3. How does your target communicate its value? How does it back up that message? Is it relevant to you?
4. What is the narrative that the website tells?
5. Is there information missing from the site that you think is important? This gets at how an Absolute target shapes the story being told about itself. For example, if you're researching nursing home companies, you may be surprised to find that there is often scant, if any, pricing data available on the websites.
6. If the entity is a public company, how is the investor relations page set up? Is it easy to navigate and are the SEC filing links provided? How difficult is it to get financial and other business or operational information on the site? How is the company's stock price presented? This will give you an indication of how much focus it puts on its share price. Is it on the homepage? Or only on an investor relations page, or not presented at all?

The right questions will vary, but the goal here is to understand how your Absolute target sees itself, and to begin to identify areas where you might want to question the target's story. Write down the answers to these questions in your AREA journal.

For example, in the summer of 2017, as part of the research for this chapter, I visited the Coca-Cola Company's homepage. The banner running across the center of the homepage consisted of a scrolling set of pictures that were teasers for a variety of general interest stories, only some of which seemed directly linked to Coca-Cola. In fact, some of the stories didn't even mention the company or its products, such as one about a cafe in Nashville, Tennessee. Coca-Cola was positioning itself as a fun lifestyle choice. The company was relying upon the universality of its original soda product even though it currently sells a much more diverse group of beverages, including Vitamin Water and a variety of bottled ice teas. A visitor to the website would have to know to search for Coca-Cola's drink products since they were not foregrounded on the homepage, which is odd because the company owns twenty-one billion-dollar brands, including Minute Maid and Dasani. The website is more in line with what one might expect from a media company dedicated to feature stories than from a beverage company selling drinks.

However, the investor tab is available at the very top of the homepage and, once there, the company features the current date's stock price and change from the prior day as well as other financial filings and presentations. There are extensive opportunities to learn about the company in terms of both documents and visual maps as well as invitations to contact investor relations and even the board of directors.

In contrast to Coca-Cola's homepage, PepsiCo's website homepage features a scrolling banner of its diverse product mix of beverages and snacks. It is more clearly focused on the company's products. Below the banner are a series of stories that closely focus on events featuring Pepsi products. The story of the homepage is of a diverse snack company, its products, employees, and its campaigns. This is not about a lifestyle; it is about the business that the company is in.

The investor tab is on the homepage and once there the content is work-a-day; it is meant for a knowledgeable investor and even prominently features a discussion defending the company's use of nontraditional accounting practices, something that Coca-Cola has as well but not center stage. PepsiCo's stock price is not available, nor are there helpful links for contacting investor relations or other shareholder services. PepsiCo's investor page is informational but doesn't reach outward like Coca-Cola's investor offerings page does.

These two companies sell very similar products, but their websites tell different stories and feature different data. One is not necessarily better than the other. It's your job as the researcher to make the qualitative judgment about how well and to whom the company is telling its story. Consider what your target's website says about the company, management, and its focus. Does the portrayal seem to make the company a better investment? Or employer? Does this positioning help them sell their products? And how might you assess that?

Reading and analyzing the way your research target chooses to present itself gives you insight into its focus and thus into how it thinks about its business (and its stock price).

Absolute: Your Target's History

Once you've gained a broad understanding of how your target presents itself on its website, you may want to dive deeper into your target's history and current leadership. Learning the history of the organization or entity can help you gain insight into its development and character.

Organizational histories provide valuable insight into the organization's sense of identity, purpose, and goals. In its most familiar form, as a narrative of an entity's past, the history will provide you with a context and explanation for change, an understanding of incentives and motivation, and insight into how a company intends to overcome challenges. For instance, does a company easily adopt new technology? A chosen technology may extend or restrict a company's opportunities.

Another example: a change in business strategy might be interpreted differently if it is motivated by challenges facing the business rather than by the perception of a new opportunity. Thus an organization's history may serve as a potent problem-solving tool. It tells of the entity's life cycle and enables you to evaluate the decisions that have been made. A start-up company will face different challenges than a company in a well-established market.

CHEETAH SHEET 8
Absolute: Your Target's History

Read the bios of the founders and the origins of your target and answer these questions:

1. Why was the organization founded?
2. What key changes have occurred in the organization's focus and values?
3. Have there been any transforming transactions (e.g., mergers or divestments)?
4. Has the organization undergone difficult or particularly good periods in the past? Why?
5. If you are researching a company, make sure you understand the company's business cycle:
   a. Are problems new or normal course?
   b. Identify where the company might be vulnerable, and its value drivers.

In the case of Sprint, Patricia learned that the company had completed a large, transformational merger with Nextel a few years earlier. The acquisition was a disaster, leading to large subscriber losses and a share price decline from over $20 to under $5. She wondered what the fallout had been for the leadership and how the problems the merger had caused were being rectified.

Understanding where an organization has come from and how it has developed will give you important insight into why it has the current leadership it does, in terms of both who is at the helm and the overall leadership structure. One type of leader and structure is not necessarily better than another. But legacy issues, corporate culture, and governance will affect current and future performance.

Begin your look at leadership by focusing on the captain of the ship. What is the leader's track record? Do the leader's strengths and interests seem to be aligned with the organization's needs? For example, a CEO who is good at identifying big-picture strategy may see that her company needs to reposition itself but may not be as well-suited as a detail-oriented leader to lead the company through the necessary restructuring. Does she seem aware of her skill set and if so how does she bolster areas where she may need support?

Moreover, it's helpful to understand how the leader came to her role, whether she has been with the organization for a long time or whether she was recruited from outside, and what her previous experience has been. This will educate and inform you about what the people who hired the candidate—whether it was a search committee or a board of directors—thought the organization needed at the time the leader was brought in.

Each leader should be evaluated individually. You may not be rattled when a CEO with a stellar track record makes an unconventional acquisition—think of the surprise move to buy Whole Foods made by Amazon's Jeff Bezos; however an untested leader making such a move would give you pause.

In the case of Sprint, in the wake of the botched Nextel deal, a new leader had been brought in. Dan Hesse, the new CEO, had worked at AT&T for over twenty years before joining Sprint to head Embarq, a wireline division it was spinning off. After a successful stint at Embarq, Hesse was hired by Sprint to fix the fallout from the merger. He was an industry veteran with operational experience.

In a similar vein, learning about what the leader perceives as his key accomplishments may give you insight into what he takes pride in. Assess whether those successes have paid off for the organization and if they've impacted the organization's bottom line performance.

Understanding the leader's compensation structure can provide you with an appreciation for her economic motivation. Does the new leader have a lot of money tied up in the entity's long-term future prospects or is her pay mostly in cash? Is there motivation to underrepresent the entity's success? If the leader runs a public company, might she have options that may soon be priced? Are equity and voting rights aligned? For example, it may not be a good sign if management owns 2 percent of the stock and yet controls 80 percent of the voting power.

Likewise it may be unhealthy for one person to own a substantial majority of a company's stock. For example, at the time of this writing, the voting stock of the temporary staffing agency Kelly Services is almost entirely controlled by the executive chairman, Terence Adderley. Adderley is the son of the agency's founder and was CEO until 2006, when Carl Camden was appointed. As the owner of more than 90 percent of the voting stock at the company, Adderley controlled the election of the company's board of directors, its advisory Say on Pay vote, and the vote to renew Kelly's short- and long-term compensation plans. Although it would seem that Adderley would have an incentive to make changes at the company in response to poor performance, when the stock fell by 60 percent in 2014, Adderley actually boosted Camden's cash compensation, perhaps to offset the hit to his restricted stock. (Camden has subsequently stepped down as CEO.)

This example, like so many in the book, shows how important it is to look behind the numbers. What else might have been going on here and how might that impact your understanding of Adderley's actions and the fact pattern?

For one more example of how revealing and potentially misaligned compensation packages can be, take Avon: Sheri McCoy joined the troubled makeup company as CEO in 2012, and even as the company's profits and share price were dogged by bad news, it revised the CEO's long-term compensation incentives when it changed its comparable company peer set, making it easier for Avon to hit its financial targets by moving the goalpost. The company removed big players such as PepsiCo and Proctor and Gamble from its peers' list and added troubled companies like Herbalife and Coty.[2]

If you're investigating a company, watch the CEO's actions in the stock market as well. For instance, is a CEO trying to explain away new operational shortcomings while aggressively selling stock? If so, this may be a red flag, raising concern both about the manager and about the company's prospects.

Some of the information about an organization's leadership will be available on their website but you may want to dig deeper. If you are examining a publicly traded company you may read management bios and their compensation disclosures in the proxy (Def 14-A) filing. If you are dealing with a nonprofit, you may choose to look at its disclosure forms on a database website such as GuideStar or Charity Navigator that pull information from the Internal Revenue Service.

At Sprint, Patricia learned that Hesse's compensation was a mix of stock and cash, with slightly more stock than cash, a well-aligned and effective package.

For Delta, Matthew noted that 85 percent of total compensation was concentrated in equity-based opportunities that vested over a three year period. Did three years make sense? Matthew noted that he'd want to consider the time frame.

Next, Matthew came upon a table that laid out how performance was measured and incentivized: it was divided among financial and operational targets as well as total revenue per available seat mile. He noted that he'd want to consider how to evaluate the operational targets but his main takeaway regarding compensation: "It appears to be very much a 'pay for performance' construct, with a substantial portion of total compensation at risk."

CHEETAH SHEET 9
Absolute: Your Target's Leadership

1. What is the CEO's track record?
   a. How effective has the CEO been at creating value for customers? For shareholders?
   b. How consistent has the strategy been and has the CEO been able to follow through on it?
2. How effective has the CEO been at capital allocation? Has the CEO deployed capital into buy-backs or mergers or dividends? If so, how successful have those decisions been?
3. How did the CEO arrive in the top spot and what might that say about her strengths and weaknesses?
4. What incentives does the CEO have to perform and over what period of time? How is compensation structured? Are her equity and voting rights aligned? Can you gauge how much of her net worth is tied to company performance?
5. Is the CEO active in buying or selling stock? What is her history of buying or selling company shares?

Absolute: Your Target's Board of Directors

Some leadership reviews will only require looking at who is at the helm, but if you are dealing with an organization with an active board you may be interested in exploring governance issues, and that may include a review of the company's board of directors. Note that how you view the board and its governance may well be colored by what you think of the CEO and that leader's performance.

CHEETAH SHEET 10

Absolute: Your Target's Governance Structure

1. What are the responsibilities of the governing members? Review the members' terms of service and how many members come up for a vote on a given year.
2. What kind of board committees are there and how often do committees meet?
3. What kind of qualifications do board members have?
4. If your target is a business, are there stock incentives, and if so, what does ownership look like at the board level? Does the company require board stock ownership? Is it given outright, or must it be purchased?
5. Do any members have consulting or other contracts with the organization that might present a conflict of interest?

Understanding your organization's board will inform you about whether the board is well aligned with shareholders and may give you insight into how seriously the organization takes having checks and balances on its leader's power. Assess whether board members are independent and whether compensation is reasonable. A board constructed of the leader's friends and family will likely be less independent and entrepreneurial than a board comprised of industry experts or people with complimentary operational skills.

Absolute: Research Reports

To finish off the basics from the Absolute perspective, I recommend searching to see if your target has published any research, policy reports, or proposals on an issue. For example, the temporary staffing company Manpower has written a series of white papers about labor issues and the workplace. One recent paper, entitled "Work, for Me: Understanding Candidate Demand for Flexibility," discusses a survey of worker preferences where "candidates discuss what matters most to them in the job search process." It's an interesting paper that concludes that "workplace flexibility as a talent management policy is no longer an option; it is an essential practice that enables organizations to attract and develop skilled talent. The practice is rapidly becoming a win-win: reflective of employee and employer needs."

Of course this a fine conclusion *and* it is also one that supports the company's business. How do papers like this play a role in how the company influences its stakeholders? How core to its strategy is conducting this kind of research and how does this factor into your understanding of the company's value proposition? After all, in the case of Manpower, in addition to providing staffing, the company also offers consulting services, which a paper like this may serve to promote.[3]

CHEETAH SHEET 11
Absolute: Your Target's Research Reports

1. Why did the organization author the study?
2. What is its stated reason for putting out the paper and might there be other incentives?
3. Is there a way to determine its impact? Are research partners credible? Where does the funding for the research come from?

Matthew located a white paper published by the Partnership for Open and Fair Skies, a US airline advocacy coalition comprised of American Airlines, Delta, and United, as well as various pilot and airport personnel labor organizations. The paper argued that subsidized competition from state-owned airlines in Qatar and the United Arab Emirates unfairly disadvantaged US carriers. For example, the paper recounted that since 1998 Qatar "explicitly or implicitly guaranteed . . . almost 100 percent of the company's term loans" and was committed to guaranteeing "Qatar Airways as a going concern." Matthew realized that his Delta research would have to take into consideration antitrust issues as well as foreign government intervention. In that respect, Delta wasn't on a level playing field.[4]

Absolute: Press Releases

Another place where your target has direct control over its messaging to the public is its press releases. These are good places to look for clues about management because the language is usually less formal than what you would find in the management's discussion of regulatory filings like the SEC documents and yet more formal than the organization's website. Here the organization knows that it may influence how it is seen or understood. For publicly traded companies, investors may trade on the news. Companies often self-promote, and most of the time this self-promotion is benign. But occasionally organizations appear to be using press releases to solicit investors while effectively skirting the SEC regulations. An example of this was Interoil, an oil exploration company that alleged it had vast resources that could not be substantiated and that it did not develop.

So how does your target use the press release bully pulpit? Might it be trying to influence share price performance by disclosing small or hard-to-verify data?

CHEETAH SHEET 12
Absolute: Your Target's Press Releases

1. How does the organization use its power to release information? Is the information specific and material or self-promotional and speculative? This gets at content.
2. How many press releases are there? The frequency of the organization's releases not only conveys how often the organization wants to communicate or how self-promotional it is, but also gives the researcher information about what news leadership considers important enough to tell the world.
3. Does the company use press releases only for major announcements or for small and seemingly marginal news as well? Is there evidence to back up the company's assertions in the releases?
4. Look at the tone and word choice of the releases. What do they convey?

Absolute: Your Target's Share Price Performance

If you are researching a publicly traded company, there is one more important bit of Absolute research you will want to do: look at a multi-year stock chart of the company's share price performance. Each stock has a different trading personality. Gaining an appreciation for what makes your investment target's share price move and how active its trading is may better enable you to assess the forces that act upon your company.

CHEETAH SHEET 13
Absolute: Your Target's Share Price Performance

1. Average daily volume: how many shares trade a day? This will contextualize the activity of the shares and help you to understand how long it might take to build a position without disturbing the share price.
2. Historical volatility: this will contextualize daily moves against historical daily moves.
3. Is there any seasonality to the share price performance? If so, why?
4. Look at insider purchases and sales. Are members of management buying or selling, and how much relative to their ownership stake? These trades may provide you with clues to where the stock may be headed.
5. What issues do the shares seem sensitive to?
6. Options market activity: is there a lot of activity on the call or put side? What is the option market predicting about volatility in the next one to three months or longer? This contextualizes reasonable volatility.
7. The stock's technical trading patterns: look at the share's trend lines, especially in relation to your investment horizon. Since stocks tend to cycle and revert to the mean, be careful to consider the shares' moving average over a reasonable length of time. Draw lines that connect major tops and bottoms. Is the stock currently above or below the trend lines? This may heighten your awareness of timing related to potential trading activity.
8. Is there a short interest in the company's shares? If so, what is the cost to borrow the stock? And what is the risk that if you borrow shares the shares might be recalled?

As always with data, look for relationships between and among different sets of information. When assessing how self-promotional a management team might be, or how influential it is upon its stakeholders, I recommend overlaying your press release data on top of the stock chart. Here you are looking to see whether press releases impact share price performance and for what kind of news. By looking at the volume of the trading you can also consider share price liquidity, its impact on volatility and how compelling a share price move might be.

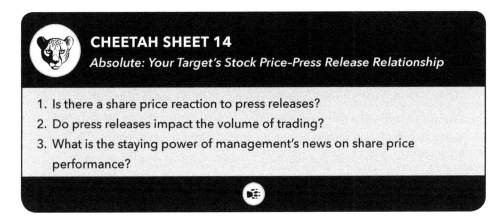

CHEETAH SHEET 14

Absolute: Your Target's Stock Price-Press Release Relationship

1. Is there a share price reaction to press releases?
2. Do press releases impact the volume of trading?
3. What is the staying power of management's news on share price performance?

You can repeat this exercise with the company's last two years of earnings releases. This will give you some insight into not only how persuasive management is, but also the staying power of its news on the share price.

Familiarizing yourself with your company's share price performance and how the stock responds to different issues and participants will help you to understand the debate surrounding the company and provide a further guide to the investigation of your Critical Concepts.

Absolute: Final Thesis Statement

If possible, try using the organization's product or service yourself. Does your experience match with the way the organization presents the user experience? It's a question that you are now well-suited to answer. Remember that the idea of perspective-taking is to see the data from the organization's point of view and to tease out its incentives and motives while also gaining the critical distance that enables you to assess assertions against evidence.

Finally, pause and craft a clear, concise, and cogent thesis statement from all of your Absolute findings that answers the question: So what? What have I learned from the Absolute perspective? What is the meaning of the company's story in its own words? This step puts together each piece of information mentioned above: the numbers, the website, the management discussion, and so on.

Patricia, as she investigated Sprint, learned that the board was primarily comprised of other CEOs from both inside and outside the industry. It was an experienced group with deep knowledge of both telecommunications and company management that likely could help CEO Dan Hesse navigate Sprint's turnaround. When she wrote her final Absolute thesis statement it read:

> *Although Sprint shares have declined precipitously after the failed Nextel merger, the company's new CEO has a track record that indicates that he has relevant experience and a strong experienced board. Initial results show that subscriber losses may be finally moderating.*

This thesis statement may seem brief but it sums up a lot of research. By pausing to answer "So what?" Patricia's thesis achieves several things in one sentence. It takes into account the company's share price performance, Patricia's understanding of Sprint's merger (a failure), her assessment that the CEO and the board of directors were competent, and her analysis that the basic business was improving. The thesis has achieved its goal—to enable Patricia to move on with a concise summary of her work to date and to provide her with a clear signpost for future research: a Critical Concept would be to understand what drove the change in customer trends and how likely it was to be permanent.

Another way to think of the formula for a good summative thesis statement that puts the disparate pieces of research together is to plug in answers for the variables placed in a sentence such as this one:

> *Company X says its business prospects are Y because A, B, and C, but/and the company's numbers undercut/substantiate that story as evidenced by D and E, which are having Z impact.*

Matthew followed a similar formula. When he came to the end of his Absolute research, he recognized that although Delta told one story to its shareholders and its customers, its white paper acknowledged a more challenging reality. As a customer, Matthew was concerned about the impact of low-cost airlines on Delta's pricing, but in his Absolute work, he didn't come across Delta discussing this new threat. His final Absolute thesis statement read,

> *Revenue passenger-miles are increasing steadily both domestically and abroad. Given Delta's strong performance with corporate travelers, a sophisticated customer segmentation strategy that drives higher revenues, and entrenched partnerships with international airlines, the company stands to benefit from this macro trend. This may ultimately narrow the valuation discount that Delta currently has versus high quality peers.*

Matthew knew this statement truly represented the story Delta told from its own perspective. He knew that when he began his Relative work, he'd want to look more closely at fuel prices, international competition, and new discount airlines as they affected Delta's dominance.

Like Matthew, you may find that your narratives conflict or tell different stories. At this point, it is important to *pause*. Why might the company tell its own story differently in different venues? What incentives might the company have to represent itself in different ways to an investor audience versus a general commercial audience?

Formulate hypotheses for why the discrepancy might occur. What problems and questions do any discrepancies raise? How might you investigate answers to them?

For example, I put together a case study on Salesforce.com, a company that sells software to help manage customer relationships. It illustrates the utility of reading footnotes and the practice of looking for dissonance and disconfirming data that the AREA Method focuses on. I had noticed that the income statement in the annual report showed revenues growing 37 percent from 2010 to 2011 and 35 percent from 2011 to 2012, indicating steady and healthy growth (see figs. 6.2 and 6.3, next page).[5]

The management discussion explains the chart by saying, "The increase in subscription and support revenues was due primarily to new customers, upgrades and additional subscriptions from existing customers and improved renewal rates as compared to a year ago. . . . The increase in professional services and other revenues was due primarily to the higher

| (In thousands) | Fiscal Year Ended January 31 | | Variance | |
	2012	2011	Dollars	Percent
Subscription and support	$2.126.234	$1.551.145	$575.089	37%
Professional services and other	140.305	105.994	34.311	32%
Total revenues	$2.266.539	$1.657.139	$609.400	37%

Figure 6.2. Salesforce.com revenue growth from 2010-11

| (In thousands) | Fiscal Year Ended January 31 | | Variance | |
	2013	2012	Dollars	Percent
Subscription and support	$2.868.808	$2.126.234	$742.574	35%
Professional services and other	181.387	140.305	41.082	29%
Total revenues	$3.050.195	$2.266.539	$783.656	35%

Figure 6.3. Salesforce.com revenue growth from 2011-12

demand for services from an increased number of customers."[6] Thus the narrative from management is that strong and steady growth is coming from new subscribers, increased satisfaction, and penetration from the existing customer base.

Yet by reading the footnotes, a researcher would see in footnote 1 that the company decided in 2011 to change its revenue recognition policy so that "objective and reliable evidence of fair value of the deliverables to be delivered is no longer required."[7] This is a critical and disturbing piece of news; the company is explaining that the method of calculating revenue in 2013 was a different and more aggressive one than in 2012, based on evidence that was not "objective and reliable."

If an organization cannot find a sound underpinning for the numbers it reports, how might a researcher have any faith that the numbers truly depict financial well-being? The Salesforce.com footnotes relay a second narrative: management is becoming more aggressive in its revenue recognition without any evidence or clear underpinnings for the change.

Already from looking only at AREA's Absolute information, the careful researcher would have discerned a different and competing thesis from the company's perspective itself *about the same set of numbers.*

So how fast are the company's revenues growing and why? It is unclear. This kind of dissonance between thesis statements might make the researcher suspect management's credibility and undercut the numbers that it provides.

Understanding that the same data may have multiple narratives is a critical part of the success of the AREA Method. It guides you through a logical progression so that you may ferret out important problems in an organization's story about its current state and its future prospects.

The Cheetah Sheet below recaps the above discussion of dissonance between data and narratives from the perspective of your Absolute target.

CHEETAH SHEET 15
Absolute: A Last Look

1. Why might the target of your research tell its own story differently in different arenas—for example, website vs. press releases?
2. What incentives might it have to represent itself in different ways to different audiences?
3. Where can you look to investigate the discrepancies that you've identified?

The answers to all of the above questions will come in the rest of your AREA research, specifically in the Relative and Exploration chapters. You may be tempted, as you work through your Absolute research, to jump the gun and start looking at other, secondary sources. Don't! By doing the Absolute research first and thoroughly, you keep your perspectives separate, which will better enable you to assess them dispassionately.

One caveat: doing Absolute research thoroughly doesn't always mean answering every question on every Cheetah Sheet. Remember that your hunt should be flexible and guided by your Critical Concepts, your time, and your resources. By completing a thoughtful Absolute investigation, you are unearthing the foundation of your research process. Your later research will help you determine if that foundation is solid or porous. But until you've unearthed the foundation, you can't begin to judge its quality.

Chapter Seven

AREA = R: Relative

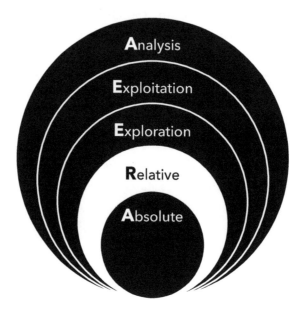

Creativity requires input, and that's what research is.
You're gathering material with which to build.
—Gene Luen Yang

There's a wonderful passage in the classic children's book *Alice in Wonderland* that exemplifies the importance of a focused decision-making process. Young Alice approaches the Cheshire Cat and asks,

"Would you tell me, please, which way I ought to go from here?"
"That depends a good deal on where you want to get to," said the Cat.
"I don't much care where," said Alice.
"Then it doesn't matter which way you go," said the Cat.
"So long as I get somewhere," Alice added as an explanation.
"Oh, you're sure to do that," said the Cat, "if only you walk long enough."

When conducting research there are so many potential sources of information and options for analysis that it is imperative to keep in mind "where you want to get to." Needless to say, time management is a critical component of doing the job well—and of the AREA Method.

The thesis statements you developed in your Absolute research are the signposts that point you toward effective Relative research. You will use them to provide a check on the Relative theses you will now create.

In the Relative phase we get a different perspective. Relative sources are sources that are connected—related—to your research target, but are outside of the target itself. These external sources offer a filtered view of your target's story and offer opinions and facts that serve to vet and supplement the Absolute phase. They may either confirm information you have gleaned during your Absolute research or expose a disconnect between your Absolute perspective and the perspective of the Relative world. Pay special attention to the debates or conflicts between these different stakeholders—these can guide your work and impact your understanding of your Critical Concepts.

The "R" category of research includes:

1. A business and industry analysis and map of your research target's competitive landscape
2. A literature review to provide an understanding of how the media and industry experts portray your organization and its salient issues

For public company research, the category also includes:

1. A review of the company's conference and earnings call transcripts, including questions from analysts and major and potential shareholders
2. A look at the company's analyst and research community
3. A look at your company's shareholder base

As you explore these facets, you will come across the names of many people who have information about your research target. They will include not only people quoted in news articles, but also the reporters who wrote the stories, investors who've asked questions on earnings' calls, research firms, shareholders, and more. Guided by Cheetah Sheet 16 on the next page, compile a list of potential sources in your AREA journal. This is a preparation for the Exploration phase of the AREA Method, where you will learn to conduct in-depth interviews and to test out some of the theses that you've crafted.

Once you've done this spadework for later Exploration, it's time to turn your full attention to the Relative phase. Begin with a business and industry map.

CHEETAH SHEET 16

Relative: Planning Ahead for Exploration

1. Record the names and contact information for each potential source.
2. Write down where you found the source's name and in what context.
3. Note how you think this person may help you understand what you've identified to be your Critical Concepts.

Relative: Mapping Your Target's Business and Industry

Now you are ready to begin your business and industry analysis and construct your map. The map will put your research target in context and help you to identify critical issues in evaluating the target's competitive position. You've already investigated your target in the previous chapter, but how does your target sit in its ecosystem? What are its competitive strengths and weaknesses? What are the important issues in the ecosystem? When you do this analysis you want to understand if there are competitors who have the potential to impact the profitability of your target and how it delivers its good or services.

For example, if you are considering working for a charity that fights hunger you may want to understand the difference between Meals on Wheels and City Harvest. How does each nonprofit do its work, for what population, at what scale, why, and with what goal? How does it evaluate its success?

Often debates will exist about the quality of an organization's business model, its competitive position, and the sustainability of those factors. Through the analysis map you can begin to identify those issues as well. The question of how management allocates capital is critical: how does it divide up the entity's financial and other resources among its people, processes, and projects?

I suggest defining the industry along geographic and/or product lines. For example, if you are researching a hospital, you would most likely want to compare it to other hospitals in the target's geographic area. That being said, if you need a specialized surgery, you may want to construct a map that looks at the top hospitals performing that procedure nationwide. You may also want to consider how the organization supplies its goods or services. For example, does the hospital you are researching draw service providers only from the local area or are they able to attract nationally recognized talent?

Every industry, including hospitals, has an industry group. These organizations often have a research arm that provides reports and useful statistics about their products and services. There are also independent research organizations that provide data by industry, such as IBIS World, Gartner Group, and others.

CHEETAH SHEET 17
Relative: Industry Mapping

1. Who are the top players in each market where your target competes?
2. What does their market share look like now? Over time?
3. What drives margins in the industry? Look at the industry's history and growth rates as well as the history and growth rates of key competitors. What's happened to margins and profitability?
4. Which organizations are growing the fastest? Who are the laggards?
5. Is one competitor taking market share or exposed to a faster growing segment?
6. How do the target's returns on capital compare to competitors? If there are differences, why? Are they driven by competitive structure or managerial ability?
7. Have any competitor companies been especially acquisitive? If so, have the acquisitions been effective or ineffective? Were they performed to create value, or just to grow the company?
8. Who is the low cost competitor? Who has pricing power? What is the pricing and volume history?
9. How quickly is the industry changing and due to what factors? Are the changes being embraced or are defenses being built? Is there any proprietary technology or privileged access to resources?
10. Can you identify why customers stick with, or switch away from, competitors? Can you identify threats that might be lurking for substitution or change in the industry?
11. Do competitor organizations recognize cost and revenues differently than your research target? Why?
12. Are there regulatory, legal, or patent issues that you need to be aware of?

Two things to keep in mind:

1. It's a competitive advantage if a company has a high and stable market share and/or can generate returns in excess of its cost of capital over time.
2. Differentiation, however, may not be a sustainable competitive advantage.

Competitive advantage is a complicated issue. For example, products that are fads (think of Crocs shoes or Beanie Babies) may become hot items that enable their parent company to earn excess returns consistently until cheap competition comes in or the fad ends, or they may be the springboard upon which the parent company launches itself to wider success and profitability. At the core, a competitive advantage should manifest itself in the ability to consistently generate superior margins relative to its market rivals. However, whether a company is able to do that in the future can be divorced from whether or not it has been able to do so in the past. There are companies with emerging competitive advantages that have to invest ahead of profits and don't show excess returns presently, but may in the future—such as Salesforce.

Your industry map should provide you with an assessment of what your target offers (e.g., products and services), when it offers it (timing, business cycles, etc.), where the entity makes those offers (e.g., markets and segments), and at what price (its competitive plan.) You want to put your target in context because it is not only shaped by its actions, but by the environment around it. Think of a world-class violinist playing with a mediocre orchestra: by placing your target in a map you can see the whole symphony.

Matthew thought from his Absolute work that Delta might be a world-class violinist, but the industry map exercise revealed that it perhaps was playing third fiddle to some upstart airlines. He developed several different industry maps. He'd already learned that air traffic revenues had been growing steadily over the past ten years, increasing from $294 billion to $557 billion—a 6.6 percent compound annual growth rate. However, as figures 7.1 and 7.2 show, this growth had not been spread evenly across all carriers. Over the previous three years, the ultra-low-cost and discount carriers' revenues had been growing much more robustly than revenues for the Big Three. American's and United's revenues had actually decreased in the previous year, while Delta's revenues increased by only 0.8 percent.

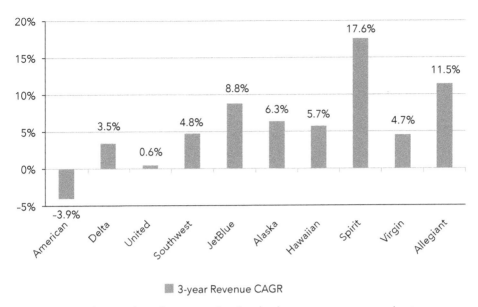

Figure 7.1. Matthew's Delta industry map showing the three-year revenue growth rate

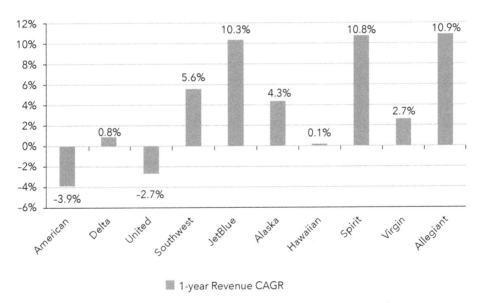

Figure 7.2. Matthew's Delta industry map showing the one-year revenue growth rate

Patricia noticed, during her industry-mapping exercise, that Sprint's margins were roughly half of its competitors' margins. In digging into why this discrepancy existed, she figured out that Sprint operated two networks, a result of the Nextel acquisition done years before, while their competitors operated just one.

This realization, derived from industry mapping, led Patricia to a key insight and a new Critical Concept: Sprint's ability to integrate its network with Nextel's and realize cost savings by transitioning to just one network would determine Sprint's future profitability.

Of course, in researching how Sprint's CEO Dan Hesse attacked cost cuts, Patricia would also be learning more about Hesse as a capital allocator. Was he someone who could demonstrate that he was increasing Sprint's value?

Patricia also read Federal Communications Commission (FCC) publications and business descriptions of competitors in their SEC filings and investor materials. She gathered statistics on the industry generally and Sprint's competitors specifically and mapped out the broader wireless industry including tower owners, handset manufacturers, equipment providers, and landline telecom companies.

She noted that although Apple's popular cell phones were then exclusive to AT&T and Verizon, most of the technology and equipment resided at third party providers, so there was a potential for the phones to become available to Sprint. She also saw that Verizon and AT&T controlled more spectrum (the electromagnetic radio frequencies that carry cellular telephone calls) than Sprint; however, not on a per-subscriber basis.

Verizon and AT&T had more than twice as many subscribers as Sprint and were adding subscribers, while Sprint and smaller players continued to lose subscribers. Additionally, Verizon and AT&T spent more than four times as much annually on capital expenditures as Sprint did. With Verizon and AT&T growing more quickly, earning higher margins, and spending more on capital expenditures, would scale be an insurmountable disadvantage for Sprint?

Once you've completed your AREA target's business and industry review, take a Cheetah Pause and write out a thesis statement for your map's narrative. Record it in your AREA journal and compare it to what you learned about your target in the Absolute phase of your research.

Patricia's industry map, written as a narrative, is available in the appendix.

She wrote the following thesis statement:

Sprint potentially has the opportunity to expand margins meaningfully as it combines its two networks and achieves cost savings by eliminating redundancies, but also appears to face stiff competition from larger competitors who may have competitive advantages due to economies of scale.

This thesis shows a nice progression in Patricia's research and thinking. When she conducted her research from Sprint's perspective—her Absolute work—Sprint touted that it was adding new subscribers. It was foregrounding growth.

Yet in her Relative research, Patricia's industry map told a different story: competitors were larger and more efficient; they had a single network while Sprint had two because of the Nextel merger. What she realized was that both the Absolute and Relative perspectives had some truth. Writing out her thesis statements captured the findings and highlighted a disconnect between them. They recorded her thinking and helped her focus her AREA process on what to explore moving forward—and they allow us, even years later, to have an audit trail of her research.

Based upon her Critical Concept from the Absolute phase—that the underlying business of signing up new subscribers was improving—Patricia's thesis statement gave her a clear direction for where to do more research. The industry map built upon the initial thesis by putting the potential for improvement into a broader context, showing that Sprint had an uphill battle facing larger competitors. Patricia's next logical research step: delve into whether Sprint's small size was a competitive advantage or liability as it integrated the two networks.

Be aware that, like Patricia's, your industry map may also reveal a disconnect from, or contradiction of, the research findings from the Absolute phase. It may hold a mirror up to what management has said in its SEC filings, or show that the business is different than those of competitors'.

For example, after the 2008 financial crisis, my student Brad, in my Advanced Investment Research class, researched Assured Guaranty, a company that provides financial guaranties (or bond insurance) on principal and interest payments of municipal debt and structured products. It was the only bond insurer that had survived the financial crisis, in part due to its inferior credit rating: it had not achieved the coveted triple A rating that its key competitors, AMBAC, MBIA, and Federal Guarantee Insurance Corporation, had, so it did not suffer the same impact from a downgrade. In researching Assured Guaranty, Brad developed an industry map that seemed to show that the company might well have monopoly status.[1]

Typically you would expect that a company with monopoly status would take advantage of the relatively limited competition to earn outsized

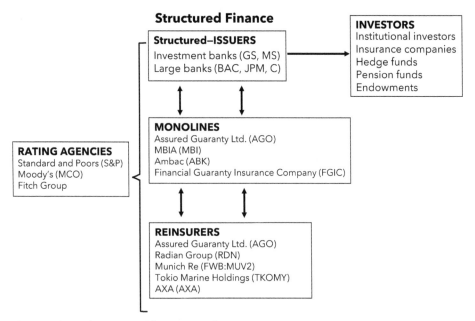

Figure 7.3. Brad's structured finance map for Assured Guaranty

returns on capital, but during the "A" phase of investigation, Brad discovered that Assured Guaranty did not have high returns on capital. When his findings in the "R" phase of research didn't match what he'd learned in the "A" phase, Brad honed in on a Critical Concept: Assured Guaranty's competitive position. He realized that he would need to locate and speak to sources in his Exploration phase who could explain this apparent discrepancy.

Literature Review

Now that you have an understanding of where your target sits in its ecosystem, you want to get a sense of how it's viewed by these entities and how it's portrayed and understood by the media. To do that, conduct a literature review. A literature review is a study of the published material about a particular subject. It's valuable because it gives you a wider lens on your research target and enables you to not only gather new information but also put older information in context.

As with your Absolute research, you may be tempted to begin your Relative research with an Internet news search. But, again, typing a search phrase into Google gives you all perspectives at once and in the order that *other* people have found valuable. It prevents you from being able to determine incentives and motivations of sources individually. That's why AREA isolates research by perspectives. Incentives matter and drive actions.

Additionally, there are other sources of information beyond Google that may be key to your understanding of your research target. What I outline in Cheetah Sheet 18 is a series of databases and other specialized sources of information that may better address your research needs than an open-ended Internet search. This allows you to home in on the literature that will best serve your Critical Concepts.

The list below is extensive and detailed to show the breadth of possible information sources. Choose ones best suited for your research decision.

CHEETAH SHEET 18
Relative: Literature Review Sources and Search Techniques

1. Set up Google alerts or filters for your target and competitors.
2. Consider mega search engines, like Google Scholar, which can search across many databases, regardless of language.
3. Search government websites for reports and statistics, especially for any highly regulated industry:
   a. Food and Drug Administration
   b. Environmental Protection Agency
   c. Comptroller of the Currency
   d. Regional Federal Reserve Banks
   e. Department of Energy
4. Check Pacer and other legal search databases like Westlaw and LexisNexis
5. Investigate industry trade organizations and publications. Include a search for industry conference websites to see what topics the target's industry is discussing. Assess who is being asked to speak at industry conferences and what organizations they work for to understand leaders in the field.

6. Look at competitor public filings and consider homing in on those organizations' management and operating structure. You can do this for segment data as well.

7. Consider answer services such as Quora and WikiAnswers, where, for a small fee, you may post questions and the site's researchers get you answers.

8. Look for academic journals.

9. Search for books about your target and its industry and check the reference section at the end of the books for footnote sources and citations.

10. Look for market data providers for your industry, such as groups that track retail sales or supermarket data.

11. Explore background check services like Accurint that collect public records and help detect fraud, verify identities, and more. These websites compile and integrate property records, credit bureau reports, legal filings, arrest records, fire arms licenses, boat licenses, phone numbers, etc. from state and local court houses, and more.

12. Explore investment and research sharing websites and message boards like SumZero or Value Investor's Club

13. Check online complaint sites such as the Ripoff Report and the Better Business Bureau

14. Visit major business libraries such as the New York Public Library's Business Library website (and physical location). Set up news feeds for your company and its competitors. Take advantage of librarians–they are online detectives.

15. Consider whether you might benefit from a Freedom of Information Act Filing (FOIA), which details specifics of government doings such as contracts, minutes from meetings, ownership structure and more. You can also find out who else might have filed FOIAs and that would clue you in to what other parties have a keen interest in your target.

As you gather articles and begin to read them, remember to continue building the list of sources that you will want to draw from for your Exploration work. This is the list that you began at the beginning of this chapter in Cheetah Sheet 16 (Relative: Planning Ahead for Exploration).

In my classes I ask my students to summarize each article in addition to tracking the sources. Matthew's literature review turned up an article about the Justice Department's antitrust case against United for attempting to purchase twenty-four takeoff and landing slots from Delta at Newark Airport. He noted that the article demonstrated again, like the white paper he found during his Absolute research, that governments play an active role in the airline industry. Even in the United States, the industry was not seen as purely a private enterprise; airlines were seen as private companies providing a public service.

The white paper had made it seem like only foreign governments were unfairly intruding and manipulating in what should be a free market. The Justice Department article and suit changed Matthew's perception. US airlines also operated in a regulated environment with government oversight. How much of Delta's destiny was its own if it could not add and sell off assets as it wanted?[2]

CHEETAH SHEET 19
Relative: Literature Review Analysis

1. What is the central point of the article? What action is the writer advocating? Why? Does it make sense?
2. Where was the article published? What kind of publication did it appear in? What is the perspective of this publication? Is it an industry magazine, tabloid, investment publication, general interest media outlet, etc.?
3. Who wrote it? What seems to be the writer's incentive? What other articles has she written and with what perspective? Do you find evidence of bias? Check word choice and tone. Is more than one view presented?
4. Does the article or report have evidence to back its claims? Do the opinions, facts, or anecdotes seem credible? How can you tell? If the article is about a publicly traded company, do these details seem relevant to share price performance?
5. How do these outside perspectives change or color your interpretation of your research target's story and your own Critical Concepts?

A literature review helps you understand how the outside world perceives your target and what issues other participants are focused on. Understanding what others are focused on can guide you to the key debates or issues impacting your target's prospects.

As you conduct your literature review, keep a bibliography of the sources of information you review, considering both the author and details from each source as you make notes. As you read widely but selectively in your topic area consider the themes or issues that connect your sources together. What seems believable and what does not?

 CHEETAH SHEET 20
Relative: Literature Review Summary

1. What does the broader world think of your target?
2. What kinds of publications write about your target? Is the organization's news mostly relegated to industry magazines or does it appear in general news outlets, or is your target tabloid fodder for having a flamboyant leader? How current is the news?
3. What topics and issues do the articles focus on?
4. How much time does management seem to be spending reacting to or participating in PR compared to operating its business?
5. If there seems to be consensus among sources do you think it's valid based upon your Absolute work?
6. Does the literature review present conflicting views or general agreement about the opportunities and challenges?
7. Are events and key people described similarly or differently across the literature?
8. What might be missing from the news stories?

The literature review summary not only enables you to recap the important information from a particular source, it also forces you to synthesize the information. It might open up new interpretations of old material, combine new material with old interpretations, or trace the intellectual progression of your target's field, including major debates. The goal: For you to uncover the target's story as it is understood by the media and other news sources and then to *pause*, evaluate, and craft a thesis statement that addresses your literature review findings.

CHEETAH SHEET 21
Relative: Synthesizing Your Literature Review

1. What are the main points from your Literature Review?
2. How does the media perception of your target differ from how your company presents itself?
   a. If the media perception is different from your company's perspective, how credible is the media's depiction of your target?
3. If you are researching a publicly traded company, how does any disagreement between media sources impact your understanding of your target's investment prospects?

In addition to the article about the antitrust case, Matthew came across a news story about a Delta flight that had gone awry. Angry passengers had spent more than thirty hours on what should have been a four-hour flight when weather twice diverted the route from the Dominican Republic to New York City and the plane was forced to land in Manchester, New Hampshire. Delta did all it could to ensure passenger safety and comfort, including transporting customs agents from Portland, Maine, to Manchester, but the passengers' experience was still a negative one. Some fell ill and required oxygen. Despite Delta's best efforts, the airline suffered reputational harm. Matthew realized that "customer satisfaction is fleeting—people are much more likely to complain about a particularly bad experience rather than celebrate an on-time arrival. Bad flights happen infrequently (particularly for Delta, which has an operational edge over its US competitors) but receive widespread press coverage."

In his Absolute research, Matthew had read about Delta's high passenger ratings. But the high ratings didn't make the airline immune from criticism. Not every negative story is a red flag, but here in what Matthew's Relative research turned up, it seemed that Delta was buffeted by forces it could not control. Passenger mile yields were falling as revenues were squeezed by foreign state-supported airlines. Fuel prices, which were at historically low levels, masked some of this pressure, but prices wouldn't stay low forever. While the company wanted to control price per average seat mile, it was also about to embark on a new set of labor negotiations that would likely demand higher wages.[3]

Matthew's thesis statement from his literature review analysis read,

> *Delta operates in a highly competitive environment and is subject to all sorts of regulations, but doesn't get any upside from the government the way foreign state-owned airlines do. Delta can't control the weather and it isn't operating in a true free market. I am less confident of Delta's investment prospects after having done the literature review.*

Earnings Calls

If you are researching a publicly traded company you'll want to listen in on its earnings calls to learn about how management presents its company and its prospects publicly when it is speaking to the investment community. In your Absolute research you developed your own internal compass about the company and its numbers, and in your Relative research you've been placing that target into its ecosystem. As a result, you have walked in the target's footsteps to unearth its incentives and motives and then assessed its competitive position through your Relative work thus far. An earnings call represents both the Absolute position *and* the Relative position.

Earnings calls, unlike press releases, are not entirely controlled by the company. Calls, while initiated and planned by the company, represent a conversation between the company (the Absolute perspective) and the Relative people who care about it—sell-side analysts, shareholders such as hedge and mutual funds, and financial journalists. The company may try to control the conversation but it is expected to address its financial picture, the broader landscape, and its strategy to compete in that environment. As a result, as participants on the call ask probing questions, nuances about the company's future performance are often revealed.

Companies generally open their conference calls to all investors, and some even provide them as free audio broadcasts over the Internet.

However, open does not necessarily mean transparent. Calls are scripted and managed. In fact, in a series of recent surveys on earnings call practices by the National Investor Relations Institute (NIRI), respondents reported that screening call participants during earnings calls is common practice. Three quarters of respondents admitted using screening tactics for such varied reasons as avoiding surprising questions, prioritizing particular callers over others, ensuring that a wider variety of analysts are given an opportunity to ask questions over the course of a year, restricting media members and employees from asking questions during a call, and meeting time constraints. Half of respondents had deleted a participant from the Q&A queue, for reasons including that the caller was unknown to the company, that the caller was not on the approved list to ask questions, that the caller was a member of the media, or because of time constraints.

NIRI also found that that most companies prepare for earnings calls, with about 30 percent beginning as far as four weeks in advance of the call. Twenty-two percent of respondents reported that during this preparatory period prior to the earnings call, they ask Wall Street analysts which topics they would like the company to address during the call. Increasingly, companies are also prerecording their financial remarks, up 88 percent in the past five years to 15 percent of study respondents. The bottom line is that companies are becoming far more proactive in controlling their financial messages and the impact is that the numbers are embedded more clearly in a sculpted narrative. For researchers there is great benefit in having done your own investigative work to know how to listen to management's presentations.

Another way companies control the messaging of their earnings calls is to limit the availability of the audio files and transcripts. While many companies do archive calls on their website, there is no SEC requirement that companies make these calls and other related materials available, and they may only be available for a short period of time. Only about half of companies surveyed by NIRI report that they archive earnings material for more than a year. If your research target lacks an earnings call archive, consider whether it could be a red flag.[4]

The majority of companies do provide their earnings calls in some format on their website, so that's the natural first place to look. Other places to look for earnings calls are at independent research firms such as Morningstar or Seeking Alpha, which offer archived earnings call transcripts.

The earnings call may help you understand the tone of the company and its management and provide clues hidden beneath the surface of its numbers. Listen to the facts, but just as carefully listen for other signals about the company's business, especially as management discusses the outlook for its next quarter and areas of potential growth and expansion. You will need to listen to a few earnings calls to get a sense of how they go and how management behaves, and to consider the extent of its transparency and openness.

CHEETAH SHEET 22
Relative: Earnings Calls

1. Is management consistent across calls in how it presents the company's strategy and metrics? Repeated changes in either might be a sign of a management that is masking challenges in its business or "drawing the bulls-eye around the arrow."
2. Pay attention to the goals management sets. Does it follow through on them? Is management aware of the challenges facing its business?
3. Consider language and tone. Are there specific quotes that seem to stand out? Does management seem pessimistic or self-promotional? Do they try to deflect questions, or are there sudden surges of emotion such as anger or frustration?

One example of a notable earnings call comes from Proctor & Gamble's August 2013 conference call, led by the company's CEO, A.G. Lafley. Lafley had been CEO for nine years, retired, and then reclaimed the helm of the consumer products giant just two months prior to the call. On the call Lafley said, "I don't think this institution or company is unique. As you get bigger and broader, you have to work a little harder to be a little more choiceful and focused and to set really clear priorities. We're just going to be more focused and we're going to begin where we ought to begin with the consumer as the boss."

The key takeaway here: the CEO, who is often the company's chief salesperson, was saying that P&G was not unique, a remarkable thing for a CEO to say. By discussing the challenges of P&G's size, he seemed to be attempting to moderate expectations. Also note that he was not talking about action, he was saying the company would be an observer. He described following the consumer's lead without discussing innovation, new products, or specific ways to improve P&G's outlook going forward. His words were not an endorsement for P&G's shares, suggesting instead that P&G would have to work hard to generate growth and an attractive return for shareholders. This 2012 call turned out to be a harbinger for shareholder unhappiness that led to a 2017 proxy fight, which P&G very narrowly won (more on this when we discuss activist shareholders).

Matthew's experience listening to Delta management showcased a confident and financially focused management team. Even before he began reviewing the calls, Matthew was impressed by the company's apparent transparency: calls were archived and available on their website going back *six years*.

Matthew reviewed five of the most recent earnings calls, and found that management consistently spotlighted a few key metrics, including pre-tax profit and earnings per share, operating margins, the company's performance relative to S&P industrials, and present and future fuel costs. In all of the calls, Delta's management appeared both focused and optimistic. Was the optimism warranted? While the content focused increasingly on competitive pressures, the tone of the calls remained professional rather than defensive, and "consistently confident regarding the direction of the business and the operational advantages that Delta had over its U.S. competitors."

Matthew was also struck by management's vocal appreciation of the company's employees: he observed that "management consistently thanks Delta employees, calling them the best employees in the industry. This happens multiple times in each call."

Matthew's thesis from the earnings calls read,

Despite the unpredictable and uncontrollable forces buffeting the airline, Delta's management projects an air of professionalism and confidence in their operational capabilities.

He noted that the calls were carefully and adeptly piloted; much of the turbulence that he'd read about in his earlier Relative work wasn't apparent on the earnings call flight-path.

Beyond management's presentation, the question-and-answer part of the call after the company has reported its news often provides the most insight into what is going on. Write down the names and affiliation of the questioners, look up their companies, and understand why they might be in the stock and on the call. This will provide clues about the company's shareholder base and how these investors see the company's share price potential in the near future. Remember that management selects whom they want to take questions from on the call.

CHEETAH SHEET 23
Relative: Earnings Call Q & A

1. How many people are queued up to ask questions? This gets at the level of interest in talking to management.
2. What types of people are on the call?
   a. Analysts: are they sell-side research only? Or are they from independent research companies? Sell-side analysts are more likely to ask softball questions because they need to have access to management.
   b. Investors: note that while most investors on a call are likely to be shareholders, they don't have to be. Consider the orientation or discipline of the investment firms on the call. Are they mostly growth funds, event-driven firms, or could they be short-sellers? The investment discipline can give you a clue to where these professional investors think the stock may go next. For example a growth fund expects accelerating growth while a value fund thinks that the share price is under-appreciated.
   c. Reporters: are they from major papers, niche industry magazines, or online sites?
3. What kind of questions are being asked? Do they focus on key areas of concern? What kinds of issues and clarification are asked about? These questions are often more important than management answers since they indicate issues that may drive the stock price.
4. Does management seem to know a lot of the callers? What does the rapport seem like?

5. How prepared is management to answer the questions? How transparent does management seem? Are they direct and factual or evasive and promotional? Are their answers specific or general? How do they respond to tough questions? Do they answer them earnestly or do they duck the question?

6. What is the tone of the call? Does your target's management sound upbeat or concerned about the business? Friendly or defensive?

7. In totality, from the calls you've listened to, how does the tone, content, and so on compare from call to call?

   a. Is one call more optimistic than others, or vice-versa?

   b. Are investor concerns similar or different across calls?

   c. Is management making progress in addressing investor/analyst concerns?

   d. Does the language management uses to describe its prospects provide clues as to the future of its business?

Just as Matthew had found Delta management in control of its financial conversation in the scripted part of the calls, when it came to Q&A, the company not only answered questions for investment professionals, it also set aside part of the call to take questions from a wide variety of press—relatively unusual in earnings call.

Not all earnings calls go as smoothly as Delta's appeared to. For example, on Salesforce.com's Q3 2013 Earnings Call, Marc Benioff, the CEO of Salesforce.com, received a tough question from the Morgan Stanley analyst Adam Holt about the company's performance in Europe. Holt asked, "You saw acceleration in Europe in a period where a lot of people are seeing deceleration in Europe. Could you drill down on what geographies, in particular split out, if any, products and really just give us more color on why your business seems to be improving there against what's obviously a very difficult backdrop?"

Benioff responded, "We certainly have a lot to be grateful [for] here at Salesforce and it's because of our relationships with all of you. So, thank you for everything that you do for us every single day and we can't say that enough at Salesforce. I think that when it comes to Europe, of course, Europe has been in a financial crisis this entire year, and you've seen us deliver really outstanding performance in Europe. And that is really based on an investment gambit that we had been making now in Europe for more than a decade."[5]

Here management first delayed answering a tough question and then provided a vague, nonspecific explanation for why the company's business accelerated in a region where others struggled, offering only that an "investment gambit" paid off without any insight into how the company's financial results were achieved and whether there is any reason to believe that the current strong results would continue.

Of course, this example, as all examples in this text, is not the complete story; it is a snapshot to illustrate the value of certain parts of the research process.

As you conclude the review of your target's calls, take a Cheetah Pause and write out a thesis statement that sums up your findings from this portion of your Relative research and again compare it against the other thesis statements that you've crafted.

Patricia reviewed Sprint's earnings calls going back four years. She noted that in the calls, Sprint's CEO consistently focused on efforts to improve customer service and reduce what the industry refers to as churn, or the percentage of subscribers who discontinue their service subscription in a given time period. She noted that the CEO repeated these goals and their progress at the top of each call.

The company had made consistent progress in both of these areas over the course of the previous four years: Sprint reduced problems per 100 calls from seventeen to less than twelve. It also improved the customer care rating assigned to it by market research company J. D. Power from 650 to 730. In line with this improvement, Sprint reduced churn from 2.5 to 1.8 percent. Patricia's thesis statement about Sprint's earnings calls read,

Sprint management earnings calls have shown consistent focus on operating goals along with a track record of execution that is increasing my confidence that management will follow through on continuing to improve the core business by integrating the two networks to boost profitability.

Analyst Community

In my class at Columbia Business School, I discourage students from using any research coverage by Wall Street analysts during the semester. I do this so students can develop their own internal compass and don't get into the habit of anchoring their own opinion to the opinion of the broader research community. However, many analysts and investigators read Wall Street research, and if you are investigating a publicly traded company, that may well be part of your research. Understanding the incentives and motives of the target's universe of analysts and its relationship with Wall Street will help you to use that research effectively.

CHEETAH SHEET 24

Relative: Analyst Research Reports

1. How large is your target's universe of analysts?
2. What kinds of firms follow the target? Major financial services firms? Independent or boutique research firms? Firms with an angle, such as those focused on short-only or bearish company reports?
3. Do any of the firms following the target have banking or other relationships with the target?
4. Are the analysts largely in agreement with one another or not?

Analysts can have a large impact on how Wall Street perceives a stock. They not only provide information but also set external benchmarks for management by forecasting earnings and making recommendations. A recent article in the *Journal of Financial Economics* found that when firms are under the magnifying glasses of financial analysts, managers can find themselves under pressure to put more resources toward routine tasks that offer quick and certain returns, potentially sacrificing longer-term goals and innovation.[6]

The study also showed the inverse: when companies lose analysts due to exogenous shocks, such as mergers between Wall Street firms, their innovations and outcomes improve. Keeping in mind that smaller, innovative companies may have smaller followings in part because they may have fewer, or less liquid, shares outstanding, the authors of the study say that the main takeaway is that companies with little coverage by analysts tend to generate more patents than comparable well-followed firms; these companies also file more important or innovative patents than their better-covered competitors.

It is important to be aware that analysts' ratings today do not have clear, standardized meanings, and analysts may have conflicts of interest that distort their opinions. Regarding ratings, one firm may have "Buy" as its highest rating, while another might use the same word to mean that the analyst likes the company but not as much as stocks it rates "Strong Buy."

Likewise, one firm's "Underperform" might mean that it expects a stock to appreciate 10 percent slower than the overall market over an eighteen-month period. For another firm, the same term "Underperform" might mean that the firm expects the stock to drop 5 percent within a twelve-month period.

Also, remember that analysts may have an incentive to curry favor with management to gain access to the company and its personnel, or they may feel pressure to help their employer gain underwriting and other commission business. Moreover, some analysts are employed by institutions with a financial stake in their recommendations. Understanding the relationship between management and Wall Street can alter your interpretation of Wall Street communication in a valuable way.

For example, one guest lecturer in my class recalled noticing that analysts on Enron's calls would address members of management by their first names and ask for input for their Excel models directly. The guest lecturer wondered about such a cozy relationship between Wall Street and Enron. His concerns were borne out in Bethany McLean's book *Smartest Guys in the Room*. McLean details a situation where Merrill Lynch's research analyst gave Enron's shares an unfavorable rating. Enron was such an important client to Merrill Lynch that when it threatened to leave over the analyst's unfavorable rating, Merrill Lynch fired the analyst.

Thus it's important to understand what business your company is doing with Wall Street in general. Is it a frequent issuer of new shares or debt? Does it do a lot of investment banking business? Companies that are active Wall Street clients may generate more optimistic research outlooks since firms may not want to offend or disrupt future business with the company.

To learn about different analysts' track records, you can either follow their recommendations over time or refer to rankings that are found in certain investor-oriented magazines, newsletters, and Internet websites such as Institutional Investor Magazine, Zacks Investment Research, or TipRanks, which has a free tool that rates sell-side analysts based upon their past recommendations.

Pause at the end of this analyst research phase: what is the narrative from the analyst community? Write out the thesis statement that best sums it up.

When I presented the case study on Salesforce.com to my class, the analyst community covering Salesforce.com was largely favorable, or bullish, on the company's growth prospects and tended not to address some of the concerning accounting issues discussed in the previous chapter. Analysts focused on the company's high rate of sales growth and hot products while touting a visionary management team. The analyst community also accepted metrics provided by management, including adjusted earnings before taxes and cash flow, which add back expenses like stock-based compensation that are part of GAAP accounting.

Yet since Salesforce.com had little in the way of earnings, the analysts valued it on a forward multiple of revenue, using the company's already rich multiple. Privately, some analysts expressed concern that the enthusiasm around Salesforce.com's growth story might wane at some point. Nonetheless, it appeared that analysts didn't want to be bearish on the stock, perhaps because they might not have wanted to risk their reputation or bonus, so long as the market believed the story. My case study showcased how incentives may influence analyst ratings.

The thesis statement that the class developed from this case study summarized the perspective of the Salesforce.com analyst community:

Analysts remain bullish on Salesforce.com, but much of their bullishness seems to be related to the company's historical performance, such as its sales growth, and the analyst community's willingness to accept the company's unconventional accounting without evidence of independent due diligence.

The thesis statement effectively gets at not only the analyst opinion of the stock but also the rationale behind that view so that the information is in context. Understanding the analysts' perspective better enables you to decide how much weight to give to their opinions as you investigate your Critical Concepts.

Shareholder Base

Next, research your target's shareholder base. Understanding who owns the stock can give you insight into how professional money managers view your target's share price prospects. Different investors have different investment approaches. For example value-oriented funds like to select investments in companies that they consider undervalued or under-appreciated. Growth stock investors select companies that they believe will grow quickly. Event-driven funds are betting that some event—a spin-off of a business unit, a merger, or even being the target of an acquisition—will occur. Investors who run concentrated portfolios—where their funds only own a small handful of large positions—are also good bets to follow. Since they have lower turnover, every position adjustment they make is that much more important to their portfolio. You can gain an analytic edge by understanding the different types of investors and funds that hold your target's shares in large quantities.

Begin by downloading the SEC 13 series filings, which include 13D, 13F and 13G filings. You can find them on the SEC website, sec.gov, or on popular financial websites or programs like FactSet, S&P Capital IQ, or Yahoo! Finance. The different 13 series filings all have a common purpose: to disclose major share ownership. A 13-D must be filed within ten days of a purchase by anyone who buys more than five percent of a company's shares. The form requires the owner to disclose any other person who has voting power or the power to sell the security. 13-F filings are quarterly filings for institutional money managers with over $100 million in assets. Companies required to file SEC Form 13F may include insurance compa-nies, banks, pension funds, investment advisers, and broker-dealers. The 13-G is also filed by anyone who owns more than five percent of a com-pany, but is intended for passive investors and requires less information. The filings not only reveal who owns the shares, but also provide contact information that gives you background information about the owner. If a large stock purchase has taken place, the filing will also show where the money is coming from for the purchase.

Be aware, however, that 13F filings may provide an incomplete pic-ture. The filings aren't required of investors who are shorting the stock, meaning that you will only get half of the story when you read them.[7] In other words, a 13F filing shows only the bullish side of a company's story. In addition, the purchase might also represent only part of an investor's

position—for example, a way to hedge exposure against another investment. This may be especially true for investors who primarily make negative, or bearish, bets on a company's stock. It's less true for typical funds,
which are net-long, and therefore a big chunk of their performance can be
attributed to their stock ownership.

CHEETAH SHEET 25
Relative: Shareholder Base

1. What percentage of the outstanding shares do the major holders own?
2. What investment discipline do they follow? Are the shareholders mostly value-oriented funds, growth funds, event-driven funds, or something else?
3. How long have the major holders been shareholders? Is there evidence that the shareholder base is changing? If so, might that signal that the company is entering a new phase of its business cycle?
4. Is there evidence of shareholder activism?

Be aware that while form 13F shows holdings at the end of each quarter
the SEC publishes the forms on its website several weeks later—around the
middle of the following quarter. Therefore, when an investor doubles his
position in a company in October, you'll be reading about it months later
in mid-February—and by that time, the investor might have already sold
the position. Still, these forms are unbiased and as such are an important
part of the investment research mosaic, especially if the relevant investor
tends to be a long-time holder.

Matthew discovered that the majority of Delta's largest shareholders
were professional investors like mutual funds, plus a few hedge funds
known for investing in large multinational companies. This institutional-heavy ownership structure meant that Delta was already a well-
known, heavily followed company with sufficient float for the largest
money managers in the world. At the time, Delta, which belongs to the
S&P 500, had a market cap of $33.5 billion, and traded close to eight
million shares per day.

Matthew's thesis statement from his shareholder base review read,

> *To a certain extent, the institutional-heavy ownership structure lim-
> its Delta's upside. Since there are so many investment professionals
> covering the name, most of the information that could move the
> stock price meaningfully has already been written about, discussed,
> and analyzed ad nauseam. More importantly, given Delta's sheer
> size, the opportunity for significant upside is more muted. It's much
> more difficult for a company to double in value when it's so large.*

Once you have an understanding of who owns the stock, you'll want
to look for letters that investors attach to the 13F series. Major holders
have the opportunity to attach letters where they may lay out the case for
a company's change in business or strategy. While initially the 13F filings
were meant as a defensive measure for companies, enabling them to see
who owns their shares and providing a warning of a new major holder,
the balance of power has largely shifted to investors, who often use the
filings as a bully pulpit, knowing that the financial media tends to publish
them. This has given activist investors a way to directly reach the public—
think of it as the investment version of Twitter. No one edits or polices
these letters besides the lawyers working for the letter writers.

Some activists think of themselves as "constructivists" and are tact-
ful and guarded in the way they approach management, while others are
more combative.

For example, Dan Loeb, a hedge fund investor and the founder of
Third Point, has used 13F filings to influence company action in a series
of colorful letters that often receive heavy press coverage. One of his classic letters, in 2012, remonstrated the Internet search engine Yahoo. Loeb's
hedge fund had accumulated a 5.8 percent stake in Yahoo and recommended four new directors to the Yahoo board: Jeff Zucker, a former
NBC Universal CEO; Michael Wolf, a former MTV executive; Harry
Wilson, a restructuring expert; and Loeb himself. Wilson, however, was
the only Third Point recommendation that Yahoo agreed to. In response,
Loeb sent a message to Yahoo's then CEO Scott Thompson, criticizing the
board for leaving shareholders out and calling their reasoning for leaving
shareholders off the board of directors "illogical."

In his 13F letter, Loeb wrote, "Am I conflicted to advocate for the
interests of other shareholders because we are owners of 5.8 percent (over
$1 billion) of Yahoo! shares (unlike the non-retiring and proposed board

members who have never purchased a single share of Yahoo! except for subsidized shares issued through option exercises and shares 'paid' by the Company in lieu of fees)? Only in an illogical Alice-in-Wonderland world would a shareholder be deemed to be conflicted from representing the interests of other shareholders because he is, well, a shareholder too. This sentiment further confirms that Yahoo!'s approach to Board representation is 'shareholders not welcome.'"[8]

Bill Ackman, Pershing Square's investment manager, has also actively used 13F filings, although, in contrast to Loeb's fire and brimstone approach, Ackman generally (although not always) tries to take a positive and inclusive tone. In the summer of 2017, Ackman acquired an 8.3 percent ownership stake in the payment processing company ADP. Unhappy with ADP's management, but hesitant to wage a full proxy fight, Ackman asked the company to add three board members, selected by him. Although ADP refused, Ackman continued to try to work with the company to move it in the direction he felt was best. In a September 7, 2017, 13F letter, he wrote, "We left the meeting with the strong impression that we could work together very effectively to build on ADP's strengths to greatly improve the company's competitiveness, profitability, and growth. To that end as we discussed in the meeting, it is our strong preference that we end the proxy contest and come to a resolution on governance. We have proposed an expansion of the board by three seats and the addition of our nominees. This would eliminate the need for us to replace existing directors and we could begin working together immediately."[9]

While both strategies may be effective, they reveal different investment approaches. Ackman's friendlier approach is consistent with an investment style that favors improving high-quality businesses while Loeb's combative approach is consistent with a style that focuses on cleaning up egregious mismanagement of a business with unlocked value. If you come across an activist, try to incorporate their approach into your analysis and consider the impact on your target. What might it mean for management's time and attention, and what might be the cost to the company?

Investor White Papers, Websites, and Letters

There are three more ways that activist investors might be trying to shape public opinion about your target: through white papers, websites, and investor letters.

An investor white paper is different from a company white paper because of the perspective of the writer. While a company white paper is generally used to highlight research, publicize findings related to the company's business and industry, or opine on regulations, an activist investor's paper is used to make an argument that the company needs to do business differently than it has been. It is a way to argue for the investor's vision of change and to present their data for why the vision is compelling.

For example, in early 2017, Nelson Peltz of Trian Partners began buying Proctor & Gamble shares, investing about $3.5 billion and acquiring a 1.5 percent stake in the consumer products giant. Peltz also began working to get a seat on P&G's board, arguing that the company needed to rethink its organizational structure. When he was unsuccessful in his initial bid for a seat, Peltz, through Trian Partners, took his case directly to shareholders by issuing a white paper and creating a website, revitalizepg.com.

In the white paper, Trian detailed how P&G had been underperforming, presented Trian's recommendations for how to regain lost market share, and argued that shareholders needed to elect Peltz to the board because "Trian has worked closely with numerous companies across the consumer landscape and has demonstrated a consistent track record of value creation with numerous corporate and brand turnarounds."[10]

Websites provide another avenue for activist investors to take their message to the public, and they have the benefit of not only hosting investor white papers but also directly guiding shareholders to action through links and other information.

Trian created a website to make the same case as its P&G white paper, writing, "Trian believes strongly in Procter & Gamble's potential, but the Company is facing challenges that have led to disappointing results over the last decade. As one of P&G's largest shareholders, Trian has a keen interest in helping P&G address these challenges. This website summarizes these challenges and explains why adding Nelson Peltz to the Board will help revitalize P&G." In addition to laying out Trian's case, the website provided a link to shareholders that offered directions on voting for board members, as well as telephone numbers that investors could call to get further help casting their vote.

Ultimately, although Peltz lost the proxy battle, P&G appointed him to the board at the end of 2017. The website dedicated to Trian's contest has been taken down.

Investor letters work as similarly persuasive vehicles as they tend to detail what the investor is buying and/or selling, why, and how she views the market and economic environment or other current events. Almost all major investment organizations put out some kind of letter at the end of each quarter and at year end. Although the letters are intended for clients or partners invested in those funds, nowadays the letters are often circulated in the public domain by financial news sites such as Bloomberg News, Value Walk, or Zero Hedge.

For example, in a 2017 second quarter letter from Baron Capital, Ron Baron used the words of the astronaut John Glenn to laud Tesla's Elon Musk. Glenn had once said about being an astronaut, "I felt exactly how you would feel if you were getting ready to launch and knew you were sitting on top of two million parts . . . all built by the lowest cost bidder on a government contract." In contrast, Baron observed, Musk did *not* buy from the lowest bidder. His argument was counterintuitive in the investment world. Musk wouldn't necessarily have the highest margins, Baron contended, but he was offering the high-quality product. If you were researching Tesla, you might want to read Baron's analysis and try to understand his thinking.[11]

CHEETAH SHEET 26

Relative: Activist Investor Communications

1. Who is the activist and what is her track record?
2. What are the information avenues being used to persuade you about a target's prospects?
3. What are the main arguments being made for change?
4. What evidence is presented to support the change being advocated?
5. What is the target's response?
6. How does the target support its response with evidence?

At times, you may come across companies whose shares are primarily owned by small, individual investors. This may offer a challenge to researchers. It may mean that there is less volatility in share price performance. News about the company may have less impact on the company's share price performance because fewer professional investors are paying attention. Not only can this be a good place for an informational and analytic edge, but it can also afford you a behavioral edge in that you may take advantage of news before it is widely understood. At the same time, the downside is that it may take longer for your research to gain public attention and thus to affect share price performance.

After reviewing your company's shareholder base, take a Cheetah Pause to write out a summary sentence summing up what you've learned here.

As with Matthew's research into Delta, Patricia's research also revealed that the majority of Sprint's holders were mutual funds and banks, some of which were index funds and others with a value style bias. She concluded that these holders were unlikely to be active on the corporate governance front. Her thesis statement read,

> *Sprint appears to have a fairly vanilla shareholder base without any big recent changes in its major shareholders. This means the business is unlikely to see much oversight on corporate governance matters or activism. Its shares are unpopular and investors might be overlooking the company.*

This thesis statement takes into account three things: first, that there is not much of interest in its shareholder base; second, that there is little evidence of the stock benefitting from a major shareholder interested in activism; and third, that if Patricia's research determined management was really executing a successful turnaround, there might be good opportunity for share-price appreciation.

Overall, what you've just done in the Relative phase of your AREA research is to challenge or confirm the results of evidence collected in the Absolute phase. You've done this by setting your target in the broader context of its industry's dynamics. Like the cheetah, you've paused in pursuit of your target, crafting thesis statements at each pause to ask yourself, "What are the Critical Concepts, how does this new layer of information further enhance my research, and how may it be tainted by the sources of information?"

Now it's time to get beyond document-based sources and travel into Exploration.

Chapter Eight

AREA = E: Exploration

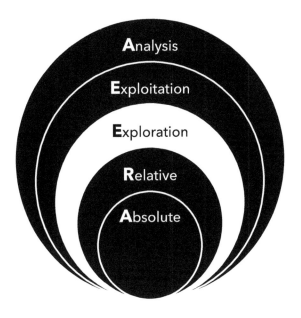

Judge a man by his questions rather than his answers.
—Voltaire

There are actually two "E's" that make up the "E" in AREA: "Exploration" and "Exploitation." One is concerned with breadth of information while the other focuses on depth; one looks for new questions, answers, and understanding, while the other challenges old or accepted certainties. They are what I call the twin engines of creativity.

Each "E" deals with creative ways to upgrade your research beyond the researcher's traditional material by mining the perspective of real people in addition to published sources of material. Exploration and Exploitation are critical components of a quality research process because they direct you to broaden your collection of information and then to carefully deepen your ability to distill what you've collected.

This chapter covers Exploration and the next covers Exploitation. In this chapter, I lay out a strategy and method for acquiring new knowledge through developing sources and interviewing. The Exploitation chapter that follows turns its lens inward on you, the decision-maker, and gives you creative tools to control for some of your own natural mental biases and shortcuts so that you can understand all of the information you've gathered.

Why do you need *more* information? You've gathered data from your target itself and from the world around your target—your target's landscape, industry, competitors, and the press. You need more information because the real, live people who interact with your target—the people who work for, with, or against it, who write about it, or who have bought and sold its products or services—have an important perspective that you can't get on websites or in documents. And, in some cases, it's a faster education: one fifteen-minute conversation where you've asked the right person the right questions might be better than three weeks of reading alone.

This chapter focuses primarily on investigative journalism techniques that I've honed over the years and that will help you do just that—get the right information from the right people by asking the right questions. There are six critical components to getting information from human sources. This chapter teaches you:

- How to identify Good Prospects (the right people) to develop sources that many researchers don't, or can't, find
- How to get valuable information from your sources by preparing Great Questions
- How to develop a call/email pitch
- How to develop an interview guide
- How to conduct targeted interviews so that you feel comfortable interacting with sources, listening to and appraising their answers, and taking notes.
- How to evaluate the quality of the information you've collected so that you can evaluate and flesh out your Critical Concepts

As Voltaire observed 250 years ago, knowledge is born from great questions. Or, to reference another great historical figure, Isaac Newton did not discover gravity because he had the right answers; it's because he asked the right questions.

The goal of this chapter, then, is give you an appreciation for, and some skills to craft, the *right* question for the *right* person so that you may elicit clear, concise, and cogent answers about your Critical Concepts.

Anyone can ask a question, but thoughtful and strategic questions take planning. That's what you'll find below: the plan to get the kind of information that's not available on your research target's website or from Wikipedia, and that hasn't been written about in the *New York Times*. It's the kind of information you can only collect from making a positive connection with another person. That's a hard thing to do—to turn a stranger into a friend in a phone conversation or via email. But it's a great way to gain an edge.

Developing Sources and Interviewing

Before getting to the hows of interviewing, I want to share a story that I think perfectly illustrates both the Exploration process itself *and* why this step is key to a thorough research process.

A few years ago, I wrote an investigative news story, published in *Foreign Policy* magazine and on ProPublica's website, entitled "Can You Fight Poverty With A Five-Star Hotel?" The article reported on the private investing arm of the World Bank, called the International Finance Corporation (IFC). The IFC, like the World Bank itself, is tasked with fighting poverty in part by spurring economic development. As part of my research I investigated how the IFC constructed its system for measuring the efficacy of its investments.

I followed the AREA Method and first read Absolute source material documents from the IFC that explained its system in its own words so that I would not bias myself with outside information. I crafted a thesis statement from the IFC's vantage point, allowing it to speak in its own words.

As part of the process, I read the footnotes of the IFC's Annual Portfolio Review. Footnote 8 said, "DOTS ratings are company—rather than project—based and use proxies (e.g., annual returns on invested capital) rather than the more in-depth evaluation methods (e.g., life-of-project re-estimated financial and economic returns) used at the evaluation stage." In other words, the IFC's measurement system, known as the Development Outcome Tracking System (DOTS), did not measure the performance of the IFC's actual investments. Instead, it tracked and measured the performance of the *whole company* that received the money, such as the Coca-Cola Company or Newmont Mining.[1]

This illuminating piece of evidence that the IFC did not really measure how its investments were performing suggested that the IFC might be potentially misleading itself and the public about its investment performance by reporting whole company data. I began the Relative phase of my AREA Method research knowing that in both my industry map and my literature review I'd be looking for sources whom I could interview to confirm whether I correctly understood the footnote, whether this was in fact the IFC's current practice, and why the IFC would measure its results this way.

Through my Relative research phase I put together a list of potential sources—people meant to benefit from IFC investments or who might live near IFC-related projects, employees at companies that received funds from the IFC, IFC personnel involved in the DOTS department, and former IFC employees, among others. I thought about my call pitch, where I outline what I want to say to introduce myself and my topic of conversation, as well as my list of questions and the order of the questions—my interview guide—so that I might be respectful of my interviewees' time and focus the conversations.

I began calling low-level sources who were not critical to my story's success but who fleshed out the IFC's investment measurement system, coached me in how to listen to the answers about the IFC method of evaluation, and helped me better understand how to converse in the IFC's language of operation. Finally, when I was ready to interview my highest-level source for this particular part of my investigation, I reached out to the chief results measurement specialist and manager of the IFC's Development Impact Department.

During our interview, he explained:

> *Once the project is complete, companies usually don't track "project" performance, but company performance.*
>
> *Think of a company with a project that's adding a 5th widget production line. After the line is installed, they care about things like capacity utilization for the company, not for widget line 5. So de facto it's very difficult to track "project" performance as distinct from company performance. Also, de facto some key performance indicators . . . only exist at the company level.*

My interviewee was trying to explain the IFC's rationale for evaluating its investments as it did, but what struck me was that the IFC didn't really know whether its investments were successful or not because it didn't track the results.

This answer (and others) confirmed two critical things. First, the IFC did not know how successful its investments were because it reported the success of the *entire company* in which the IFC might only have a tiny investment. Second, and equally problematic, was that my interviewee's answer confirmed that the IFC relied on companies' self-reporting and did not do its own due diligence.

In other words, Exxon Mobil, DuPont, and other companies the IFC had invested in essentially set their own metrics for what would be measured, paid for their own reports, and told the IFC what the results were. Then the IFC used the whole companies' returns on its investments in its tracking system.

Without knowing how its investments fared, how could the World Bank and countries that support it, including the United States, know that the bank was spending its money well and fulfilling its mission of fighting poverty? This question became even more important based upon further research that uncovered that the IFC was increasingly funding investments—including luxury hotels, high-end shopping plazas, and cinemas—that did not seem directly tied to its mission of fighting poverty.

By following the AREA Method, particularly Exploration, I uncovered a financial story that hadn't been told. To read the whole story, go to my website, **areamethod.com.**

But you don't have to uncover a story of financial misrepresentation to benefit from the Exploration stage of AREA. My student Tom, investigating Chipotle after the restaurant chain was linked to a series of illnesses, needed to conduct extensive Exploration research because the situation with the company was so new: no Absolute or Relative data existed about how the company's new food handling procedures might be affecting food quality or customer wait times and satisfaction. Tom's real-time "gumshoe reporting" helped him not only develop an informational edge, indicating that that the new food safety procedures would slow through-put (as described in chapter 4), but also gave him the confidence and conviction he needed to understand a fluid situation.

Now it's time to for you to start your Exploration. The first step is to nail the formula. The most effective interview is a simple formula:

$$GP + GQ = IQ$$
Good Prospects plus Great Questions equals Interview Quality

This formula means that you identify relevant and interested sources who are qualified to answer your targeted questions, and you ask them the best questions you can formulate to arrive at a quality interview.

Good Prospects

How do you find the right people to talk to? That will depend on your target's ecosystem and on your Critical Concepts. What do you need to know and who out there might know it already? And who knows you and your intentions and blind spots? Who might be an expert on *you* as an interpreter of information and as a decision-maker? Cheetah Sheet 27 provides an overview of some of the best places to look for Good Prospects.

Who are the people you're looking for as you conduct your research? Insiders might want to sell you on the target—but they might not. Outsiders might not have the "inside scoop" but they might provide important distance. One student, Adam, assigned to investigate the online travel review and booking site TripAdvisor, spoke to a travel consultant. This Good Prospect had deep industry knowledge and was able to provide context and background to Adam on both his company-specific research and the industry landscape. However, Adam didn't want to assume that this expert represented how customers perceived the company, so to understand user-experience he created a survey for his fellow MBA classmates. He wanted to get both sides of the story. The students gave a much more mixed picture of the company, and conveyed that when they were booking hotels, price was more important than TripAdvisor's brand.

Patricia, researching Sprint, identified the viability of Sprint's network integration plan (remember, Sprint had two networks) and its ability to survive against Verizon and AT&T as her two most important CCs. To explore these issues, she attended a wireless industry conference hosted by an industry trade journal.

At the conference, Patricia met several potential sources, including the CEO of a private wireless phone company, a vice president at one of the tower companies, a local wireless engineer and a vice president at one of the large equipment providers. She got their business cards and had follow-up calls with the sources, learning about things like the cost of different kinds of equipment, the characteristics of Sprint's previous and future network technologies, and the equipment needed to operate a network.

CHEETAH SHEET 27

Exploration: Finding Good Prospects

1. Industry journals and trade conferences
   a. Even if you don't attend, some conferences will list speakers and attendees on their web page
   b. Most companies will list events or conferences they have spoken at on their investor relations website and also issue press releases announcing their presence at various conferences
2. Universities and colleges
   a. Look for both professors and PhD students who are well versed in critical industry knowledge and contacts
3. Trade associations
4. Old annual reports or the S-1 (prospectus)
   a. Look for retired directors or executives who are listed
5. LinkedIn
   a. Most industries have associations that can be a valuable source of potential contacts
   b. You can search by company to find potential contacts
   c. You can also identify relationships between people in the industry even when they are not at the same company
   d. Note that your LinkedIn searches are not private. Sometimes people can see that you've looked at their page.
6. Industry reporters. Contact them and ask them who likes to talk about the industry
7. Expert networks. They may be pricey but are meant to save time.
8. Employees' unions
   a. Ask to speak to current or former members
9. Twitter
   a. Search @company or @industry and see who is talking about the industry
10. Companies like D&B Hoovers, DiscoveryOrg, and others provide company capsules listing officers and directors of the company and its competitors, including employees below the C-suite
11. Lawsuits and the entities named in them, which you can find through court filings

CHEETAH SHEET 28

Exploration: Finding More Good Prospects

1. Employees at competitor companies
   a. Private companies can be especially valuable. They may be more forthcoming than publicly traded ones that are burdened by Regulation Fair Disclosure (Reg FD). Reg FD requires all publicly traded companies to release nonpublic information in a "full" and "fair" way to prevent selective disclosure.
   b. Employees at suppliers
2. Independent contractors
3. Government officials and regulators
4. Insurance representatives
5. Customers of your target
6. Students, alumni, and professors in the industry
7. Private investigators
8. Headhunters who cover the industry (their whole job is networking)
9. Major shareholders
10. Real estate brokers, clerks in assessors' offices
    a. Contact a commercial real estate broker from the area
    b. Local inspection groups or authorities are a great source of knowledge on real estate
    c. Look at county clerk's office filings for tax assessment filings
11. Lawyers who have worked for or against the company or industry and people named in related lawsuits
12. Accountants who specialize in the industry
13. Strategy consultants
14. Employees in support positions such as executive assistants, payroll, processing, and IT professionals

This new information allowed Patricia to build out her own model of what Sprint's network integration would look like. It enabled her to develop a deeper understanding of the actions, and associated costs and benefits, needed to integrate Sprint's network. She was able to vet this against Sprint's cost estimates and determine that the company's estimates were, in fact, reasonable.

She also learned that competitors who used the technology on Sprint's first network and competitors who used the technology on Sprint's second network were integrating their networks with the same next-generation technology that Sprint was transitioning to, indicating the technical viability of Sprint's targeted transition.

Patricia also looked within Columbia University for sources. She found a business school professor who focused on the telecom industry and was able to give her data on the industry cost curve. She found an alumnus who worked at an industry company and a student who interned as an industry consultant. In her conversations with them, she found that the industry cost curve was much flatter than she expected. Providing nationwide coverage was a fixed cost, but adding capacity to a network was variable and most wireless companies were well into the "capacity" phase.

Patricia was able to make great contacts through visiting just one trade show and tapping her university network. But don't limit yourself. Interesting information can sometimes turn up in unexpected places, including from sources that might seem dry at first glance. See Cheetah Sheet 28.

If you're looking for experts in a field but don't have a name, try job websites like Monster.com, Vault, or Ladders.com. You can search resumes for experience and of course get employee reviews of companies and salary searches on sites like Indeed.com or Glass Door.

Three other great resources when you need someone to help with a foreign language or when you'd like someone else to help out with your research are listed in Cheetah Sheet 29.

Lastly, it is worth identifying interview prospects who are not necessarily experts on the target or the issue but who are experts on *you*—people who deeply understand your interests and values, your default biases and blind spots. Try to identify one or two people who know you well and who you'd want to consult as you absorb and make sense of all the information you gather from other sources.

CHEETAH SHEET 29

Exploration: Getting Help with Your Search

1. Phone companies. Many have translation calling services, which are helpful if your target speaks a foreign language.
2. Freelance reporters. They can help with finding sources and/or conducting interviews. Look on websites such as Journalismjobs.com or MediaBistro.com.
3. Librarians

Valuing Your Sources

Once you've identified a list of potential sources to contact, write them down in your AREA Journal and rank them in order of the likelihood that you think they may provide important information about your Critical Concepts. Consider what you think the sources might be able to help you to better understand and then put the sources in order from least important, or lowest level, to most important.

The low-level sources can provide you with background and help you to better flesh out your understanding of your target. By contacting lower-level sources first, you also have a chance to practice your call pitch, a loose script of what you plan to say to introduce yourself and your task, and perfect your questions. As you progress up the interview chain, you will be more polished and more knowledgeable. By the time you've reached your high-level sources you will not only have a good sense of context, but will also have a "truth-meter" running that can help guide the way you listen to the answers provided and identify incomplete or potentially misleading information.

For example, as you read above, I already knew the answer to the question of how the IFC reported its data before I interviewed my sources. This enabled me to nicely push back when I received information that I knew might be incomplete.

But it's not time to make those calls or send those emails yet. First, you need to develop your Great Questions.

Great Questions

Before crafting any questions for interviewees, *pause.*

CHEETAH SHEET 30

Exploration: Great Questions Roadmap

1. What kind of *answers* do you need? Be targeted on your Critical Concepts.
   a. What do you want to find out and why?
   b. What difference would that information make?
2. How do you expect to use the information you gather?

If you can't specify how you will use the information before you have it there is little reason to expect that you'll be able to figure out how to use it after the findings are in. The goal is to use both your time and the time of the people whom you are interviewing wisely.

Once you've settled on what you want to know to address your research target's CCs, think about what kind of a response you want to elicit. There are four major kinds of questions that are commonly asked.

CHEETAH SHEET 31

Exploration: Types of Great Questions

1. Behavior questions—what someone does or has done. These kinds of questions will yield descriptions of actual experiences, activities, and actions.
2. Opinion questions—what someone thinks about a topic, action, or event. These questions will tell us about people's goals, intentions, desires, and values.
3. Feeling questions—how someone responds emotionally to a topic. These questions elicit information about the emotional responses of people to their experiences and thoughts.
4. Knowledge questions—what factual information the respondent has about your target and your CCs. While you may argue that all knowledge is a set of beliefs rather than facts, the issue here is to find out what the person being questioned considers to be factual.

In designing your questions you want to determine precisely what type of information you need from your interviewee. Do you want to know about her behavior, opinions, feelings, or knowledge? By deciding what is important, you will write questions that clearly communicate to the interviewee what kind of answer you're looking for and avoid confusion.

As with all parts of the AREA Method, think about where and how you might be making assumptions as you write your questions. Often the best questions are the most basic and elemental. Basic does not mean obvious, it means central—focused on your Critical Concepts so that you may solve your specific research decision.

CHEETAH SHEET 32
Exploration: Great Questions: Direct, Broad, and Theoretical

Direct questions:

1. How does the target achieve its goals? How does it make money?
2. What is the biggest contributor to profitability?
3. Can you describe an average day? This might be a day for the person, or for the role he plays inside the organization. The question can reveal the interviewee's priorities. At times what someone does means more than what the person says.
4. Do you have any concerns about the target?

Broad questions:

1. What should I know about the industry or sector?
2. Is there a way to bring data to bear on this topic?

Theoretical questions:

1. If you had to do it over again, would you do it differently and how so? Why?
2. If you took money out of the equation, would you still make the same decision, or take the same action? (This question focuses on getting beyond the economics of the issue.) Follow up with:
3. Is there more than one possible answer to the question?

Here is a classic example of asking a basic question that made all the difference in one money manager's research into an investment opportunity. The manager, a guest speaker in my Advanced Investment Research class, recounted how he was researching a pharmaceutical company whose stock price had soared based on the prospects for an erectile dysfunction gel the company was developing. The company had run clinical trials showing that their gel was more effective than a placebo gel applied to a control group. Our guest speaker interviewed people who had seen the research conducted and asked a vital question, one that at first blush might not be so obvious and yet turned out to be basic and essential to understanding the study's results. His question: "Who applied the gel to the people in the study?" He learned that while a female applied the company's gel, the placebo gel was applied by a male. The results of the study were indeed statistically significant, but they had nothing to do with the gel.

In terms of what to ask interviewees, many of your questions will come out of the work you've done in the Absolute and Relative phases and will be specific to your target and decision. However, to help you think about the kinds of questions to ask, below I've culled a list of what I've found to be good questions over the years. These general questions focus on getting interviewees talking about basic, important qualities about an organization.

As an example, if you are evaluating the management training program of a commercial bank you might consider questions like:

1. Who are the clients for the program? (Direct, Knowledge)
2. Describe a typical trainee day. (Direct, Behavior)
3. What is the retention rate of the program? (Direct, Knowledge)
4. Where do trainees go after the program? (Broad, Behavior)
5. How has the program changed over time? (Broad, Opinion)
6. Describe the program's measure of success and a successful program graduate. (Broad, Knowledge)
7. If you could change one thing about the program what would you change? (Theoretical, Opinion)
8. If the program disappeared, what would happen to the company? (Theoretical, Feeling)
9. Do you think changes to the program would improve the retention rate? (Theoretical, Opinion)

Once you've written your questions, *pause* and look carefully at the way that you've worded them. The way a question is worded is one of the most important elements determining how an interview subject will respond. Are you asking leading questions? Are you providing a context for your questions, or simply firing them off one after another? An interviewee will be impacted by different question formats.

For example, if you're interviewing someone in the management training program, or someone who has gone through it, you might not want to ask: "Did you like the program?" That question is both too leading and potentially too personal. It also may only elicit "yes" or "no" answers. Instead you might consider rewording the questions to ask: "What kind of person would benefit from this program and why?" This version is softened and has more of an objective tone to it. Despite the fact that the answer will get at the same information—whether the person liked the program enough to recommend it to someone else—the question's format has the psychological effect of distance, allowing the interviewee to be removed from the question. This format might help to get at more objective and useful information.

At times during an interview, you may be puzzled by or unclear about something your interviewee has just said. Although you can't plan out clarification questions ahead of time, do take some time to practice these types of questions so that you'll be comfortable interjecting them when necessary. Make sure to be open and honest when you need clarification and convey the notion that the need for greater understanding is yours, and not a failure by the person being interviewed. You don't want the interviewee to feel inarticulate.

 CHEETAH SHEET 33
Exploration: Great Clarification Questions and Feedback

1. I'm not sure I follow what you just said. Would you please explain it again?
2. Could you give me an example or anecdote so that I may better understand (or visualize) the concept that you are explaining?
3. It's really useful to have such a clear statement about . . .
4. You're bringing up a lot of important points.
5. I really appreciate your willingness to express your feelings (or share your expertise) about that. That's really helpful.

You'll also want to give the interviewee reinforcement or feedback during the interview about how the interview is going. Words of support, thanks, and praise make the person feel appreciated and encouraged.

It's important to maintain control of the interview. Time is precious and sometimes answers may be long-winded or irrelevant. You need to have a sense of what you want to find out and recognize when responses don't provide the right data so that you can get the interview back on track. This may take direct feedback.

For example, simulation questions like "What happens when you meet with the sales team?" are particularly effective when you want to learn about how a process unfolds, whether that process is returning merchandise, moving products from one area of a warehouse to another, or understanding how an ER assesses a possible stroke patient. Often, however, interviewees will respond to a simulation question with what they *hope* will happen, or what should *ideally* happen, rather than what actually happens. In this case, try reframing the question to get your interviewee back on point: "Okay, so you're motivating the team. Take me into the sales meeting. What does the room look like? What would I see and hear? What are you saying?"

It's hard to interrupt an interviewee. We've all been taught to be polite and not speak when someone else is speaking. However, it's respectful to make good use of the short time available to talk. Below are some techniques to keep your conversation on track.

CHEETAH SHEET 34
Exploration: Techniques for Staying on Track

1. If you know how much time is allotted at the outset, tell the interviewee upfront that since there is only so much time, you might need to interrupt a response to keep the interview moving.
2. Here are some ways you might gently interrupt the interview when needed:
   a. "Let me stop you here for a moment. I want to make sure that I fully understand something you touched upon earlier" (then ask a new/more targeted question)
   b. "Let me ask you to pause for a moment because some of what you are saying I want to get at a little later on. First I'd like to find out . . ."

As you ask the questions, write down the number of the question being answered next to your notes on the interviewee's answer so that you know what you've asked without having to note the specific question.

At the end of the interview, ask the interviewee the following questions:

CHEETAH SHEET 35
Exploration: Great Closing Questions

1. What else should I be asking?
2. Who else do you recommend I speak with as I continue my research?
3. What organizations do you belong to that might be useful sources of information?
4. What is the best way to follow up with you in the future?

You don't want your wording to limit your response set. You simply want to provide a framework that allows your interviewee to best express his own understanding, in his own terms, allowing him to select from his full repertoire of responses without bias. All of the above discussion provides examples of open-ended, not closed, questions. Refrain from "leading the witness." If you lead the witness, you won't know what she might have said.

Watch your word choice and tone when you ask a question so that you do not put ideas or words in the interviewee's mouth. You don't want to suggest, you want to receive the person's unvarnished, authentic answers.

For example, this question leads the interviewee: "Do you have any problems with your manager?"

This question negatively frames the employee-employer relationship as one that might have problems and leads the interviewee to think about his relationship in terms of the problems it may have. This type of wording might bias your interviewee. Instead, a more objective question would be, "Tell me about your relationship with your manager."

One way to write a neutral question is to use an illustrative example format, letting the person you are interviewing know that you have pretty much heard it all—the good, the bad and the ugly—so you're not particularly interested in something sensational; you're really interested in what that person's experience has been. Here is what I asked a series of customers about their experience at a store where they tried to return merchandise: "How did the company handle the return? Some of the people that I've interviewed said that they were treated nicely and their money returned easily. Some people said they felt bullied into keeping the item. Others told us that they had to spend nearly an hour on the phone with the company before the customer service person agreed to the refund. When you think about how you were treated, what kinds of things come to mind?"

With this format, by giving multiple extreme examples of responses I let each interviewee know that there is nothing that he can say that will surprise me. The critical thing to avoid here is asking a leading question that might give the interviewee a hint about a desirable answer.

While ideally every interview should build upon the previous one, expanding information picked up earlier, moving in a new direction, and seeking clarity and elaboration, that doesn't mean always asking different questions to different people. Instead at times you may want to have standardized questions so that you ask your interviewees the same questions in the same order.

By following a script that's exactly the same for all interviewees you can avoid extrapolating from a single anecdote or having a fragmented set of insights. You won't have points all over the place and you won't falsely derive meaning from a sample of people that is incomplete.

For example, Matthew's Exploration work included interviewing an airline industry expert and investor relations managers for Delta and two discount airlines, asking everyone the same question: what are the sustainable competitive advantages for airlines? By standardizing this fundamental question Matthew was able to make comparisons across the interviews and match them to his own understanding of the industry. Matthew also knew to consider the bias of his sources. He knew that investor relations professionals are meant to represent the viewpoints of the companies that they work for.

As you build your questions list, this is a nice place to recall the earlier discussion about edges and pitfalls –that is, what do you think might go well in your interviews and where might you run into a challenge? By identifying these assumptions, you can also consider what interview style may work best. I think of my interviews as falling into three personas: the Scientist, the Consultant, and, used sparingly, the Interrogator.

The Scientist is focused on collecting technically sound data. She's on a truth-seeking mission. I usually use this approach with early-stage low-level interviews where I ask the interviewees to explain how or why something is done.

The Consultant wants to build consensus and clarify information. He's already collected the data and is partnering with the interviewee in understanding it. I've used this approach with mid-level interviews as a way to share and to check the quality of the information amassed.

The Interrogator is a detective investigating a crime—of sorts. She's probing, and at times aggressive (which doesn't mean she's unkind or rude). When you need information that could make the interviewee feel defensive or uncomfortable and need to ask some tough questions, this approach is needed. For example, if you were writing a news story about the credit scoring company Equifax just after it revealed that it had been the victim of a massive cyberattack, you'd need to ask about the security breach. Use this approach sparingly, as a last resort, and near the end of your interview, after you've established a rapport with your interviewee. For a more in-depth look at how to use these personas, individually and in concert, see the discussion in the appendix.

There is no one right interview approach. The approach that will feel right will be the one that will elicit information that is relevant, appropriate, and useful, and that you couldn't have gotten simply by reading Absolute company documents or Relative source material. It's the approach that will yield information about the broader context, the research target, and a specific set of issues and questions vital to your Critical Concepts.

Remember: in interviewing, you are driving a discussion. You're not just reading words on a page. You are engaged in dialogue with a thinking, feeling, and opinionated person. Interviewing, after you reviewed Absolute and Relative documents, gives you a different angle and insight. At the same time, you gain important distance on your own thoughts and feelings. This allows you to check your biases and reassess *your* research behavior.

Juan, one of my Advanced Investment Research students, was assigned to study Brookfield Asset Management, a Canadian company with a variety of global assets spanning real estate to renewable energy. Published reports that Juan found in the Relative phase of his research referred to the company's CEO and his investing style as the "Warren Buffett of the North."

Like Buffett's Berkshire Hathaway, Brookfield owns pieces of many companies, yet early on in the Exploration phase of his research, Juan discovered that the CEO of the company was also the head of the company's distressed real-estate fund. Juan wondered whether management might face some conflicts of interest between the different branches of the company but was unsure how to research his concern.

Juan updated his interview script and questions going forward to try to investigate this particular issue. He reached out to current major holders of the company's shares, industry experts and current and former employees of the company. One interviewee said this: "How will [the executive] manage his fiduciary duties to Brookfield shareholders and to limited partners? Follow the fees to see where he puts the assets."

This insight was valuable for a few reasons. It not only pointed Juan where to look for evidence that might support or refute allegations of a potential conflict, but it also tipped him off that other people close to the company might be doing similar due diligence, suggesting the seriousness of the issue. It also contradicted the rosy picture of the company painted by the press in the Relative phase of Juan's research.

Based on his Exploration work, Juan developed a path forward: He wouldn't assume the worst, but he would look for evidence to verify or challenge the assumption of conflict.

Timing Your Interviews

It seems that we're all overbooked these days. Be thoughtful about that as you reach out to interrupt someone else's day to benefit your own. In other words, a critical factor in making a good question list is a consideration of how much time you think you may actually get with any one person, or how long it may take them to respond to your questions in an email you've sent. If you're asking for a phone call and you think you may only have fifteen minutes, make a comprehensive list of questions but then whittle it down to only the most essential ones—the ones that will help you collect information to better examine your Critical Concepts. Make each question necessary, clear, and concise, and craft it so it moves the interview forward from the prior one.

If you're asking for a written response to emailed questions, you'll also want to make sure that you've pared your questions down to only the essential one or two. If the interviewee responds, you want to thank her, and that may be a great opening to ask to continue your discussion on the phone.

CHEETAH SHEET 36

Exploration: Vetting Your Great Questions

1. Are you writing the same question in multiple forms and being repetitive?
2. Are there extraneous questions that you may delete?
3. How can you improve the clarity of your questions?

Assess: what do you really need to have answered in the time allotted?

The Interview Guide

Once you've developed a list of Great Questions, it's time to *pause* and create your interview guide. How do you want to the interview to proceed? Where should you place the most important questions you need answered? What follow-up questions will be important to ask, based on the answers you get?

An interview guide is a roadmap that lays out the framework for the interview so that you can control the timing and momentum and navigate the path to make sure you're able to ask your most critical questions in the time you think you will have with your interview subjects.

As you'll see in an example from Matthew below, the most effective interviews don't move in a straight line from "easy" questions to "hard" ones, nor do they only address the most salient points you're researching. You are dealing with a human being and you're having a dialogue—not an interrogation (even if you'll need that approach). The goal is to reduce the "distance" between you and your interviewee.

To make your interview guide compelling and to craft a logical progression for your interview so that it best resembles the normal flow of conversation, it's useful to think of having your questions follow a story-board with a beginning, middle, and end.

Matthew's interview guide for talking with Delta's investor relations manager follows. Note that the parentheses after questions are his notes on what he believes to be true. They allow him to have his "truth-meter" running; they are not part of his questions.

1. What are the sustainable competitive advantages for airlines?
2. Critical Concept 1: What are the barriers to entry for an ultra-low-cost carrier (ULCC)?
3. How do slots work for airports that don't have the slot designations?
4. Critical Concept 1: How does Delta react when an ultra-low-cost carrier enters a route?
5. Critical Concept 1: Will the discount carriers act rationally if we are in a sustained low fuel cost environment?
6. What determines the price of Delta's stock? (i.e., what are the key metrics that investors are looking at and that this company/industry trade on?)
7. What are Delta's most promising growth opportunities?
8. Critical Concept 2: Has Delta considered locking in current fuel prices longer term? Is that an option?
9. Critical Concept 2: How is Delta thinking about upcoming labor negotiations with pilots' union? (Can you really meet goal of flat—+2% cost per average seat mile ex-fuel? Excludes profit sharing)
10. Critical Concept 3: Competition from Middle Eastern airlines? (Big policy item for Delta. Blessed with distance? Bigger deal for European carriers?)

Matthew's guide begins with a general question about the broader airline industry, making the investor relations person comfortable and allowing him to share his industry knowledge as the expert he is. Matthew's second and third questions are also straightforward, establishing a friendly student-teacher type of relationship.

Questions four and five get into a touchier area and ask the investor relations person to move from sharing knowledge to offering opinions and forecasts. Here, Matthew is being an Interrogator, taking a "surveillance and compliance" approach to check out and verify data he's collected. Note that in question six, Matthew backs off to reestablish a friendlier, Consultant-style rapport. He wants to hear how the investor relations person might describe the company's talking points about the forces that impact its share price performance. This ebb and flow is important because his final three questions zero in on Critical Concepts related to possible rising costs as well as competition from discount carriers and subsidized airlines from the Middle East.

CHEETAH SHEET 37

Exploration: Storyboarding Your Great Questions

1. Begin with a brief introduction that explains who you are, what you are researching and why.
2. Open with some nonconfrontational and relatively easy-to-discuss questions that have concrete answers and that are not controversial.
3. Lead into your Critical Concept questions, the meat of your concerns about your research target.
4. Wrap up the conversation with closing questions: "What haven't I asked?" "What am I missing?" Then thank the interviewee, ask how best to get back in touch for any follow-up, and ask for recommendations of other people to contact for your research

People generally like to talk about their work, but in order for them to truly share their thoughts, feelings, and evidence they need to get comfortable with you—a stranger—whether the interview is being conducted over the phone, in person, or via email. From the journalist's perspective, it's always better to speak to someone directly, but there's been a generational shift and today many people are more comfortable with email. The key thing is to take the time to put yourself in the place of the interviewee and consider how you and your questions might come across to a stranger.

The underlying theme: have an idea of what you want to find out and then design questions and the order in which they will be asked so that they give you the information you think you need. You have a better chance of getting good information if you are able to conceptualize and structure your interviews well.

Rehearse your interview. How do your questions sound out loud? Put some evidence of your own research into your questions so that the interviewee knows you've done the work and that you have some familiarity with the issues, giving them confidence that you are not wasting their time. This will better enable you to have a conversation, not just an interview, because you will show that you are be able to share data and insights.

Finally, do a bit of background research on each person you intend to contact. Your goal isn't to learn *everything* there is to know about your interviewee but to find *something* in common that will help you to build rapport and that will give you better insight into the interview subject. Your research may be a basic Internet, Facebook, and LinkedIn search to see whether your interviewee has written articles, where she may have been quoted, and what personal interests she may have that will allow an easier introduction.

For example, when I was researching a counterterrorism story for the Council on Foreign Relations I wanted to contact a specific military advisor who had been on one of the missions I was writing about. He was an important and high-level person who could put me in the room. Putting him at ease with me was key. During my background research I discovered that he and I were both affiliated with our local town's sports league. So, early in the interview, when it was appropriate to share a little bit about me, I was able to work in our connection and it helped the relationship and conversation.

An Interview Guide in Action

Below I provide an example of an interview guide from an interview I did with a chief executive of a waste management company. I was focused on the company's ability to handle its debt load. It had the highest leverage in its industry and the industry's highest operating margins, meaning that the company's solvency was at risk if margins were unsustainable. My goal was to focus on that CC.

After my initial opening questions, which set a friendly tone, I wanted to make clear to the CEO that I was prepared and had researched the company. I then moved into my Interrogator persona, delving deeply into the business to understand the company's debt dynamic. My interview guide incorporates both my questions and the data I had previously gathered so that I could compare the CEO's answers to my own, allowing me to conduct "surveillance and compliance." My data are italicized and in parentheses.

1. Are you comfortable with earnings estimates for this quarter of about 30 cents per share, and are you on track for earnings of about 90 cents per share for the year? Follow up: How much could earnings decline before potentially tripping your interest coverage covenant?

2. What do you think the stock price reflects that the market is focusing on? How do you explain the company's recent stock price performance? How do you think it understands your company's refinancing issues?

3. What is the company's biggest challenge now? How might you regain the market's confidence?

4. Explain the change in your operating model. *Looking for a discussion of how expansion aids field operators' flexibility to manage profitability.*

5. How much debt is scheduled to be repaid for the rest of year? (*Estimate is $275 million due this year.*) How much free cash flow will you generate then? Is EBIT (earnings before interest and taxes) in excess of covenant requirements? If so, how much? (*Estimate $131.1 million at end of second quarter.*) How many other recent refinancings have you done, plan to do? (*Company did two in last 18 months, $750 million at 11%, $600 million at 11%*).

6. When do you foresee trying to tap the bond market again? How do you explain to investors what happened in September when the company pulled a deal for $250 million at 9%? (*Terms.*) At what interest rate is a refinancing neutral to the company's earnings and cash flows? (*Estimate 9% according to sources.*) How much debt do you expect to issue or pay down over the next 16 months? (*Estimate $1.3 billion*)

7. What % of earnings growth is tied to deleveraging? Interest expense? (*Estimate from sources: 80%.*)

8. What is happening with margins? What in your estimate accounts for the company having the highest margins in industry? How much are they being pressured in the current environment?

9. How much does the company's debt level limit flexibility?
10. What is your goal for the company's debt to capital ratio? (*Estimate: 65%, now 83%*) By when?

Note the arc of this guide. Here I chose to delve into my main topic of interest—the company's debt situation—then ease off and circle back to it. My goal was to listen to whether the answers were consistent and whether they matched up to what I'd earlier uncovered in my research. I didn't plan on divulging what I'd written in parentheses, but having my answers there allowed me to quickly consider how I might want to press on his answers based upon how they matched up with what I'd already learned. It's critical to have your data handy and well organized with your questions so that you may assess both the quality of what you think you know and whether management is forthcoming, well-informed, and honest in their answers.

My questions had a somewhat loaded tone and language in an effort to discover whether the CEO agreed with the market's concern or rejected it. For example, I asked him about the debt level "limiting" flexibility. Would he accept this categorization of his company's opportunities or not, and why? I was letting him know that critics were concerned about the impact of his company's debt load on the company's future prospects.

Note that while I often have multiple questions in a section, I only ask one question at a time so that I am not giving someone a chance to only answer part of a question and also so that I may reevaluate what I need to ask as the interview progresses.

During the interview, I was impressed with the CEO's comfort and command of his company's numbers. He easily handled complex details and strategy questions. Although I was asking about tough topics, he seemed calm and prepared, suggesting that he knew the company's challenges. To see the story that resulted from this interview, *Out of the Dumps*, visit my website, areamethod.com.

An interview guide allows you to carefully use the limited interview time available. You may only get this one chance to speak with the interviewee, even if she says you may call her again. However, I recommend crafting two sets of questions: one for the time allotted and a second set with questions that you'd like to have answered if you receive more time than expected. In this way, you will be well prepared to anticipate every contingency.

An organized guide makes data analysis much easier because it is possible to locate each respondent's answer. And, importantly, it allows for replication: if you or someone else wants to check your work, they will know exactly what was previously asked.

If you are not sure that you've come up with the right questions, this is a good place for you to reach out to collaborate. Consider collaborating with groups or constituencies that:

- Have an interest in your findings
- Have authority/power/influence
- Believe the interviews are worth doing
- Care how the results are used

At times, academicians, regulators, or other researchers might have an interest in your findings and add good questions to your list. Also, if there is someone who will need to sign off on your research, discussing your CCs and question list beforehand might make it easier to incorporate her concerns at this critical juncture of your research.

The Call Pitch

Once you're ready with your interview questions, you need to get your interview target on the phone. This is no easy feat, and a considerate call or email pitch can make all the difference. What is the short "elevator" speech that you plan to use?

While there is no one right way to reach out to someone, I recommend that, whether it's by email or over the phone, you do three things: Be educated, be compelling, and be urgent in your cause. You need the person to respond to you now—or soon. If you're making your pitch by email, give it a once-over before sending it to consider your tone, grammar, and mechanics. If you're making a call, write it out and rehearse it as well.

Here's a call pitch template:

Hi, I'm Cheryl, a research analyst, calling from Y. We are an [investment firm, media outlet, business] that focuses on Z, and I've been assigned to better understand A and B [main concepts you want to discuss that show some of your research].

I'm reaching out to you because C [something about why you chose the source and why he/she is specifically the right person to get answers from]. I'd like to ask you [your first question]. Have I reached you at a good time?

For example, one of my call pitches on the counterterrorism story was to a Department of Defense researcher who had written a paper criticizing the current counterterrorism policy. I wanted a better sense of her sources and her perspective. Was her analysis controversial and what did she hope to achieve by challenging the status quo? Here's my call pitch:

I'm reaching out to you because I read a recent paper of yours about the implications of US military responses to terror threats in Northern Africa. I thought your discussion about the militarization of counterterrorism policy response was thoughtful. I'd like to ask you about how you compiled the data for your study and what kind of response the paper has elicited. Have I reached you at a good time?

If the time you called doesn't work, make a date for something that works at the source's convenience, stressing that you are flexible and can work with your source's busy schedule.

When constructing your pitch, choose a job description for yourself that sounds friendly, represents what you do, and conveys a sense of science and objectivity. Refrain from industry lingo or jargon.

Now get ready for rejection. Recent statistics show that only about 5 percent of voicemail messages are returned. The best way to improve your success rate is to get a referral. Then your chance of connecting jumps up to 40 percent—and can be even much higher if the referral comes from within the organization you're targeting. However, this still means that more than half of the calls you make will go unanswered.

The stats for emails aren't any better: 80 percent of sales emails—emails from strangers who seem to be asking for something—go unopened.

Don't be discouraged, though. As was the case for my World Bank story, just one good connection with someone knowledgeable can be a game-changer. What follow are a few tips to increase the odds of making a successful connection with a stranger.

For phone calls: be brief, compelling, and upbeat in your tone. Survey data shows that the optimal length of a voicemail message is between eight and fourteen seconds. However, don't sacrifice tone for brevity. *How* you leave your message –the tone—is actually more important than what you have to say. So be succinct, but animated and interesting; it's up to you to spark the curiosity, compassion, or interest of the other person.

For email, make sure your subject line is short—three words is ideal. Anything over that and the likelihood that your email will be read drops by 60 percent. Pay attention to when you send your email: data from Mail Chimp, an online marketing service, show that the best open rates for emails are on Tuesdays between 2 and 5 pm. The worst open rates are first thing in the morning and late on Friday afternoon. And don't forget about time zones: if you're sending an email from California at 4 pm, your recipient in New York may have already left the office. Remember that your email is your call pitch: be credible, specific about why you want to learn from the person you are contacting, and compelling. If you're asking questions in the email, use bullet points—and keep your questions short. Finally, make sure you check—or, ideally, have someone else check—for typos and tone.

Plan to follow up. Just like you, the people you're reaching out to are busy. And while it's tempting to move on, don't. About 80 percent of successful "sales" come after five or more follow-up calls. While you may not think you're selling something, you are selling an opportunity to connect with you.[2]

Avoiding Material Nonpublic Information

If you are working for an investment firm you want to be careful that you're not asking your interviewee for confidential information, which is nonpublic information that gives you, as an investor, an unfair advantage over other investors. For example, if during an interview an executive told you that the company sales had suddenly slipped and it might miss its next earnings target, you would be in possession of knowledge that other investors don't have and that could impact the company's financial results. In those interview situations, I'd add the following caution at the end of your interview pitch:

Just to be clear, I'm not looking for confidential information from you because I work for a trading firm, but I am hoping that you'll be

*able to give insights about A and B to the extent that you are allowed
to share your views with me.*

In this way, you are clearly stating at the outset that you do not want the interviewee to give you information in breach of a legal duty, which could give rise to problems under insider trading regulations. This will set the right tone for the conversation from a securities law compliance perspective and minimize the chances that the interviewee will unexpectedly give you material nonpublic information that could inhibit you or your firm from trading.

Three other notes on this important topic:

First, it is always dangerous to financially compensate sources for their information. Whenever there is a clear quid-pro-quo, it increases the chances that a source could be viewed as having breached a duty by giving you information for a "personal benefit," which could create insider-trading issues.

Second, be especially careful if the source is a close friend or family member, which creates an added risk because such relationships can be seen as creating a built-in motivation for sources to breach their duties by sharing too much information with you.

Third, know that there is a critical safe harbor in what the SEC calls material nonpublic information according to the "mosaic theory" of research. The mosaic theory is a legal principal that says it is legally acceptable, as a researcher, to gather pieces of nonpublic information for trading purposes, provided no single piece of information is in and of itself material. When you put these nonmaterial pieces of information together and gain some new insight or something that you think may not be known or understood by the market, the mosaic theory postulates that you would be in the clear; the "mosaic" does not constitute material nonpublic information.

Rules around material nonpublic information change over time and are complex so the above paragraphs are neither the total picture nor the final word. Do not rely upon them. Be diligent and work with a compliance officer to make sure that you are following all current policies and practices.

Interviewing

Congratulations! Now you're ready to start interviewing. Essentially, conducting an interview is about multitasking. It is much more than just listening. It requires interacting easily with people, generating rapid insights, taking notes both on the conversation you're having and on your interview guide, and formulating new questions quickly and smoothly while guarding against asking questions that impose interpretations on the situation and reading clues such as tone and pauses to respond to what is not being said.

If you think it's tiring just to read this list, know that it is even more tiring to conduct a successful interview. Don't conduct an interview on an empty stomach and make sure that the time you allot for the interview includes time for your "after-interview" process, which should immediately follow the end of the formal interview.

Keep in mind that employees at different levels have different experiences. If you're talking to a low-level employee, understand what it feels like to have a boss coming down on you. If you're talking to a mid-level contact, appeal to her desire to help and her desire to feel important. If you're talking to a high-level contact, showing that you're well versed in your topic may yield deeper conversation.

Once you have someone on the phone, remember the sage advice given by Zeno of Citium in 300 BC: "We have two ears and one mouth so we should listen more than we say." While this is difficult, it is important to recognize that different people have different styles of speaking and you will do best if you are able to learn to adjust to each of your interview subject's personal mannerisms. Leading a good interview takes practice. It is not just about data collection, it is also about interaction and thus relationship building. The purpose of interviewing is to find out what is on someone else's mind. It is not to put new ideas into someone's mind, but to access the perspectives of the person being interviewed.

It's your responsibility as the interviewer to provide a framework within which people may respond comfortably, accurately and honestly to open-ended questions. You are in the driver's seat and the quality of the information that you receive depends upon how you steer the interview.

Thus while you want to be able to rapidly get down to business to accomplish the necessary tasks, you really want to be both sufficiently directive to get the job done *and* sufficiently nondirective and open to allow interview subjects to feel that their input is meaningful and substantive. You may want to unlock and stimulate conversation in the people you are speaking with and then figure out how to be reactive, adapting to the conversation as it progresses.

If you are conducting a face-to-face interview, reading nonverbal communication is important. Write down nonverbal cues, or a subtle change in behavior or demeanor, that may indicate a "tell," a clue that perhaps you've stumbled upon a topic that the person is uncomfortable with, or where the interviewee wants to say more but is hesitant or still formulating her thoughts.

Whether you are interviewing in person or on the phone, I recommend not interrupting a pause and allowing the silence to hang so that the interviewee may want to fill it. Allow the interviewee to decide how to fill her silences.

Taking Notes

If you're conducting a phone interview, aim to wear a headset. This will prevent your interviewee from hearing you typing while he is speaking, which can be uncomfortable for a source. You don't want to put the keyboard between you and your source; it changes the call from a natural conversation to an interview.

If the interviewee is speaking too quickly, try slowing it down by either repeating what the person said as a question as you write it down, or by asking her to repeat it. You might also consider saying, "May I have a minute? You made an important point there and I want to make sure that I have it down in my notes."

Develop shorthand. I often just drop the vowels so that I can type faster. Cheetah Sheet 38 offers some tips from the field that can help you develop your own shorthand and make the process effective and efficient.

You may be tempted to record your interviews. However, be aware that one-way recording is only allowed in some states. Check the rules for yours. And even if you do record, take notes. Note-taking is active listening and a filtering system. Taking notes by hand or typing them makes it easier to locate something someone said in the tape of the interview and will facilitate later analysis. Another important benefit of taking written notes is that sometimes even the best recording systems fail; it's always good to have a manual backup.

If you are recording and taking notes, write the time of the beginning of the interview on the top of your notes. Then, every fifteen minutes or so during the conversation, record the time code in the margin.

CHEETAH SHEET 38
Exploration: Taking Great Notes

1. Only use quotation marks during note-taking to indicate full and actual quotations.
2. Develop a system to indicate interpretations, thoughts, or ideas that occur. For example, I use brackets to set off my own ideas from the interviewee's. I use the margins to record nonverbal notes such as whether the person seems angry about a specific topic or issue, or seems to know more than she may be indicating.
3. Keep track in your notes of the questions you ask as they are answered by writing down the number of the question as it corresponds to your interview guide.

When the interview is over, immediately take a few quiet minutes to read through all of your notes. Use this "after-interview" time to make sure that you've recorded the number of the question next to the corresponding answer and to fill in and flesh out answers that you recorded quickly while the interview is still fresh and you can record more comprehensively.

Be careful to note if you change or add in things that may not accurately reflect what the interviewee said during the interview, so that you don't confuse what was said in the interview with your notes after it. Record your impressions of how and why the person said what he said in important places. Indicate if you thought someone was not being fully truthful or forthcoming and why you had that impression, or if, through verbal and nonverbal cues, someone seemed worried about sharing information with you. By staying with the interview after it's over and reading your notes immediately, you will be surprised at how different the notes may be from what you thought they were.

Always add your interview sources to your contact list for future follow up, along with notations about the content of the call and how useful the interview was. In so doing, you will have a better context for knowing how and when to call upon the person in future investigations and you will be able to remind the person when you last spoke and what you discussed. Also note who else the interviewee recommended that you contact so that you may use that connection later. Then send a thank you note or email to leave your interaction in a good place.

Finally take a Cheetah Pause and develop a thesis statement from your interviews. I find it useful to sum up each interview separately and then craft a final thesis statement from all of my interviews.

One of my students, Remi, was assigned to research Tejon Ranch, a company with 270,000 acres of land just sixty miles north of Los Angeles. The company was interested in developing this land, and at first blush it seemed like a pretty good idea to Remi.

In the Absolute phase of his research, Remi read the company's reports, which revealed that the company held other assets in farming, mining, oil extraction, and other businesses, but that these assets didn't generate much cash. He also learned that Tejon Ranch didn't talk to investors, hold conference calls, or give much detail regarding its projects, so the Relative and Exploration phases of research would be critical.

In the Relative phase of research Remi located an environmental impact report and learned that Tejon had given up a lot of land to environmental groups in return for the right to develop the land they still held. The remaining land would not be easy to develop as it was in a mountainous area. Still, to Remi, this did not seem like a bad deal.

In the Exploration phase, Remi was surprised to hear, again and again, that Tejon Ranch's land was "in the middle of nowhere."

How could land only sixty miles—ninety minutes—from LA be in the middle of nowhere? When Remi asked this follow-up question, his sources explained: it was ninety minutes from Los Angeles *without* traffic. *With* traffic, Tejon Ranch could be nearly *three hours* from LA—thus, in the middle of nowhere. Very few people would be willing to commute three hours each way.

Moreover, although he had read that the area was mountainous, his interviews put the problem of the terrain into perspective. Exploration sources helped him to estimate that it might cost $3 *billion* to grade and prepare the land for development, as there was also little if any infrastructure support there.

As a result of his interviews Remi got a read on the true value of the land. His ability to understand the source of disagreement over the land value was critical to his ability to get an edge on his target.

By thoughtfully developing his sources and using different interview approaches, Remi was able to develop the other side of this seemingly straightforward company narrative.

For Patricia, researching Sprint, the Exploration phase of research unearthed two important insights. The first was informational. Her interviews made her much more comfortable that Sprint was a viable company and that the technology that it was transitioning to would work on both of its networks. She also got more comfortable with the company's associated costs to combine the networks, collecting good information about possible future cost savings. These findings ultimately led her to believe that going forward Sprint's cost structure would be similar to that of Verizon and AT&T.

Patricia's second insight, no less important, was behavioral, and was something that she could only get from interviewing: she read her interviewees' verbal and nonverbal cues. Her interviewees were upbeat in their tone and word choice. They came across to her as confident that Sprint would be competitive going forward.

Her thesis statement from her interviews read:

My interviews indicate that management's network consolidation plan is viable and that it would make Sprint competitive with AT&T and Verizon. If management can execute on schedule and budget, the company's stock is cheap.

Patricia concluded from her thesis statement that there were three CCs going forward. One involved Sprint and two were about her own assumptions and judgments, as well as her research process and her ability to correctly read the tea leaves (or, in Sprint's case, get the signal):

1. What might impede management from executing on-plan?
2. Where might I be wrong?
3. What mistakes might I have made?

Like Patricia, by the end of your Exploration work, you too should be refining your Critical Concepts. You've carefully explored the outside world from the perspective of your Absolute target, from its Relative sources, and now in Exploration through interviews. In the next chapter, your process turns inward. Where might you be making assumptions and judgments about your data? Can you back up all assertions with evidence? Let's find out.

Chapter Nine

AREA = E: Exploitation

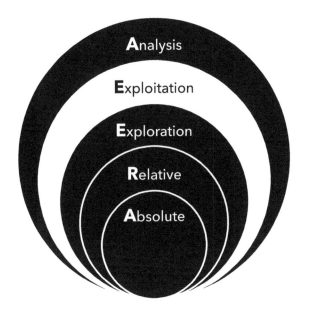

Habit is habit, and not to be flung out of the window,
but coaxed downstairs a step at a time.

—Mark Twain

Look at this image.

At first glance, what do you see? A face? We often believe the first thing we see and don't always ask ourselves, is that all? Might there be more? At times our thoughts, like our eyes, limit us.

Or make liars of us. Can you see the word "liar" embedded in the face?

While our eyes transmit information to the brain, our brain interprets that information—

often incompletely, because the brain interprets information based upon prior experiences.

Let's try another one and see this phenomenon in action again. Read the following paragraph.

"Aoccdrnig to rscheearch at Cmabridge Uinvervtisy, it deosn't mttaer in waht oredr the ltteers in a wrod are, the olny iprmoetnt tihng is taht the frist and lsat ltteer be at the rghit pclae. The rset can be a ttoal mses and you can sitll raed it wouthit a porbelm. Tihs is besauae ocne we laren how to raed we bgien to aargnre the lteerts in our mnid to see waht we epxcet to see. The huamn mnid deos not raed ervey lteter by istlef, but preecsievs the wrod as a wlohe. We do tihs ucnsoniuscoly wuithot tuhoght."

Surprising, isn't it? You're finding meaning in a mass of jumbled letters. How is this possible?

When information enters the mind, it self-organizes. New information fits itself into existing experiences and familiar patterns. Even if much of the information the mind is receiving is new, the mind will default to patterns previously activated and automatically "correct" and "complete" the information received.

In the paragraph above, your brain takes a bit of information (the first and last letters) and activates the "word" channel—and you see and understand the word. This is why when we try to have new ideas or solutions we often instead keep coming up with the same familiar ideas; information flowing down the same channels, making the same old connections, produces the same old ideas over and over again. Our brains are almost like personal judicial systems, making decisions based upon precedents. We have a (well-meaning) incentive *not* to learn new things.

The AREA Method readily acknowledges our cognitive shortcomings and is crafted to help you identify the source and perspective of your information so that you can not only develop a healthy skepticism about the information you gather, but also spot new, or *dis*-confirming, data. Noting that all information is influenced by its authors, the second section of "E" moves from "Exploration," or broadening your research by listening to others, to "Exploitation," or evaluating *your* perspective and understanding *your* information and ideas.

The exercises in Exploitation are meant to break down your information and your thought processes so that you can study the elements and structure of both. It will help you *evaluate* your work and then ascribe *value* to it, while closely reining in your cognitive short cuts. It may lead you to collect more information and to do more work.

In the next chapter, Analysis, you will process the data you've gathered, interpreting it all and taking a final Cheetah Pause to ask, "What does it all mean?"

Evaluation and interpretation are two discrete ways of thinking that we often combine into one. Evaluation is an assessment of something. Interpretation is your opinion of what it means. By separating them, the AREA Method challenges us to slow down and to think about our thinking. For in the end, at the conclusion of the Analysis chapter, you will again have to rely upon your own judgment.

To begin the evaluation phase, Exploitation provides you with a set of creative tools and techniques that come from experts in journalism, intelligence gathering, and psychology. These tools will help you to improve your analytical skills and will protect you from avoidable errors of bias that impede sound decision-making about your data. For while our instinct to piece things together from incomplete information can be both good and bad, in our research, we want to avoid the bad.

Just as you can train your brain to experience the "liar" optical illusion as two pictures—a face and a word—rather than just one, so too may you learn to read a set of information or data in multiple ways. The goal: to gain new insights, original ideas, and solutions.

Insight comes when new information enters the brain and connects with information previously stored there to craft a new understanding. It may be achieved by active study or by presence of mind. The exercises in Exploitation will help you to achieve insight by activating these connections. These creative exercises are meant to:

- Help you challenge and cross-examine your judgment
- Guide you to look at the same information or data as everyone else but see something different
- Promote thinking beyond the boundaries of already established fact
- Encourage you to connect dots and derive insights across your research
- Encourage fluidity of thought

Remember that the truth can rarely be reduced to certainties. The following exercises embrace uncertainty to try to lead us toward a clear, insightful appraisal of the situation. As Richards Heuer, a former Central Intelligence Agency analyst, wrote in his book *Psychology of Intelligence Analysis*, "Major intelligence failures are caused by failures of analysis, not failures in data collection."[1]

The way that Heuer and others teach us to prevent such failures is *not* to simply confirm things that you already believe, but instead to *disconfirm* them.

One prominent method of disconfirmation is something many of us learned in an early science class: the scientific method. Dating back to the seventeenth century, the scientific method teaches scientists to focus on proving that they can't reject their hypotheses rather than trying to prove that they can confirm them. It has four simple steps:

1. Define a problem
2. Formulate an educated guess or hypothesis
3. Design an experiment to test the hypothesis
4. Analyze the results

Like the scientific method, the goal of the exercises in this chapter is to provide an objective, standardized approach to testing hypotheses that minimizes the influence of bias. You have already created several hypotheses with your thesis statements from the Absolute, Relative, and Exploration stages of your research. In this chapter, you will develop and test additional hypotheses, moving your research story forward by scaffolding onto earlier hypotheses, in the same way a scientist follows the scientific method to refine her hypothesis. By using a standardized approach in investigating your hypotheses you will have better comfort and confidence that you can stick to the facts and limit the influence of personal, preconceived notions.

Yet even with such a rigorous methodology in place, we'll still make mistakes from time to time. We might fail to accurately account for errors, such as problems with measurement or data selection, or we may mistake a hypothesis for a factual statement.

For example, think of the terrible mistake in 2003 when the United States invaded Iraq based on the Bush administration's assertion that the country was stockpiling weapons of mass destruction. This was not a statement of fact, but rather a hypothesis.

A theory may be correct without foolproof evidence. For example, the theory of relativity predicted the existence of black holes long before there was actual evidence of black holes. However, one of the goals of science—and of this section—is to remember that even when you think you are on to something your goal is to try to disprove it.

The key point here is to focus not only on finding information that confirms your hypotheses, but also on demonstrating you can't disconfirm them. It's a more robust process that will lead to fewer errors. Having twenty reasons to follow a certain path may not matter if there are two insurmountable roadblocks.

Charlie Munger, Warren Buffett's partner at Berkshire Hathaway, is fond of using such techniques and has been known to paraphrase mathematician Carl Gustav Jacobi, saying, "Invert, always invert."[2] By inverting our thinking we take conscious control of it. This may sound easy, but is hard to do in practice because we are *wired* to jump to conclusions. The AREA Method reconciles abstract thinking with observation and begins by working backwards from a conclusion.

Medical research is often approached this way. For example, doctors have made big breakthroughs in developing drugs to fight AIDS not by trying to eliminate the virus, but instead by focusing on confusing the process by which the HIV virus converts to the disease of AIDS.

What follows is a discussion of four exercises to help you question your thinking and your data. While you may want to pick and choose among the exercises and the various ways to view the evidence you've gathered, these exercises are not interchangeable. Rather, they are interrelated. They work to get you out of your own perspective and to gain some distance from your own biases because, while each exercise is sensitive to the data you choose to test, each exercise evaluates data differently. Together and separately, the exercises are channel blockers that push your thinking and decision-making habits out of their well-worn pathways and into new patterns. Ideally, each exercise allows you to see your decision in a new light, so that you build a layered understanding of your decision.

Pro/Con Analysis

This useful analysis tool has been in use for centuries. In 1772, Benjamin Franklin recommended the approach in a letter to his friend Joseph Priestly, who was wrestling with a thorny problem. The exercise asks you to begin to combine your disparate pieces of research into two different coherent and cohesive narrative arguments about the organization you are researching to understand and analyze two different futures, one positive and one negative. For example, if you are considering a job opportunity at an organization, your Pro/Con might be the arguments in favor of taking it and against taking it. If you are evaluating an investment opportunity, your Pro would be that your Absolute target is a good investment and your Con would be that the target would make a poor investment (which in turn might make it a good investment on the short side).

CHEETAH SHEET 39

Exploitation: Pro/Con Analysis

1. Begin by writing out two brief memos, one that is framed in the affirmative, the positive side of your decision, and the other statement making a case for the negatives, against the decision.
2. Next, write two separate narrative essays, one to support each thesis, and list all of your reasons and evidence for each case. Be careful that both the Pro and Con cases are responsive to all major arguments addressing each point for both theses. If you make a specific case for your decision in the Pro case, respond to it in the Con case. This will help you to see where the argument might be flawed.
3. When you're done writing each compelling case, write up an analysis of your findings.

The goal of the Pro/Con exercise is not to develop a view, but rather to step into the shoes of both views to develop a more complete understanding of the arguments in favor of and against your decision relating to your research target. The outcome should not only illuminate "the other side of the trade," but also provide a guide for further targeted research to investigate the answers to the questions that the Pro/Con exercise brings to light.

Below is Patricia's Pro/Con analysis written for Sprint. Her Absolute, Relative, and Exploration research brought forth several different views on the company's prospects. On the one hand, she'd learned that independent market research firms reported that Sprint had higher customer satisfaction ratings on its network performance than competitors, yet on the other hand, experts in the industry were concerned with the issue of

whether Sprint could profitably compete against larger rivals AT&T and
Verizon.

Patricia's Pro/Con exercise investigated these two statements:

Pro statement: *Sprint is selling at a cheap price and could
dramatically increase profitability by combining their two
networks*

Con statement: *Sprint is heavily indebted and competitively
doomed. They appear optically cheap, but are actually expensive if
you take into account deferred capital spending.*

These were her write-ups to address each statement:

Pro

*Sprint trades at just 4.5 x EV / EBITDA after their Clearwire stake.
They are not only cheap, but their network improvements will be
realized in future subscriber growth. The high operating leverage
to new subscribers will drive profitability growth going forward.
They might be the #3 player, but they provide the second best service according to JD Power & Associates, offering evidence of their
ability to compete with larger players. Furthermore, service is the
most important factor for subscribers, and Sprint's network quality should be reflected in their long-term subscriber counts. Sprint's
excess spectrum offers a meaningful advantage since AT&T and
Verizon are capping data, but Sprint does not have to. The ability
to offer unlimited data to users means that Sprint has an advantage
with heavy data users. Their debt might be high, but they have the
liquidity to pay off almost half of it and all maturities through the
next two years.*

Con

*Sprint is a heavily indebted and unprofitable company with long-
term solvency and competitive issues. Recent reductions in churn and
improvements in the network are just a result of shifting customers
from the antiquated iDEN network to the CDMA network. Sprint
still meaningfully lags Verizon and AT&T in spending for Capital
Expenditures, placing them at a long-term disadvantage in terms of
serving customers. While JD Power & Associates, a market research*

firm, found that Sprint customers were more satisfied with their ser-
vice than competitors, the high ratings are on a small base. Sprint has
far fewer customers and thus network traffic than the competitors.
Sprint's network quality might collapse if the company was actu-
ally able to add more customers. Furthermore, the AT&T / T-Mobile
merger increases Sprint's competitive issues due to their competitors'
growing scale. Free cash flow is overstated since the company has
spent all of its upgrade capital expenditures through Clearwire and
the company is barely profitable. Furthermore, the long-term value
of spectrum is negligible. The "spectrum crunch" is overstated and
based on long-run projections that are unknowable. Also, cell site
technology improvements will drive down a buyer's willingness to
pay for spectrum. In such a capital-intensive and competitive busi-
ness, it is only a matter of time before they have solvency issues,
given their lack of profitability and high debt load and capital needs.

The Pro/Con exercise forced Patricia to flesh out and consider both
sides of Sprint's investment story equally. It evaluated her understanding
of her Critical Concepts:

1. Did Sprint have a defensible competitive position?
2. What was the company's future earnings power? This answer
   was dependent upon two things: Sprint's ability to combine its
   networks and the company's normal capital expenditures. On a
   free-cash flow basis the stock looked cheap. But was the number
   inflated because Sprint was not reinvesting enough money to
   maintain the business?

The exercise raised several new questions regarding how Sprint might
view and address the above issues. It also led Patricia to consider what
evidence she had collected to support or refute the options. She hadn't
previously considered that Sprint could be understating its capital expenditures by diverting capital expenditures through Clearwire, whose financials statements were unconsolidated, so the exercise forced her to think
through the bearish argument on that topic.

Were the expenditures so low because Clearwire was doing Sprint's
capital spending? Patricia later said it was "really valuable to realize that
possibility," a direct example of the value of the exercise.

Her concluding thesis statement from the Pro/Con exercise read:

The Pro/Con exercise crystallized the importance of understanding how much Sprint needs to spend on capital expenditures. This issue will not only determine the company's cost structure and ability to compete with larger rivals, but also clarify valuation.

To help her answer her new questions, Patricia moved on to the next Exploitation exercise, the Competing Alternative Hypotheses exercise, so that she could lay out all of her evidence for and against her hypotheses.

Matthew, researching Delta, had a similar Pro/Con experience to Patricia's. The exercise pointed out clear pluses and minuses and helped Matthew to hone in on important questions that needed to be answered, funneling him back into AREA's earlier steps to collect missing data points.

Here are the statements Matthew developed for his Pro/Con exercise, with a detailed narrative for each, followed by a chart where he laid out how his Critical Concepts would play out in the contrasting Pro/Con scenarios (fig. 9.2).

Pro: *It's different this time*

Delta's competitive moat is comprised of unparalleled operational excellence, a best-in-class corporate travel program, and dominant market share in several of the country's most profitable markets that have unique barriers to entry in their own right. Delta will never be the low cost provider—and it doesn't have to be.

Con: *Same as it ever was*

Delta is operating at peak earnings in a cyclical industry, with significant capacity coming on board from ultra low cost carriers that exhibit a structural cost advantage. Delta is also in the midst of a contentious negotiation with its pilots' union that will increase expenses, and faces challenges from state-subsidized airline operators overseas. Even in a muted fuel price environment, this will result in lower ticket prices, higher operating expenses, and weaker profitability. An increase in fuel prices will only weaken the company's operating condition as it is unlikely that Delta will be able to pass on the full impact of price increases to consumers given the increased capacity across the industry.

Topic	Bull Perspective	Bear Perspective
Industry Capacity	Large network carriers are finally addressing capacity rationally, taking out older aircraft and judiciously adding capacity. Smaller airlines are increasing capacity at a much higher rate, but they're just a blip on the radar screen. Southwest and JetBlue are larger concerns, but a lot of the capacity increase is utilization increase as opposed to new aircraft.	Although the Big 3 are only increasing capacity 2–3%, capacity increases industry wide are starting to become a major concern. Spirit increased capacity 30% in 2015, Allegiant 18%, Frontier expected to increase capacity by 20% in 2016. Southwest intends to increase capacity by 6% and JetBlue 10%+. For the latter two, this will result in a significant increase in the available aircraft, utilization, and available seat miles.
Ultra low-cost carrier ("ULCC") Competition	ULCCs are basically increasing the size of the passenger universe as opposed to taking market share from other airlines. ULCCs are for consumers who had previously decided not to fly, rather than consumers who are switching from another airline. They are also taking the spillover passenger on the margin—again, not a large concern. The network carriers have also introduced tiered pricing as a way to directly compete with these airlines. Also, the ULCCs still need to obtain gates/access which is challenging in most major metropolitan markets.	ULCCs have a superior cost structure and have been growing rapidly. These airlines have just scratched the surface of the number of markets / routes that they can enter because of the lower cost structure. In order to compete in the markets where ULCCs enter, network carriers will need to cut price significantly which will compress margins and profitability. I am skeptical that tiered pricing will be successful given that it takes away the primary benefit of flying a network carrier (no frequent flyer miles).
Brand equity	For the past five years, corporate travel managers have named Delta their favorite airline. Delta also ranks substantially higher than its competitors (4.19 vs 3.31 for 2nd place on a 5 point scale), indicating that the difference is quite large. Delta's average ticket is ~114% of the industry average domestically, demonstrating that customers make a conscious choice to fly Delta in spite of price. This is a long term and sustainable competitive advantage.	While not a perfect commodity, airlines are a fairly commoditized product for the leisure traveler. Price is the ultimate determinant for a purchase decision.
Fuel	There is currently a supply-demand imbalance in oil that favors airlines. Based on the futures curve, oil is priced to increase gradually to $52 by 2024. With the current cost structure airlines should continue to be extremely profitable at those, levels.	Fuel is a commodity, and most of the airlines have taken off most of their fuel hedges for the next few years. Assuming no airline has unnatural skill in hedging oil, a changing fuel environment really shouldn't benefit anybody over the long run. Today's current profitability will be competed away by increased capacity and lower revenue per available seat mile, because airlines will assume that if they don't fill the additional capacity, someone else will.
Valuation	On the surface, Delta and its airline counterparts are cheap. Delta trades at 4.0x EV / Forward EBITDA and a P / Forward EPS of 7.1x. The median EV / Forward EBITDA and P / Forward EPS for the industry are 3.9x and 9.3x, respectively. Both Delta and the industry are trading far below historical averages on both metrics. There's a huge margin for error when trading at these depressed multiples.	We are experiencing peak earnings, so of course valuation metrics are near trough levels. Current EBIT and net profit margins are multiples of what they've been historically, so if we assume a reversion to the mean then these stocks might actually be expensive at these levels.

Figure 9.2. Matthew's Delta Pro/Con exercise: the bull and bear perspectives

The Pro/Con exercise brought up a few questions for Matthew. He realized that he didn't understand whether the passengers who flew discount airlines were the same passengers who flew Delta. Were discount airlines getting a new population of passengers and growing the market, or were they poaching from Delta? He also realized that he didn't know what happened to pricing in markets when a discount airline entered. Would Delta need to lower its prices? And if so, by how much? Matthew also wanted to get a handle on how wide Delta's moat was for corporate travel and how protected it was by its reputation.

To answer these questions, he went back into earlier AREA steps to collect new data and then he plugged the key pieces of evidence into the Competing Alternative Hypotheses exercise, which follows below, to assess different hypotheses for how Delta's future could play out, given the environment it was operating in.

Competing Alternative Hypotheses

The Competing Alternative Hypotheses (CAH) exercise was developed by Richards Heuer, a forty-five-year veteran of the CIA. In the 1970s, Heuer ran the agency's methodology unit in its intelligence operations department. During his tenure, Heuer realized that most CIA errors were the result not of insufficient data, but rather insufficient ability to process data correctly because of human biases. He penned the manual *Psychology of Intelligence Analysis,* which details some of his thinking about problems of human perception and their manifestation in analytical errors.

Heuer believed that we all face inherent difficulties in processing complex information, but analysts could offset these psychological shortcomings by creating a system to manage them. In developing the CAH exercise, Heuer wanted to provide researchers with an unbiased process of analysis to avoid some common analytical pitfalls like ignoring evidence that conflicts with an existing hypothesis or rejecting an alternative hypothesis without thorough evidence. By forcing you to systematically work through evidence and its implications, CAH avoids the errors of oversight that occur in a bias-influenced process. The CAH exercise, like the cheetah pauses where you craft your thesis statements, creates an audit trail. Seeing your key pieces of data matched against your hypotheses brings your assumptions and your evidence face to face.

Two key elements distinguish CAH from conventional analysis. First, CAH starts with a full set of hypotheses rather than the most likely hypothesis for which you seek confirmation. For instance, if you were leaning toward snapping up Facebook shares in the wake of the data privacy scandal because they suddenly seem cheap, the CAH would push you to test all possible hypotheses rather than your favored one. By laying out all of your hypotheses and your data together, the CAH exercise systematically evaluates the impact of your data against each hypothesis. By giving all hypotheses equal time and attention you keep from succumbing to bias. You won't only match evidence against what you deem to be your most likely hypothesis. This ensures that alternative hypotheses receive equal treatment and a fair shake. Using CAH enables you to ferret out key connections between data and hypotheses that are not always obvious or intuitive. You don't want to run roughshod over an unexpected insight.

Second, while conventional analysis generally entails looking for evidence to confirm a favored hypothesis, CAH often reveals that a particular data point can support multiple hypotheses, which means that data point is not be as useful as initially expected. A data point that supports a particular hypothesis might seem compelling, but if it supports every hypothesis, it actually has very little diagnosticity. Something that is true is unlikely to have disconfirming data but something that is untrue might well have supporting information. Thus in CAH it's more important to focus on the negatives than the positives. The result is that the most probable hypothesis is usually the one with the least evidence *against* it, not the one with the most evidence *for* it.

In the 2016 US presidential election pundits were saying Donald Trump was unelectable because he was "outside the norm" and not a "typical" candidate. But Hillary Clinton was also "outside the norm" as the first woman to run for president as a major party candidate. This data point—outside the norm—equally supported the unelectability of both candidates and therefore had little diagnosticity.

Thus the CAH exercise discourages you from what decision scientists call "satisficing," or picking the first solution that seems satisfactory, rather than going through all of the possibilities to identify the best solution. For while it might be of small consequence to "satisfice" when choosing, say, a particular brand of cream cheese at the grocery store, it can be very costly to do so when the decision will affect your earning potential and job satisfaction for years to come.

By going through all possible solutions, you're less likely to be led astray by trying to confirm only one hypothesis that you think is true. You won't run the risk of having just enough evidence to support a favored hypothesis while failing to recognize that most of that evidence is also consistent with other hypotheses. You may also bring to light previously unconsidered ways of interpreting evidence.

In focusing more attention on alternative explanations, CAH brings out the full uncertainty inherent in any situation that is, in Heuer's words, "poor in data but rich in possibilities." Such uncertainty can be frustrating, but is likely a more accurate reflection of the true situation. As Voltaire said, "Doubt is not a pleasant state, but certainty is a ridiculous one."

How do you determine which data points to use? Your Critical Concepts should guide you.

CHEETAH SHEET 40

Exploitation: CAH Exercise Directions

1. Identify the possible hypotheses that merit detailed examination.
2. List significant evidence and arguments for and against each hypothesis.
3. Prepare a chart with hypotheses across the top and evidence down the side. Analyze the evidence against each hypothesis. Identify which pieces of evidence confirm each hypothesis, which are disconfirming, and which may need more research to be able to tell whether they confirm or disconfirm the hypotheses.
4. Refine the chart. Reconsider the hypotheses and delete evidence and arguments that have no diagnostic value.
5. Draw tentative conclusions about the relative likelihood of each hypothesis. Proceed by trying to disprove the hypotheses rather than prove them.
6. Analyze how sensitive your conclusion is to a few critical items of evidence. Consider the consequences for your analysis if that evidence were wrong, misleading, or subject to a different interpretation.
7. Report conclusions. Discuss the relative likelihood of all the hypotheses, not just the most likely one.
8. Identify milestones for future observation that may indicate events are taking a different course than expected.

By focusing attention on the few items of critical evidence that cause the uncertainty or that, if they were available, would alleviate it, the CAH exercise can guide future collection, research, and analysis to resolve the uncertainty and produce a more accurate judgment.

The CAH process has eight steps grounded in basic insights from cognitive psychology and decision analysis. Subsequent discussion can then focus productively on the ultimate source of the differences. In the appendix, you will find a detailed explanation of the following outline.

This exercise requires you to clearly delineate your assumptions as hypotheses and compare them to your evidence.

Matthew, who was researching Delta, had been particularly impressed by business travelers' loyalty to the airline. For the previous five years, corporate travel managers had ranked Delta higher than its competitors even though Delta's average ticket price was about 114 percent of the industry average. If Delta could continue to charge premium ticket prices while its costs remain steady, the company's returns would exceed its costs of capital. However, ultra-low-cost carriers were changing the ticket pricing landscape. Matthew developed three hypotheses around this central issue:

1. Delta's returns will exceed its cost of capital
2. Delta will earn returns commensurate with cost of capital
3. Delta will earn returns below cost of capital

Matthew's CAH is mapped out in figure 9.3.

Note that Matthew was only testing out one Critical Concept, but it is the one he deemed most important to understanding Delta's investment prospects.

The CAH changed how Matthew understood Delta's value proposition. By looking at the data all laid out against the hypotheses several things became clear. First, no hypothesis is a clear winner; every option has some downside. Second, one of Matthew's key "plus" data points—that Delta's operational excellence had been, and would continue to be, a real competitive advantage—didn't look so special when laid out alongside other data points. Although this point was a negative for Matthew's hypothesis that Delta would earn below its cost of capital, the bearish hypothesis actually had the least disconfirming data, which

Evidence	Competing Alternative Hypotheses		
	Delta's returns will *exceed* cost of capital	Delta will earn returns *commensurate* with cost of capital	Delta will earn returns *below* cost of capital
Market has significantly consolidated. Top 4 players now own almost 70% market share domestically. They are incentivized to act rationally and have demonstrated capacity discipline thus far.	+	+	-
Fuel costs recently were about 50% lower than they've been over the past five years. There is no evidence that airlines will be able to raise prices commensurate with the cost of fuel to sustain margins.	-	N/A	+
Ultra low-cost carriers are increasing capacity significantly. While still a small portion of the overall market, these new routes will likely be in markets where the Big 4 are earning outsized returns.	--	-	+
Delta's operational excellence is a real advantage for the business traveler. For the past five years, corporate travel managers have ranked Delta higher than competitors and Delta's average ticket is about 114% of the industry average.	+	+	-
Revenue per Available Seat Mile fell last year and companies have guided to further declines this year.	-	-	+
Spirit and other ULCCs claim their entrance into a market actually increases the total addressable market and does not take share from current participants.	+	+	+
Cost per Average Seat Mile ex-fuel will come under pressure from increased labor costs, particularly for larger carriers who cannot grow capacity to moderate wage increases.	--	-	+
International competition is increasing, particularly from state-funded airlines in the Middle East. Capacity from these airlines is also increasing substantially.	-	-	+

Key: (+) Indicates evidence support hypothesis; (-) Indicates evidence refutes hypothesis

Figure 9.3. Matthew's Competing Alterative Hypotheses exercise for Delta

made it the most likely. This exercise reoriented the way Matthew understood and prioritized his facts.

Here is Matthew's thesis from his CAH:

Low cost carriers are increasing capacity significantly, and although they are a small portion of the overall market, these new routes will likely be in markets where the Big 4 are earning outsized returns, which may well pressure Delta's ticket prices. It is unclear whether Delta's operational excellence is strong enough to withstand these competitive pressures, especially in the face of increased labor and fuel costs.

Patricia, investigating Sprint, approached the CAH differently than Matthew had. Where Matthew tested three hypotheses related to one Critical Concept, Patricia developed three different hypotheses, one for each CC. In her mind, the CCs all had equal weight as to their importance for Sprint's value proposition so she wanted to think about each of them. Patricia's CAH represents a more complex analysis, more reflective of the real world, and enabled her to see how the different CCs stacked up against her most compelling data points.

Patricia found the CAH exercise valuable in that it forced her to systematically evaluate each hypothesis and data point. In her Exploration work, a source at Verizon had estimated that 50 percent of Verizon's capital expenditures was related to subscriber growth. If the source at Verizon was correct, Sprint's spending was roughly in line with Verizon's in a steady-state environment. Could that be the case? Patricia's CAH exercise is illustrated in figure 9.4.

Patricia's findings showed that her hypothesis about Sprint underfunding its network had the only negative evidence—it was the *least* likely to be true. If so, and if customer satisfaction and reduced churn were indeed linked with capital expenditures, as her interviews recounted, then perhaps the market was incorrectly valuing Sprint's shares. But by how much? She returned to Exploration for additional interviews to estimate the capital expenditures required to maintain and upgrade a network. The estimates then enabled her to judge Sprint's maintenance capital expenditures needs "from the ground up." The result supported the hypothesis that Sprint was *not* underinvesting in its network.

In addition, Patricia found solid evidence that Sprint's network consolidation was viable and that Sprint could compete with AT&T and Verizon,

Evidence	Competing Alternative Hypotheses		
	Network consolidation is visible	Sprint can compete with Verizon and AT&T	Sprint has been underspending on Cap Ex
The "good" network has lower churn and is adding subscribers	+	+	-
Sprint has historically lost subscribers to Verizon and AT&T	N/A	N/A	N/A
Clearwire has Spectrum and is building 4G network	N/A	+	+
Source at Verizon says 50% of its Cap Ex is related to subgrowth	N/A	+	--
Sprint has higher network ratings than AT&T	N/A	+	-
T-Mobile and PCS have same cost per sub as Verizon and AT&T	N/A	+	N/A
Conversations with engineers, tower operators and execs support management estimates for network integration	++	++	N/A
Hesse has reduced churn since taking over	+	+	-

Key: (+) Indicates evidence support hypotheses; (-) Indicates evidence refutes hypothesis

Figure 9.4. Patricia's Competing Alternative Hypotheses exercise for Sprint

but more important, she did not encounter evidence refuting those hypotheses. She realized she could disregard historical subscriber losses because many of them were tied to the "bad" network. In her judgment, it was more of a lagging indicator than a leading indicator.

Furthermore, four of Patricia's data points—competitors' per subscriber costs, network quality ratings, "good" network subscriber trends, and channel checks on network integration—didn't refute the hypothesis that Sprint could consolidate its network and compete with Verizon and AT&T. She concluded with the thesis statement:

Based upon the CAH exercise, it appears likely that Sprint is not underinvesting in its network, the network consolidation plan is viable, and Sprint can compete effectively with Verizon and AT&T.

Visual Maps

Approximately three-quarters of our brain's sensory resources are dedi-cated to vision. That leaves only one quarter for all the other senses combined. According to Dual Coding Theory, a memory theory that explains the impact of imagery on the brain, we process verbal and visual information with different parts of the brain. In other words, when we work only with words, we're not even using a quarter of our brain.

Since learning depends on both hemispheres of the brain—left hemi-sphere (verbal, logical, sequential, analytical) and right hemisphere (visual, emotional, intuitive, nonlinear, big picture, synthesis)—one of the creative exercises that I ask my students to undertake is to put their visual thinking into play by using pictures to help them think about their Critical Concepts for their research target.

Translating visual thinking onto (virtual) paper is visual mapping. It combines words and images to create a visual record of your thoughts, lit-erally revealing the "big picture." It helps you think about complex issues by demanding pictorial translation.

I have included three visual maps of the AREA Method in this book. Each one is distinct and explains a different aspect of AREA. The visual map on page ii of this book, the AREA Method Cheetah Sheet, portrays an overview of the whole AREA system. The visual map in chapter 1 (fig. 1.1, page 8) shows how AREA separates sources of information and acts as a feedback loop as depicted by a series of concentric circles, starting by zooming in on your target's perspective and then telescoping outward to investigate how other storytellers understand and evalu-ate your target. The third visual map, in chapter 2 (fig. 2.1, page 13) explains AREA's value proposition.

Another example: an international company like Coca-Cola Company has a diverse set of products in its portfolio. How can it quickly and eas-ily communicate its breadth and depth to potential investors, customers, competitors, and partners? The company thought about this problem and developed a compelling visual map that lays out the company's diverse product lines as well as its competitive advantages (fig. 9.5).[3]

In its color version, while its product logos are all different colors and shapes, the composite results are presented in Coca-Cola red.[4] It's a story that conveys the company's depth and breadth all without using words.

Research shows that 65 percent of the population are visual thinkers, but one hundred percent of us benefit from receiving information visually,

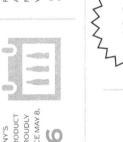

Figure 9.5. Coca-Cola's product portfolio visual map

a statistic borne out by the vision-related metaphors we use all the time.[5] *Do you see what I mean? I get the picture.*

Here are some more interesting statistics related to the value of relaying information visually: 70 percent of all of our sensory receptors are in our eyes. Almost half of our brain is involved in visual processing. In .01 seconds (before you have finished reading this sentence) your brain can read a visual situation.[6]

When I introduce visual mapping in my classes, students often push back, arguing that it's silly or reductive. But when they complete the exercise and pictorially portray their investment puzzle, they regularly comment that it forced them to get creative and that seeing a picture of their material helped them *see* their research process anew. This isn't surprising. A study by researchers at the University of Minnesota found that "presentations using visual aids were found to be 43% more persuasive than unaided presentations" in part because "attention, comprehension . . . and retention are enhanced when presentation support is used compared to when it is not."[7]

There is no one right way to make a visual map, but there are many benefits to doing so, including fostering creativity and imagination and sparking dialogue with others, as well as helping you to better internalize trends and connections—so consider how you might visually display some of your research. Students have made compelling maps over the years that include cartoons, pie charts, bar charts, line graphs, mind maps, Venn diagrams, memes, and infographics.

CHEETAH SHEET 41
Exploitation: Visual Mapping

1. How might you display your research target's "big picture" and/or details?
2. Can you connect your new information to existing knowledge in a chart, table, or graph?
3. Can you craft questions that you still need answered?
4. Consider using a website and app that can turn data into visual representations, such as Piktochart, Tableau, and Visually, among others.

Put your map(s) in your AREA Journal.

Following are two samples of visual maps. The first map (fig. 9.6), by Cari, a student of mine who was assigned to research General Motors during its restructuring, uses visual representations of the analysis, development, formulation, communication and implementation of the car company's strategy, both for the "old GM" and the "new GM." The second map (fig. 9.7) follows Matthew's Delta research honing in on where the airline industry was in terms of peak operating margins so that he could see Delta's performance in context against its peers.

The General Motors visual map displays pictorially the strategic changes that GM management undertook to transform the carmaker, particularly the transformation in its balance sheet and cost structure. It does this by giving the viewer a snapshot of the "old" GM and the "new" GM, with fewer brands, plants, employees, and dealers. In the section that details the changes in the union contracts, Cari visually lays out the financial ramifications of these changes: less debt, reduced scale of operations, which lowers the company's fixed costs, and auto sales at a cyclical low. The picture here is worth a thousand words. Cari has shown that GM has a dramatically different risk profile than it did before bankruptcy and the industry might be in a cyclical trough as well.

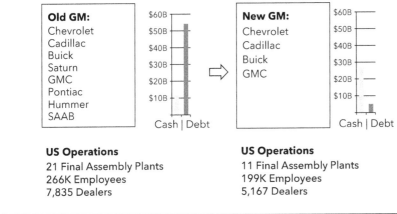

Figure 9.6. Cari's General Motors visual map: the impact of GM's restructuring

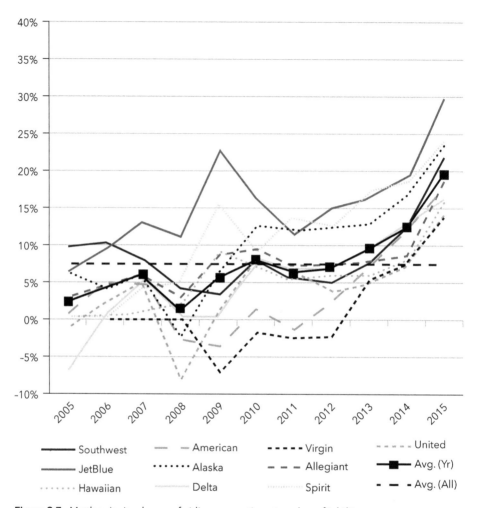

Figure 9.7. Matthew's visual map of airlines operating at peak profitability

Above is Matthew's Delta visual map (fig. 9.7).

One of Matthew's Critical Concepts dealt with assessing where Delta was in its cycle of earnings. His line graph clearly shows that the industry was experiencing a significant upward trend in its earnings, far beyond previous performance. In fact, the big three carriers—American, Delta, and United—all began their ascent in operating profit at about the same moment in time. However, while Delta had been participating nicely in the upturn, it was unclear whether the high profits in this long-cyclical industry were part of a new normal or if it might be nearing a cyclical peak. It suggested to Matthew the need to determine whether the industry might be nearing an inflection point.

Matthew's thesis statement related to this Critical Concept, one of the four he had, postulated that Delta had done an excellent job of catering to business travelers based on pricing, customer service, amenities, and overall value. As a result this was his thesis:

In order for Delta to flourish in this industry, airline services cannot become a commoditized product. Business travelers will always be restricted by location, however, in choosing an airline partner. Delta's operational advantage at this point is unclear and the visual map suggests that Delta's market opportunity might be saturated at this point.

You can find Patricia's visual map for Sprint in the appendix.

Scenario Analysis

Scenario analysis is another decision-making exercise to consider possible outcomes and their implications after a given period of time. It is a risk-assessment technique that does not try to show one exact picture of the future, but instead envisions several alternative futures based on key factors that would affect an organization going forward, such as changes in interest rates or whether or not a company is able to execute on its proposed strategy. It is not predictive, but meant to manage uncertainty. It's different from the Pro/Con exercise because Pro/Con starts with binary outcomes—two sides of the same coin—and looks for all supporting data for each outcome while scenario analysis starts with all of your data points and turns them into three possible outcomes—an upside, a neutral outcome, and a downside. The goal with scenario analysis is to visualize and explore different ways forward.

A good scenario analysis shows not only a range of possible future outcomes but also the development paths leading to the outcomes. It does not need to rely on historical data and does not expect past observations to be still valid in the future, yet it tries to consider possible developments and turning points that may be connected to the past. Note that scenario analysis assesses different outcomes from independent sets of assumptions. As a researcher you may also consider testing sensitivities within outcomes of each scenario.

CHEETAH SHEET 42

Exploitation: Developing a Scenario Analysis

To complete the scenario analysis, imagine three versions of your decision outcome.

1. Upside: the first story might have everything proceeding normally, with things falling into place and a happy ending, but should remain pragmatic and feasible. Tell the story in detail, laying it out step-by-step to reach the best possible outcome from your decision. Keep asking yourself: *And what happened next?* Resist the temptation to skip to the end of the "story" without imagining the challenges or journey on the way. By describing the steps to a successful outcome for your research target you may generate even more scenarios for what might occur and when. If you can't figure out how to get from A to B, maybe B isn't as realistic as you thought.

2. Downside: tell a negative story about your decision outcome. This time imagine a bleak future, where things go wrong and unexpected challenges impede the progress, thwarting and derailing success. This scenario imagines the process being a struggle with a bad ending. Through this story, you may come to understand where the real challenges lie and how the decision might unravel.

3. Base: the final version is in the middle, neither great nor terrible. Perhaps it is a mediocre outcome, nothing disastrous yet no triumph. How does that scenario unfold? Which things work out and which don't? Again, fill in as much detail as possible.

The scenario analysis will likely reveal new elements you need to consider that you may not have articulated and questions you need to find answers for. For example, are some factors less independent than you thought? Which factors matter, which don't, and what will actually affect those that matter enough to change the scenario?

The exercise should reveal not only key choices that the organization may need to make and important turning points that may make the difference between the outcomes, but also how your research target's value would be impacted by the various scenarios. Once you have written out a complete scenario analysis, consider the following questions.

CHEETAH SHEET 43

Exploitation: Scenario Analysis Assessment

1. Which of the three scenarios has the most evidence to support it?
2. What do you see now as most critical for the outcome of your target?
3. Which variables matter enough to change the scenario?
4. To be successful, how does your target need to act? What does it need to avoid?

Matthew's scenario analysis focused on his four Critical Concepts and how they impacted Delta's future: competitive threats from low-cost and other large carriers; ongoing labor negotiations; fuel prices; and broader economic factors. Matthew did a good job considering the key variables and how they might play out differently, but ideally he would have tied these analyses to their impact on Delta's overall profitability. Matthew's scenario analysis appears in the appendix.

For Patricia, investigating Sprint, the base case seemed most likely once she had carefully conducted the full scenario analysis. However, the downside case highlighted the risk that higher spending could pose. Patricia realized that she needed a better read on Sprint's spending. What level of capital expenditure would Sprint have to maintain?

Here is Patricia's scenario analysis:

Upside
Here there are two possibilities. First, Sprint gets acquired as the industry consolidates. At similar values to the T-Mobile acquisition, Sprint is worth $15–$20 per share, representing 3x–4x upside. In the second case, Sprint integrates in line with management estimates and exits the integration with $10 billion in net debt and roughly $5.5 billion in Enterprise Value / EBITDA—MCX. With an improved network, Sprint improves subscriber retention and trades a multiple of 11x EBITDA—MCX, reaching a value of roughly $15 per share, representing 3x upside.

Base Case
Sprint implements the network vision plan successfully, but it costs
$10 billion instead of management's $5 billion estimate and saves
$2 billion instead of management's estimate of $2.5 to $3 billion.
Normal capital expenditures are $4 billion, at the midpoint of the
Sprint analyst's estimates. In this case, post-integration, Sprint
would have net debt of roughly $15 billion and earn roughly
$4.5 billion in earnings before taxes minus MCX. At a multiple of
10x EBITDA—MCX, Sprint would be worth roughly $8 per share,
offering roughly 60% upside.

Downside
Sprint's maintenance capital expenditures (MCX) are above the high
end of the analyst's estimate at $5 billion. In this case Sprint cannot
cover its interest and bankruptcy is a risk. However, with spectrum
licenses worth $10 billion and $35 billion in subscriber replacement
value, Sprint still has enough value to cover its $15 billion in net
debt. Sprint gets acquired for $10 billion, roughly one third of the
replacement value of its assets, and shares are worth roughly $3, rep-
resenting a 40 percent loss.

  Patricia's scenario analysis thesis statement reads as follows:

Sprint shares appear to offer favorable risk / reward as shares offer
upside of 3x–4x with downside of roughly 40% based upon a liq-
uidation analysis of the company's assets, and a base case upside of
60% assuming the company's successful integration plan. The most
important factor might be the appropriate level of Maintenance
Capital Expenditures for Sprint.[8]

As you can see from Patricia and Matthew, the four exercises described in this
chapter work in concert by revealing different insights. Matthew's Exploitation work pushed his thinking about Delta. The exercises worked together
to deepen his understanding of the challenges the airline carrier faced. His
Pro/Con showed him that he needed to better understand whether discount
airlines were poaching Delta customers or growing the total market. His
CAH further explored this question and revealed that Matthew had placed
too much weight on one of his key data points: that Delta's relationship with

business travelers had allowed it to maintain premium pricing. Had he just done the Pro/Con and CAH it would have still been a game-changer. But by also completing a visual map he realized that Delta's stellar operating profits were not theirs alone; Delta was moving in concert with competitors. The scenario analysis then pushed his thinking even further: While he'd been focusing his research on a few Critical Concepts like fuel prices and wages, there was a lot more that was unpredictable. The exercise helped him zoom out and in effect showed him that he had been assessing his CCs almost in a vacuum. Together, these exercises made Delta seem less unique, the market more volatile and Delta's moat more vulnerable.

Before you move on from your Exploitation research, it's important to recognize that smart people can fool themselves about what they're finding. This final section turns its lens from how you the researcher may play tricks with your thinking to how organizations may try to trick you—legally or otherwise.

Plots and Ploys

There are many ways that a company or organization may misrepresent its own financial results. Financial data may obscure the real value of underutilized or poorly understood assets, or management may engage in financial chicanery. What follows is first an overview of some of the ways in which financial statements might misrepresent an entity's value, followed by a discussion of some possible red flags that you will want to be aware of to spot signs of deception and fraud.

There are several ways that data can get obscured. At times management is incentivized to keep the stock price low, for example during restructurings and spin offs, when management is waiting for options to be set and prefers the lowest stock price possible. At other times, management is forced to understate the value of their assets—for example, when the existing accounting rules diverge from the economic value of the assets. And, of course, investors may not appreciate or recognize assets of economic value. All these scenarios may enable the stock price to diverge from the fundamental value of the entity.

A classic example of mismatched incentives impacting financial results occurred when Liberty Interactive, a media company that owned the television and Internet retailer QVC, split off Liberty Ventures into its own trading stock in early 2012 to "reflect the separate economic performance of the business and assets," according to the company's press release.⁹ Liberty Ventures represented Liberty's minority ownership stake in a series of publicly traded companies, the largest of which were Expedia and Trip Advisor, along with some unusual legacy debt.

Although Liberty Ventures listed negative book value under generally accepted accounting practices, the value of the assets was dramatically higher in two ways. First, the Trip Advisor and Expedia equity stakes were listed at historical cost, but due to appreciation in these shares since the time of Liberty's investment, the equity stakes were worth hundreds of millions of dollars more than their carrying value.

Second, the legacy debt carried some unusual tax characteristics that provided Liberty Ventures with cash they wouldn't have to repay for almost two decades while incurring no interest. The right to borrow money for twenty years at a 0 percent interest rate surely had economic value, but this was ignored by general accounting standards.¹⁰

The result was that while Liberty Ventures listed a book value of less than zero, it had assets that were worth over $2 billion. An investor who recognized this could have enjoyed an increase in the stock from $40 at the time of the spin off to almost $120 two years later.

On the flip side, if you are researching a hospital and it has uncollected bills, it may be claiming that it can receive 100 percent of the money owed it when in fact some percentage of those bills will almost certainly remain uncollected. Is your research target realistic and how does that change its financial picture?

Below are some places to look where accounting standards may cause assets of value to be underreported or overreported. The first two in this list were relevant in the case of Liberty Ventures.

CHEETAH SHEET 44
Exploitation: Plots and Ploys Hidden Value

1. Equity stakes (held at historical cost instead of market value)
2. Tax assets (in this case arising from unusual debt). This can include net operating loss (NOL) carry-forwards if the entity has taken a valuation allowance against them. (The valuation allowance reduces the book value of the NOL. Entities often will take a valuation allowance against

the full amount of their deferred tax assets if they have reported a cumulative loss for the last three years. Entities also take a valuation allowance if they deem it more likely than not that they won't use their net operating carry-forwards before they expire.)

3. Contracts—for example, contracts guaranteeing revenue or contracts giving an entity the right to operate something

4. Patents—for example, Google spent $12.5 billion to purchase the telecommunications equipment company Motorola Mobility based largely upon the value of its patents. Motorola was, after all, the inventor of the very first cell phone.

5. Legal recourse—for example, the digital video recording company Tivo collected $500 million from a lawsuit against its rival DISH.

6. Mailing lists that allow you to contact potential customers and generate sales leads.

7. Licenses—for example, for wireless spectrum or public broadcast rights.

8. Unprofitable subsidiaries that are salable, like Barnes & Noble's Nook division. Barnes & Noble eventually sold a stake in this business to Microsoft, resulting in a one-day increase of 52 percent in the company's stock price.

9. Inventory. Take the case of Rockwood Chocolate: Cocoa prices spiked in the midst of a shortage, but Rockwood used LIFO (last-in-first-out) inventory accounting. As a result, its cocoa bean inventory appeared to be worth much less than it actually was. Rockwood could have sold its cocoa beans, but it would have had to pay tax on this gain. However, the transaction would be nontaxable if it was used in a partial liquidation of the business. Rockwood initiated an arbitrage opportunity, selling stock at $34 per share that could be bought back for $36 in beans. Warren Buffett did one better: he famously bought Rockwood stock but ignored the offer to sell his shares for beans. He held the stock and ultimately, when he sold, Buffett pocketed $58 a share; the arbitrageurs had only made $2 a share.[11]

10. Use rights, such as air, water, mineral, or timber

11. Order production or backlog

12. Current revenue deferred to a future period, such as an acquiring company not recording revenue before a merger or acquisition

No list of potential sources of hidden value will be comprehensive. Essentially what you are looking for are instances where the economic value of an asset—specifically, its ability to produce cash—diverges from the accounting treatment of that asset. In assessing the value of these assets, pay attention to both the reliability of the asset's value and your ability to estimate it. For example, although Motorola's patents were extremely valuable, it's generally tougher to understand the value of a patent than the value of a parcel of land. Land has comparables and patents generally don't.

Other "hidden" assets might lie on the balance sheet but be under-appreciated by investors because they represent a seemingly unrelated line of business that may be valued differently in the market than the company's core business. For example, Penn National Gaming, which owned nineteen casinos across the United States, announced at one point that it would spin off its real estate (which was owned, not leased) into a real estate investment trust, or REIT. Investors suddenly valued the real estate that they had previously ignored at metrics for comparable REITs, causing Penn National's shares to appreciate by roughly 30 percent.

In the case of Penn, investors had underappreciated the value of the real estate Penn owned because it merited a different valuation multiple than the gaming business and seemed unrelated. Real estate is one of the most common assets that can be a hidden source of value on a company's balance sheet. This is partly because as stable sources of recurring revenue, real estate earnings merit high multiples, and partly because a REIT structure reduces taxes, increasing the distribution of the business's earnings.

Value can also be distorted during the bankruptcy process, when a company may use "fresh start accounting" to revalue the assets on its balance sheet. One example is the Howard Hughes Corporation (HHC). HHC was spun out of General Growth Properties (GGP) as GGP emerged from bankruptcy. After writing down the value of several of its assets during bankruptcy, HHC emerged with a book value of roughly $2 billion. However, the valuation methods used to write down these assets included assumptions, such as a 20 percent discount rate, that appeared to be excessively conservative. An asset-by-asset appraisal of HHC's assets indicated that they were likely worth somewhere between $4 billion and $6 billion, meaningfully above the company's estimate and the share price at the time.

Understanding the potential proceeds from a sale of these kinds of items may provide evidence of underappreciated value. The easiest way to value such assets might be to consider whether they have an identifiable stream of revenue or cash flow, such as the proceeds from an equity stake in a sale or the earnings power of real estate as a separate entity. Be careful to consider whether the benefits from such assets are short- or long-lived, or if the value may change as the market does. Make sure hidden assets are actually able to be separated from the rest of the assets and can be realized.

Hidden value may lurk when accounting standards understate a business's earnings. In other words accounting earnings (i.e., net income) and actual free cash flows (FCF) may be dramatically different. Consider the case of Crown Castle, a cell phone tower company. GAAP required Crown Castle to depreciate its towers over a time period that ranged from one to twenty years. However Crown Castle had lease renewal options for decades into the future. While these assets were depreciated over twenty years or less, the towers, which consisted of galvanized steel planted in cement, had useful lives of forty to fifty years, if not longer. The result was that while Crown Castle recognized depreciation charges of 35 percent of sales, it spent less than 0.1 percent of sales on maintenance capital expenditures. Accordingly, the company appeared deeply unprofitable on a GAAP basis, even though it had substantial free cash flow on a recurring basis.

Excess depreciation is a common way in which a company's earnings might be understated. But it's not the only way. Here are four other possible places to look for hidden value: noncash amortization arising from past acquisitions; noncash restructuring charges; noncash provisions that are overly conservative, for example the loan-loss provision at a bank could substantially reduce earnings; write-downs of assets.

Just as a financial statement may hide value, so too may it hide risk. Consider J. C. Penney in 2012. The business had just seen steep decreases in sales after disastrous turnaround efforts by the CEO at the time, Ron Johnson, and was trying to stabilize itself. Free cash flow was a negative $900 million and their balance sheet listed $930 million in cash and $2.2 billion in total liquidity, or just over two years of cash to burn.

The footnotes, however, disclosed a different picture: the company increased free cash flow and liquidity by $1 billion through liquidating inventories, changing vendor payment schedules, deferring vendor payments, taking advancements from their private-label credit card program, and stretching accounts payable. All of these actions would have to be undone to operate on a go-forward basis, and after adjusting for them, the company was burning $1.9 billion in cash with just $1.1 billion in liquidity, or only half of a year's worth. Sure enough, the company had to raise capital within a year, and, when it did, it was at a meaningfully lower share price.

There are many ways that companies might inflate or mischaracterize their financial positions.

CHEETAH SHEET 45
Exploitation: Plots and Ploys That Pad Value

1. Stretching out payables, as J. C. Penney did.
2. Financing payables. Like the plot to change the timing of operating cash flows, this method enables a company to use a third-party financial institution to pay vendors in the current period while the company is paying back the bank in a subsequent period.
3. Securitizing receivables. Here a company may muddy both true cash flows and earnings by packaging their receivables and transferring them to a financial institution. Under GAAP, the company then shows that it's sold the receivables in the operating section of the cash flow statement. Problems may occur as companies choose how much and when to securitize accounts receivable and then where on the income statement any gain from the sale may be recorded, since GAAP does not require specific placement.
4. Gain on sale transactions. When a company sells an asset and reports a sale, it should be broken out in another line item below operating income, clearly identifying it as a one-time event. However, some companies add it to revenue or deduct it from expenses, inaccurately characterizing it as a recurring event. Both may be considered aggressive.
5. Creating unusual transactions to generate a gain or loss, such as failing to record unearned revenues like customer prepayments.
6. Recording revenue prematurely or recording revenue of questionable quality.
7. Recognizing a future recurring expense, such as an advertising cost, as a one-time charge.
8. Capitalizing software or other research and development costs.

Having a heightened sense of awareness to where and how accounting problems may manifest themselves will help you to better appreciate whether your research target uses aggressive or conservative accounting policies.

Take, for example, Autonomy, a high-growth British software company that sold itself to Hewlett Packard (HP) for close to $10 billion in 2011. HP later revealed that Autonomy had been increasing sales by buying computer hardware and selling it to customers below cost. They would book the sales, increasing revenue growth, and count the losses as sales and marketing expenses. They effectively masked the fact that revenue growth was not coming from sales of their software, but instead from sales of hardware that were executed solely for the purpose of inflating their reported financial results. In fact, in 2018 Autonomy's former chief financial officer Sushovan Hussain was found guilty on sixteen charges of artificially inflating the firm's financial position before it was sold in what prosecutors claimed was an "unsustainable Ponzi scheme."[12]

It may seem overwhelming for you to look in all these nooks and crannies and to figure out whether you are seeing possible financial misrepresentation, but there are some warning signals that even a novice researcher can use to uncover financial plots and ploys.

Spotting Fraud

Assessing your target's assets for strength or weakness may enable you to see through misrepresentations and properly assess the true value and condition of the entity you're researching. It can provide comfort or raise concerns about the target's financial foundation. However, what I've outlined above is predicated upon the idea that the entity is operating legally. Uncovering plots and ploys in an entity that is deliberately behaving fraudulently needs a different lens. Even in this situation, though, there are some clues that will help you determine whether or not you've uncovered an instance of fraud.

CHEETAH SHEET 46
Exploitation: Plots and Ploys Warning Signals

1. Incompatibility. Are the accounting rules or regulations applied differently by your target than they are by its peers? For example, might the company be depreciating its plant or equipment at a different pace than competitors? (e.g., ten versus twenty years)
2. Goodwill or distorted value from mergers and acquisitions where a transaction may mask results. For example, assets and liabilities that have been repriced due to corporate finance transactions
3. Recent changes in accounting policies or auditors.
4. Recent changes in working capital. Are inventories or receivables growing materially faster than sales? This can be a sign of channel stuffing or aggressive revenue recognition.
5. Cash taxes. If the company is reporting earnings, but isn't paying cash taxes, is it a sign that they aren't reporting earnings to the IRS? This can be a warning signal that earnings are overstated.
6. Free cash flow vs. net income. Is the company generating cash matching its GAAP earnings? If cash flows are materially lower, this can be a sign of poor earnings quality.
7. Capital expenditures vs. depreciation and amortization. Are capital expenditures materially higher than depreciation and amortization? Some entities committing fraud have capitalized operating expenses. For example, in the Securities and Exchange Commission complaint against WorldCom the SEC alleged WorldCom improperly reduced its operating expenses by recharacterizing certain expenses as capital assets.[13]

In my work as a financial journalist I began to notice some commonalities among entities that perpetrate fraud. What follows is a Cheetah Sheet that outlines some questions you should ask of your investigation if you suspect that there may be foul doings. I initially developed these questions as a template for myself but later worked them into a case study that I wrote entitled "Spotting Signs of Fraud and Deception" for my course in persuasion at Columbia Business School.

Below the Cheetah Sheet you will find an excerpt of how the Cheetah Sheet played out across three of the biggest frauds in recent history: Bre-X, Enron, and Bernie Madoff. Madoff, a money manager, orchestrated the largest Ponzi scheme ever, costing investors $60 billion. Enron, an energy company, was the biggest instance of corporate fraud ever, leading the seventh largest US company into bankruptcy and erasing $60 billion in shareholder value. Bre-X, a gold mining company, was the biggest mining scandal of all time, costing investors $6 billion. The similarities between the scam artists are shockingly consistent.

When assessing the overall possibility of a company or organization engaging in chicanery, begin by asking yourself:

1. *Are there undue pressures for performance that may potentially affect the reporting of financial results?* Pressure may manifest itself as a tone coming down from the top of a company, or the explicit, or implicit, messages that executives send to employees. Where is emphasis placed? How frequently is the emphasis mentioned and in what ways is it reinforced? A tone that places a heavy emphasis on the stock price and/or financial results may unwittingly send a message that seems to encourage cutting corners.
2. *Does the way the company operates cause concern or stress?* And where might those stressors manifest themselves? How may concerns be hidden?

If your answer to the above two questions is "no," you almost certainly won't find fraud. If your answer to those two questions is "yes," it still may not be fraud, but it is time for Cheetah Sheet 47.

Fraud is not that common. And a tough manager who is laser-focused on results doesn't always generate a workforce that feels compelled to perform at all cost. But if you are finding *most or all* of the warning signs below for your target, you may have uncovered an entity that has too much in common with Bre-X, Madoff, and Enron.

Let's look at two indicators of fraud and how they played out for Bre-X, Bernie Madoff, and Enron.

1. *Controlled access to evidence. Is your target closely guarding who has access to it, when, and how? Are independent observers truly independent? Are records missing or destroyed?*

Bre-X controlled which gold samples could be evaluated. The company refused to allow reputable mining competitors like Placer Dome and

CHEETAH SHEET 47

Exploitation: Plots and Ploys Corporate Deception Warning Signs

1. **Controlled access to evidence**
   a. Is your target closely guarding who has access to it, when, and how?
   b. Are independent observers truly independent?
   c. Are records missing or destroyed?

2. **Results are subject to management estimation**
   a. Is your target using generally accepted accounting principles?
   b. How verifiable are its estimations?

3. **Authority bias**
   a. Does your target make its case by affiliating its reputation with known entities and big name outsiders who have credibility and influence?

4. **Profitability calculated in an unconventional way**
   a. All profitability ratios focus on the bottom line, but each variation reports it from a different perspective. Does your target's reporting seem reasonable?

5. **Inconsistencies in evidence**
   a. Is your target's business or operations too complicated to easily explain?
   b. Do discrete pieces of data conflict with one another?
   c. Have other entities been able to replicate or validate results?

6. **Focus on the stock market**
   a. Is your target overly focused on its share price performance?
   b. Does management blame short sellers for poor share price performance?

7. **Results are too good to be true**
   a. Are financial returns unnaturally smooth?

8. **Management egotism**
   a. Does your target's management have boundaries between their interests and their company's?

9. **Use of force or threats**
    a. Is your target involved in a lot of lawsuits?
    b. Are tough questions permitted? Are analysts who have skeptical or unfavorable reports cut off?
    c. Does the target's management blame outside factors or individuals for organizational weaknesses?

10. **Is management making repeated statements that any lack of clarity will soon be resolved?**

11. **Shady personnel history**
    a. Is the target affiliated with individuals with a questionable past, such as bankruptcy proceedings, stock promotion, or other?
    b. Is the target staffed with family?
    c. Does the target seem to heavily employ people from government or its regulators?
    d. Does management eliminate internal resistance through firings?

12. **Management fails to follow procedures**
    a. Are there unusual disclosures in the entity's documentation?

Barrick to do their own drilling. Moreover, a mysterious fire destroyed Bre-X's records. When an independent observer was hired by the company, it had to use data provided by Bre-X, but Bre-X provided crushed gold samples, preventing easy source analysis. There were other unfortunate events that made access to evidence difficult—for instance, Bre-X's exploration manager committed suicide

For Madoff, auditing and return calculations were performed in-house and the business was never audited by a recognized auditor. Still, few questioned Madoff in part because Madoff was a figure of authority in his industry's regulatory organizations, including the NASDAQ, and the Securities Industry Association.

Enron kept specifics on how they made money secret for "competitive reasons." The company paid big fees to its accounting firm, the now defunct Arthur Andersen, and at one point Andersen shredded documents.

The company had similar sway over its Wall Street bankers, who became dependent upon fees generated from Enron's business.

> 2. *Authority bias. Does your target make its case by affiliating its reputation with known entities and big-name outsiders who have credibility and influence?*

Bre-X was able to get credible people and companies, including Barrick Gold Corp and copper and gold producer Freeport-McMoRan, to invest even after bigger miners (such as the government of Indonesia) passed. It had blue chip backing from J. P. Morgan and the now-defunct Lehman Brothers.

Madoff was chairman of the NASDAQ and more. He sat on the board of Yeshiva University, and, through a family foundation, doled out millions of dollars to well-known charities.

Enron won accolades from the media—for instance, it was rated the most innovative company by *Fortune*. It had a top-end audit committee (including a former head of the Commodity Futures Trading Commission). It had ties to George H. W. Bush and to Robert Rubin, a former secretary of the treasury.

Although I only detailed two of the Cheetah Sheet warning signs here, all three of these organizations had *every one* of the warning signs of fraud listed on the Cheetah Sheet. For a full detailing of all the warning signs for each of the three companies, please turn to the appendix.

Exploitation has been about zeroing in on your perception of your target through different creative lenses to try to counter your own cognitive biases and inject a healthy sense of skepticism. Think of trying to get the perfect photograph of a view from the mountain you've just climbed: you try different frames and different focal points, with the goal to get the best picture you can, and every shot captures something about the view, but at the same time, each is limited by its focus and frame. In the same way, each Exploitation exercise has an upside—you can capture something that is not readily visible—but it also has limitations that keep you from capturing the entire scene.

In the next and final AREA chapter, on Analysis, your focus will shift to take in that entire scene by putting all the snapshots of your research together, reconciling your many thesis statements and deciding whether you have conducted the best research process possible. In effect, you will ask yourself whether you have taken the right path to the top of the mountain.

Your thesis statements are more than still pictures, however. They have something to say to you and you have been listening and evaluating each in turn. In the final chapter, you will bring all the data and the perspectives you've researched into the conference room and sit around the table together, to try to come to conviction.

Chapter Ten

AREA = A: Analysis

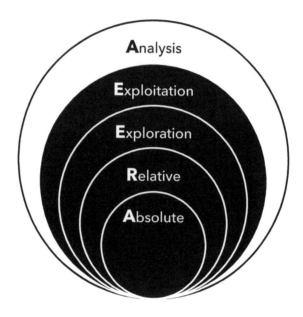

Not everything that can be counted counts,
and not everything that counts can be counted.
—Albert Einstein

In the Midrash, an ancient commentary on the Hebrew Bible, there is a story about young Moses being tested to determine his level of understanding. Moses's adopted father, Pharaoh, loved him so much that he would kiss and hug Moses, who would then grab Pharaoh's crown and put it on his own head. This worried Pharaoh's magicians: would Moses eventually try to take Pharaoh's crown?

Jethro, one of the men of Pharaoh's court, argued that Moses did not understand his actions and so suggested that Moses be tested: place a piece of gold and a hot coal before Moses. If he reached for the gold, he had understanding and should be killed; if he reached for the coal, he had no understanding and he should live. Moses grabbed the fiery red-hot piece of coal, burning his fingers and his tongue.

At this moment in your AREA research, you are both Moses and the men of Pharaoh's court: *you* are trying to figure out if *you* have enough understanding. Are you reaching for a piece of gold, or might your research target amount to a lump of coal? You've gathered data from a variety of perspectives, you've evaluated your own understanding of the data, and now you are ready to interpret it all. Yes, you've been consistently pausing to analyze your findings through your many thesis statements, but through the process outlined in this final stage of the AREA process, you will determine whether your data yields gold or merely coal.

Before asking yourself "What does it all mean?" the first step in analyzing your data is to decide if it is complete, if it is accurate, and if it can lead you to a decision. To do that, this chapter will explore solvability and fallibility: might it be too hard to fully answer your Critical Concepts, and might your work have gone awry? Once you've determined what your data can and can't tell you, you will use the Analysis process to reconcile the many thesis statements that you've crafted throughout your AREA work so that you may make a thoughtful, well-researched, and confident decision.

Solvability

By now you've identified which puzzle pieces of your Critical Concepts are important and knowable, and which aren't. Are there any that may not be solvable by analysis or that may be too unpredictable? You might wonder why solvability is addressed here in the AREA Method as opposed to at the outset—the reason is that it's important to prevent upfront assumption and judgment about what is solvable and what data and information exists related to your decision. While it is vexing to determine that there are "unsolvable" problems, many problems that appear unsolvable aren't.

There is no systematic method of testing puzzles to determine whether they are solvable or not. It's not merely that the test has never been found; no such test can ever be found. Different people have different comfort zones and different skills when it comes to problem solving. While the exercises laid out in chapter 9, on Exploitation, are meant to help you in taking a fresh look at your information, at times you will have to determine your own ability to judge the critical factors at hand, and you may have to either move forward without all the answers or reframe the problem.

For example, many students heading off to college don't know what they want to do or be when they finish college. In other words, they are going in without knowing their specific goal or its solvability. But not knowing what major you want to pursue or even what career you're aiming for doesn't mean you shouldn't go to college: college graduates on average earn more than people who don't go to college. Therefore even if you don't know what you want to do with your college degree, you can know that a good next step is to get one.

On the other hand, if you are researching a rapidly evolving technology, it may be impossible to know what its market opportunity will look like in five years. How would you decide you can get an edge on a 3-D printing company? It could be really tough to figure out how that technology is going to evolve, in which case you might determine that this critical concept is "unsolvable."

Patricia, studying Sprint, had to solve for an unclear future as well: how valuable was the company's Clearwire stake? Clearwire was basically a publicly traded allocation of spectrum. What was the value of that resource, which was, in part, a function of relatively new wireless technology? How much wireless data might people use in the future and how efficiently could it be processed? Even the best wireless engineers wouldn't have known the answers.

Yet Patricia was able to come to conviction about whether or not to recommend buying Sprint's shares without being able to answer those questions. How? She was able to determine that the value of the spectrum was not a critical concept. Specifically, she determined that the company's undervaluation did not depend on the value of its spectrum.

In general, if a company is dependent on a technology you can't predict, but you can figure out that the technology is worth more than zero and the company trades below its net cash, then perhaps the "investment" is solvable even if the technological issue isn't. The ultimate goal of thinking about solvability is to avoid spending a lot of time on things you're never going to figure out. There is nothing wrong with putting something in the "too hard" pile if it is indeed too hard.

Matthew, researching Delta, realized that he was never going to achieve certainty about all four of his Critical Concepts. But through his AREA process, he came to believe that Delta was operating at peak earnings in a cyclical industry with results that were aided by historically low fuel costs, favorable labor agreements, and industry consolidation. But the competitive dynamic was shifting. Low-cost carriers were beginning to compete aggressively against Delta on some of its most profitable routes and new labor agreements were likely to result in higher operating costs. Delta's stellar reputation, in Matthew's analysis, wouldn't be able to overcome all of these headwinds.

One more example: my student Maya researched a business development corporation (BDC) called MVC Capital. MVC traded at a discount to net asset value (NAV), but the validity of the company's NAV calculation was uncertain because the majority of the businesses MVC owned were private and BDCs had a reputation for overstating the value of their businesses.

Maya looked at historical sales of MVC's holdings and found that they typically occurred at prices above book value, indicating conservative valuation. However, she was not able to get far beyond that to get comfortable with an analysis of how accurately the company marked its investment portfolio. She could not prove that the company wasn't harvesting its successes and hiding its failures. She did not know how timely it was in marking up or down changes in valuation and whether the marks were conservative or not. She couldn't come to conviction and opted to pass on the investment.

Thus when you look at a well-defined problem (one that you think you understand), there is one question to consider regarding whether or not there is an explicit solution to the problem: *Can the problem, whatever it is, be solved analytically?* If not—if the information or data don't make sense, or there are too many different elements that make it impossible to solve—there is nothing wrong with moving on.

Thinking about Mistakes

Beyond countering our adaptive ignorance and mental shortcuts, which is tackled in depth in the previous chapter, on Exploitation, where else might you face research flaws? Might you be making a mistake in your analysis or might you be facing a failure of data? The power of discovering a mistake is not only that it gives you something concrete and detailed to fix, but also that it allows you to advance your knowledge.

For example, skill at statistical analysis and skill at drawing findings from the data are often two different things. Statistics are often subject to error, and problems such as improper research sample size may obscure relevant results. To prevent such problems, consider Cheetah Sheet 48.

CHEETAH SHEET 48
Analysis: Getting the Data Right

1. The Rule of Three: does your data come from *at least* three different people? By collecting data from three unrelated sources you can be more certain that your information is valid. Be aware of groupthink. When sourcing contacts, it isn't enough to have three sources if they are too closely related or depend upon the same data set. For example, my student Raj researched Iridium, a satellite communications company that was optically cheap and growing quickly but had to expend significant capital over the next several years to launch a new satellite system. Raj focused on what Iridium's valuation might be after the satellite system was constructed. He came to view Iridium's long-term growth rate as a CC. While management told Wall Street analysts that the company would likely realize high single digit growth in voice subscribers, Raj's AREA research indicated growth would be slower. He found two industry consultants, two handset distributors, a major holder, and a competitor who estimated future growth in voice subscribers would be anywhere from flat to mid-single digits, below management's estimation in all cases. In this case, Raj achieved a quantity and diversity of sources to compare against management's estimates that made him comfortable having conviction in his data.

2. Base Rates: we all tend to ignore base rates, which are the underlying percentages or the actual likelihood of an event occurring. This tendency can lead to poor decision-making. For example, millions of people play the lottery every day in spite of overwhelming odds against winning the jackpot because media stories about winners–the exceptions to the odds–are more salient and memorable than the odds themselves. Despite an extremely low payout rate, the lottery is the most successful form of commercial gambling because we all rely too heavily on memorable events rather than base rates. We also all tend to overestimate our ability to beat the odds.

3. Data Fishing: while it is useful to identify patterns and relationships between data, be careful to avoid data fishing, which occurs when you look for data to support a belief you already have. So if, for example, you've decided that you feel great when you drink coffee, you might decide that it's healthy without a firm hypothesis for why this is so. If you

start looking at coffee studies to find variables that correlate health with coffee, it's highly likely that at least one variable *will* correlate. However, you've data fished your result.

4. Comparing Apples to Apples: review how the data was selected. Make sure you understand how a study was designed and conducted. If you are researching an oil drilling company, it might not be relevant to assess the number of drill holes needed in the North Sea by looking at data in the Gulf of Mexico.

In addition, mistakes can be made when numbers are reported in a vacuum. A customer churn rate of 20 percent is a meaningless statistic by itself. Is that high or low and why? Does it present improvement or deterioration? Numbers need to be in context to be evaluated.

Errors may also stem from choosing the wrong basis of comparison. For instance, there are many ways to compute profits: return on sales, return on investment, profit in absolute dollars, percentage profit over five years, profits this year compared to last, expected versus actual, and so on. All of the figures are quite different. Consider which comparisons are appropriate, preferably *before* collecting your data, so that by the time you are here in the Analysis phase, you have focused information that will provide a clear basis for action and decision.

At times, companies themselves will give Wall Street multiple ways to think about their earnings. In 2017, General Electric was providing four different earnings calculations, including plain net income and "Industrial operating plus Verticals earnings." None of the four convinced analysts that multiple measures meant transparency—or profitability.[1]

Pre-Mortems

One useful tool to assess potential pitfalls and mistakes is the pre-mortem. It's the hypothetical opposite of a postmortem, often used in medical settings to allow health professionals and the family to learn what caused a patient's death. The joke is that with a postmortem, everyone benefits—except, of course, the patient.

A pre-mortem, by contrast, is implemented before a decision rather than after it, so that the decision-making can be improved rather than autopsied. Unlike a typical critiquing session, in which project team members are asked what *might* go wrong, the pre-mortem operates on the assumption that the "patient" has died, and so asks what *did* go wrong. The task is to generate plausible reasons for your research target's failure.

According to researchers from Wharton School of Business of the University of Pennsylvania, Cornell University, and the University of Colorado, prospective hindsight—imagining that an event has already occurred—is said to increase your ability to correctly identify reasons for future outcomes by as much as 30 percent. The exercise also sensitizes you to pick up early signs of trouble even after you've made your research decision.

To conduct a pre-mortem, begin by imagining that your research target has failed to perform in the way you expected. Write down in your AREA Journal all the reasons that you think it might have failed, including reasons that are less obvious, or seem to have a low probability.

CHEETAH SHEET 49
Analysis: Pre-Mortem

1. Begin by imagining that your research target has failed to perform in the way you expected.
2. Write down all the reasons that you think this failure could occur, including reasons that are less obvious, or seem to have a low probability.
3. What actions might you take if one or several of the events that could cause failure begins to play out?
4. What assumptions are you making about your target and the events that may cause failure?
5. Can you set up a construct to prevent your research decision from failing in the way you've identified it might?
6. At what point might you need to reevaluate your understanding of your findings, and perhaps your research target itself?

Exercises like the Pre-Mortem will make you less likely to fall prey to mission creep or to ignore bad news as it occurs.

Patricia, studying Sprint, identified two reasons the company might fail to perform as she hoped: one was an adverse event that could impact the company's liquidity and the second was whether Sprint could compete against AT&T and Verizon, which were both larger than Sprint. Patricia's CAH had already led her to look deeply into Sprint's capital expenditures so she chose to focus her pre-mortem only on Sprint's competitive positioning, figuring that her concerns about a liquidity issue had been put to rest.

Ironically, in the months after Patricia researched Sprint, liquidity issues almost derailed Sprint's turnaround: the company's shares fell by 50 percent after the company signed a large purchasing agreement with Apple for the iPhone. This textbook case shows that in conducting your pre-mortem, one reason for failure may not be enough. Make sure to consider all of the issues that plague your CCs so that you may have an expansive view of potential future pitfalls.

Below is Patricia's thesis from her pre-mortem on the competitive landscape. In this exercise she played out her autopsy on Sprint's death by imagining it was too small to compete.

Although the cost advantage that Verizon and AT&T have is not as big as analysts think, it does exist, and if pricing in the industry declines, it could limit Sprint's flexibility, making it difficult for the company to compete against larger, better-capitalized rivals.

In her pre-mortem Patricia told a story of failure, even though she thought it unlikely. However, the pre-mortem helped her think through red flags that she could watch for if she bought Sprint's shares. She identified three: she could track prices competitors offered relative to what Sprint offered; she could keep an eye out for a shift in the industry's advertising focus on service to being more about pricing; and she could monitor margins for signs of pressure. For this last point Patricia noted that she'd want to keep in mind how management might characterize a change in margins. Might management be using pricing to gain market share or, might management be responding to negative pressures that pricing was becoming difficult or unsustainable?

Advocacy/Adversary Teams

One of the guest speakers in my Advanced Investment Research Class spoke about his office's policy of having researchers defend their investment analysis before a "Contra Team" that formalized antagonistic roles to ensure that alternative evidence would be considered. The Contra Team's job was to research the investment with the goal of making the case against the recommendation. This kind of advocacy-adversary model is a good way to acknowledge that a single researcher or evaluation team may not easily be able to maintain neutrality and objectivity throughout the research process and to give fair attention to both negative and positive findings. You've already completed a similar Pro/Con exercise in your Exploitation work, but doing this exercise with another person or persons may enable you make sure that both sides of your target's research are given careful consideration.

One caution: this kind of approach is only as effective as the presentation style of the advocate or adversary. A way around such a downside might be to apply this kind of "debate team" approach to data analysis, where different people might represent different viewpoints about the data's findings.

For example, one team might be formed to focus on all the findings that appear to lead to negative conclusions, another to look for positive findings, and a third to look for a balanced perspective. If you believe people have a predisposition to either the positive or negative findings, it would be enlightening and useful to assign those with negative predispositions to the positive side and vice-versa. This may force people to examine their predispositions carefully and to tease out nuances in the data. Additionally, by directly involving others you may increase their understanding and commitment to the evaluation findings.

Checklists

While this book is filled with checklists in the form of the Cheetah Sheets, there is another useful kind of checklist to analyze your research: the "mistake" or "don't do" list.

The "don't do" list helps you avoid mistakes that you already know are mistakes. In a complex process like investigative research a "don't do" list is as valuable as a good "to do" list.

As the Nobel Prize-winning psychologist Daniel Kahneman writes in his book, *Thinking, Fast and Slow,* "Humans are incorrigibly inconsistent in making summary judgments of complex information."[2] Avoiding mistakes that you don't already know are mistakes will be really difficult, but avoiding mistakes that you *do* know are mistakes is doable through a checklist. By studying other researchers and learning from their mistakes, you can expand your checklist and reduce your "miss" ratio.

Many well-known investors use checklists, including Mohnish Pabrai, managing partner of Pabrai Investment Funds in Irvine, California, and Guy Spier, who runs the Aquamarine Fund.

When I interviewed Pabrai about his preinvestment checklist, he told me that he'd put together his ninety-eight-question list by studying the mistakes of investors he admires. One example of an investment he studied: Warren Buffet's rare loss in Dexter Shoes, a company that was operating in an industry without a real barrier to entry and that therefore did not have a way to protect itself from competitors. Pabrai's checklist has questions on everything from debt and leverage to labor coming from foreign sources.

Pabrai told me that he believes that most errors center on five main issues. Below are Pabrai's five issues, supplemented with questions that I've written to help you as you look at your data.

CHEETAH SHEET 50
Analysis: A Fundamental Investment Checklist

1. Valuation: are you only interested in the research target because it is a cheap investment?
2. Leverage or risks associated with borrowing: have you properly understood the target's leverage and borrowing?
3. Management and ownership: do you understand management's incentives and ownership structure?
4. Moats: how well fortified is this business against competition?
5. Personal biases: have you truly used AREA's perspective-taking process to control for and counteract biases?

Pabrai advises, "Rub your nose in your own failures. Avoiding the mistakes you've made in the past will take your error rate way down in the future."

Final Analysis: Reconciling Your Thesis Statements

Now that you've assessed the solvability of your Critical Concepts and the fallibility of your process and your data, congratulations! You're ready for one more Cheetah Pause.

Your thesis statements have provided you with clear signposts for completed sections of work and suggested your path forward for what to investigate next. They have also given you a way to document your process so that you can look back at your thinking as you move forward. Now is the time to pause once more, to bring them all together to serve as learning and teaching tools.

Thinking about the thesis statements this way—as learning and teaching tools—harkens back to the first chapter, where I discussed process and content; content provides substance to the process, but is also derived from the process. A good process encourages good content.

You may want to look back at Cheetah Sheet 1 to ensure that your thesis statements combine the follow ingredients: your findings, interpretations, judgments, and recommendations for moving forward.

Now is the time to bring them together. Write the thesis statements down side by side in your AREA Journal. When matched up, they should provide the scaffolding for understanding the complex issues you've investigated. Are the thesis statements consistent? Do they reconcile or diverge? Do they progress so that you are moving forward toward a fuller understanding of your research target? Do they capture the evolution of your thinking?

Taken together, do your statements suggest that you should circle back, do more work, and rethink your CCs, or are you ready to come to conviction about your research decision?

For example, my student Amanda researched Hologic, a medical equipment company focusing on mammography and women's health, and was not able to reconcile her thesis statements, particularly her statement from her Exploration phase.

She reported that her calls "revealed a tepid reception of the new technology on the part of radiology groups," which conflicted with her other work extolling the virtues of 3-D mammography, the company's latest high tech advance.

Amanda ultimately decided that the incompatibility was due not to poor research but rather to the fact that the company had not clearly articulated its new technology's value proposition. Would it? Did the company's sales team need more time? The takeaway is that the AREA process made her realize that the company was not at that point a high conviction research target either way. She could not determine that there was a strong demand for Hologic's 3-D mammography technology "given a lack of understanding regarding what patient outcome benefits actually are."

CHEETAH SHEET 51
Analysis: Appraising Your Thesis Statements

1. Do the thesis statements address your Critical Concepts?
2. Do they represent what you have learned, understood, evaluated, and concluded about your target? If they don't, revisit and rework your thesis statements until they are specific, factual, and actionable.
3. Are there unresolved issues or conflicts in your thesis statements? If so, it may be worth revisiting those issues.
4. Are the perspectives accurately reflected so that the motives, considerations, and incentives of each source are clear in the thesis statements? If not you may want to vet the information from that source.
5. Do the thesis statements reflect your own confrontation of your assumptions, judgments, and biases?

Below are the eleven thesis statements that Patricia developed as she researched Sprint.

1. **Absolute: After reading the SEC documents**
   "While Sprint's aggregate results are unimpressive, the company is losing subscribers, and profits are declining, the

more technologically advanced CDMA network is a bright spot and is becoming a larger part of the business."

2. **Absolute: Management and board composition**
"Although Sprint shares have declined precipitously after the failed Nextel merger, the company's new CEO has a track record that indicates that he has relevant experience and initial results show subscriber losses may be finally moderating."

3. **Relative: Business and industry map**
"Sprint potentially has the opportunity to expand margins meaningfully as it combines its two networks and achieves cost savings by eliminating redundancies, but also appears to face stiff competition from larger competitors who may have competitive advantages due to economies of scale."

4. **Relative: Earnings calls**
"Sprint management earnings calls have shown consistent focus on operating goals along with a track record of execution that is increasing my confidence that management will follow through on continuing to improve the core business by integrating the two networks to boost profitability."

5. **Relative: Shareholder composition**
"Sprint appears to have a fairly vanilla shareholder base without any big recent changes in its major shareholders. This means the business is unlikely to see much oversight on corporate governance matters or activism. Its shares are unpopular and investors might be overlooking the company."

6. **Exploration: Interviewing**
"My interviews indicate that management's network consolidation plan is viable and that it would make Sprint competitive with AT&T and Verizon. If management can execute on schedule and budget the company's stock is cheap."

7. **Exploitation: Pro/Con exercise**
"The Pro/Con exercise crystallized the importance of understanding how much Sprint needs to spend on capital expenditures. This issue will determine not only the company's cost structure and ability to compete with larger rivals, but also clarify valuation."

8. **Exploitation: Competing Alternative Hypotheses exercise**
"Based upon the CAH exercise, it appears likely that Sprint is not underinvesting in their network, the network consolidation

plan is viable, and Sprint can compete effectively with Verizon and AT&T."

9. **Exploitation: Visual map**

   "The visual map shows that Sprint's investment proposition varies widely depending on what the real level of needed capital expenditure is. It highlights the importance of the factor and also Sprint's sensitivity to it."

10. **Exploitation: Scenario analysis**

    "Sprint shares appear to offer favorable risk /reward as shares offer upside of 3x–4x with downside of roughly 40% based upon a liquidation analysis of the company's assets, and a base case upside of 60% assuming the company's successful integration plan. The most important factor might be the appropriate level of Maintenance Capital Expenditures for Sprint."

11. **Analysis: Pre-Mortem**

    "Although the cost advantage that Verizon and AT&T have is not as big as analysts think, it does exist, and if pricing in the industry declines, it could limit Sprint's flexibility, making it difficult for the company to compete against larger, better capitalized rivals."

Together, these statements show a truncated path of each part of Patricia's entire AREA research process, giving her not only the most important takeaways from each part of her research, but also her analysis, conclusions, and implications for further research. The statements also show the evolution of her Critical Concepts: At first she was concerned about the company's small size relative to its competition and its state of disarray after the failed Nextel merger. She realized though that the key to Sprint's future success was whether it had a handle on its costs and necessary investment. Once she believed that Sprint was better capitalized than investors understood, she could zoom out again to solve for the feasibility of Sprint's consolidation plan and subscriber growth.

Patricia's statements read like a story—an investment story—and without even having read the ending it's clear that she's come to conviction. You know what will come next: the logical progression of her AREA work led her to write one final concluding thesis statement recommending buying Sprint's shares:

Sprint's network consolidation plan is viable from both a technical and executional perspective, given management's track record.

Sprint is the 3rd strongest competitor in its market, but the competition appears manageable on both a cost basis, as they implement the network consolidation, and a subscriber retention basis, as they shift to the CDMA network. Accordingly, the stock is cheap based upon the business's projected earnings after the network consolidation plan.

This thesis statement has all four of the above recommended facets: it has Patricia's findings, interpretations, judgments, and recommendation. It builds from her prior work and she has defended it in thinking about where she might have made mistakes and in her pre-mortem. At the time she made the recommendation, Sprint's shares were selling for $5.33. A year later they were changing hands at $6.67, about 25 percent north of where they were when Patricia made her "buy" recommendation. The shares continued to rise for the next two years, which is the investment timeline that I ask my students to plan for.

Not every AREA research project will have such a "happy ending," but Matthew's did in the short term as well—and quickly. Over the course of the Spring 2016 semester, Matthew watched Delta's stock slide steadily south. In late April it was trading at about $47 a share, and in the month after the course ended, it fell even further, to $36 a share. His final recommendation was to sell Delta's shares, which, in the short term, had an immediate payoff. If Matthew had actually made this investment, he may well have been able to close out his position at a tidy profit.

Matthew's final thesis:

Delta is operating at peak earnings in a cyclical industry, with results that have been aided by historically low fuel costs, favorable labor agreements, and industry consolidation. However, the competitive dynamic is shifting due to significant capacity coming on board from discount airlines that will lead to increased competition on many of Delta's most profitable routes and labor expenses, which are increasing sharply, and will further highlight that Delta operates at a structural cost disadvantage relative to its peers. Even in a muted fuel environment, this will result in lower ticket prices, higher operating expenses, and weaker profitability.

However, by November of 2016 Delta's shares had climbed back above the price at which Matthew had made the sell recommendation. The volatility and unpredictability in Delta's share price reflects the Critical Concepts Matthew focused on. None of them have gone away; fuel and labor costs in particular have been on the rise. But the confidence that Matthew heard from Delta management in the earnings calls as well as from the large institutional investors who were holding Delta stock has actually been the more compelling narrative long-term.

In its first quarter 2018 earnings conference call, Delta's CEO Ed Bastian repeated a refrain Matthew had heard often on the calls he listened to: "More customers than ever are choosing Delta because of the great service our people provide and the reliability of the product that we deliver. Not only are we seeing record numbers of passengers, we're also seeing solid improvements in our customer satisfaction scores."[3]

There are many different paths that your research can take, but by following the AREA Method, like Patricia and Matthew, you will be better able to articulate your goals and your vision of success. You'll have recorded the "what," the "why," and the "how" of both the work and the thinking behind your decision in vivid detail. That AREA audit trail will serve not only as your research story but also as something that may resonate with others who will be able to follow and learn from your process. The goal: to turn your good ideas into great solutions.

Chapter Eleven

Warren Buffett and Untangling
Your Plate of Spaghetti

As I was wrapping up this book, I sent a copy of my general interest decision-making book, *Problem Solved,* to Warren Buffett. He responded with a lovely note of encouragement and had this observation: "It always amazes me how many seemingly intelligent people have trouble thinking clearly. Their thoughts get tangled into a plate of spaghetti."

Mr. Buffett is so eloquent, and so clear thinking. He's right, of course. We do get tangled, and spaghetti is a wonderful—and apt—metaphor.

When we're faced with a complex problem—financial or otherwise—what we think we know about the problem is tangled with other problems, thoughts, and perspectives. We don't have a process for separating out the strands—how we think and feel about the problem, what we actually know, and what others are recommending and why. It's a hot mess. Still, we too often simply grab a few strands and twirl them together; it impairs our decision-making.

Because I have used the AREA Method for so many years now, it feels intuitive and natural to me; it has become my go-to operating system. But each spring, when I lay out the method in my Advanced Investment Research class, my students tell me how unique and how valuable the method is, both in organizing their process and thinking and in giving them the skills and confidence that they need to conduct original, unbiased research.

Even students who have worked in financial research prior to taking my class find the AREA Method eye opening. In 2018, one of my students, Arjun, told me that he had spent six years working for a hedge fund yet did not have confidence in his research skills or system. "I was looking for a process or framework to structure and round out my thinking. Practically, as a hedge fund analyst, I would be looking at four to six companies at the same time, researching twelve to fourteen hours a day. It was overwhelming to track and control all the data I was looking at."

When Arjun was assigned to research the cosmetic chain Ulta Beauty in my class, he found himself completely out of his comfort zone as a researcher. I had selected Ulta because it had good tension in its investment story—there were both bulls and bears on the stock—but the world of American women's cosmetics was something that Arjun, a male from India, was completely unfamiliar with.

As an experienced analyst he knew how to read numbers, so he began his Absolute work with comfort. But he quickly became overwhelmed when he realized the sheer complexity of the cosmetics field: Ulta was selling 20,000 units per store and Arjun knew nothing about mascara, lipstick, nail polish, and the myriad other beauty products Ulta offered.

The literature review Arjun conducted in his Relative work led him to an article about the most popular cosmetic purchases of the prior year (in *Cosmopolitan* magazine, no less), which not only gave him a crash course in the ecosystem of beauty products but also provided some insight into how women used and assessed cosmetics. Then the breakdown of different kinds of questions assembled during his Exploration work gave him the courage to go into Ulta and competitor Sephora stores to interview customers and employees about their makeup preferences, purchasing habits, and loyalty programs.

By the end of the semester, Arjun had learned the foreign language of cosmetics, could speak it fluently, and was confident in his knowledge and judgment of Ulta as an investment opportunity. He told me, "Going forward, I believe the AREA Method is a way I can silo the work and document all my findings, so I can come to valuable conclusions without missing out on the big picture." He concluded that "this method is a MUST for long term fundamental investors. It definitely gives you an edge in your research process."

My student Harry, researching Snapchat, observed, "Original thinking is the most valuable thing an analyst can add but also something that very few do. The main benefit of AREA is the process of 'segmenting' the research by its sources, A, R, E, E, and A, so that, in the Absolute stage, I was forced to think for myself without any outside interpretations. It is tempting to look at other opinions but once that happens you can never be unbiased again. I always go straight to the financials now whenever I look at a new company, and haven't used sell-side research in weeks."

Mateo, another experienced financial analyst, examined iconic motor-cycle manufacturer Harley Davidson in my course. He commented that before he took the course, his research process consisted of "reading a couple sell side reports and looking at comps." AREA, he said, improved his research because of its emphasis on beginning with original primary research and its focus on eliminating bias. "The main benefit was the clearly delineated process that constantly kept accounting for the possibility of biases. The entire process seems to have been designed with the idea of really having an original and unpolluted thinking process, which I think is the only way to gain an edge in investing."

Mateo also noted that, even as an experienced financial analyst, he had no background in interviewing, so he found the Exploration section "the most valuable part of the method."

Like my students, most of us don't have a methodology for investigating complex problems, financial or other. We have so much on our plates that the tangled mess of ideas and information becomes overwhelming. Too often, instead of taking dedicated time to examine our big decisions mindfully, we rely upon our preconceived notions, our assumptions, and our judgments to guide us. We decide whether, how, and how deeply to research a company the same way we eat spaghetti: we stick our fork into the tangled mess of (our own and others') thoughts and take whatever is picked up.

In other words, we "swipe right" on our decisions. Mimicking the popular Tinder dating app that originated the term, we view our decisions as things that should be made quickly, on the basis of a gut reaction. We "hook up" with a decision rather than thinking carefully and rationally about whether it's the best decision we can make to further our goals. By simulating the omnipresent, fast-paced technology devices in our lives, we end up relying upon our biases, missing the opportunity to empower ourselves, to commit to becoming experts in our lives, and to vet our ideas with evidence.

But we don't really want to keep making mistakes—and, heaven forbid, the same old mistakes. We want to confront our mental shortcomings and prevent ourselves from making poor decisions out of a poor decision-making process.

That's the idea behind AREA: to give you an operating system that both mentally prepares you for problem solving and then gives you the tools to enable you to solve your problems so that you can better achieve your goals.

When you are ready to invest in yourself and your decisions, AREA gives you the spadework to get it done. It begins by helping you clear the mental space you need, heightening your self-awareness and your sensitivity to the incentives and motives of others. This enables you to confront your biases and assess your problem's edges and pitfalls. You are preparing your mind for the problem solving you are about to do.

AREA then gives you the tools to pull apart the strands of your decision and to bring in new strands to look at and organize the situation anew. Finally, it helps you knot the strands back together. Instead of a plate of spaghetti, you can transform those strands into a sturdy rope, carefully woven together into a strong, evidence-based decision.

Once you understand the AREA system and have applied it, it's yours to keep. And like a muscle, the more you use it, the stronger it gets—and the more mindful you become. You're not only seeing and solving problems differently, you're building your internal compass as a researcher, an investor and a financial sleuth.

Not every research problem or decision requires a full AREA investigation. You, like the cheetah, can determine the length, intensity, and complexity of your hunt. Pick and choose from AREA's offerings to make your work *work* for you.

Our daily lives and our technology may be telling us to make big decisions faster. But faster is not always the goal. Many of us want something that is far more fulfilling: the process and the skills to make big decisions better.

Appendix

1. Sample AREA Journal from Matthew's Delta Airlines Absolute Work.

The best AREA Journals I have seen share a few similar qualities. They are organized into one long journal so that all of the researcher's work and thinking is captured in one place. Each entry is dated and there are subtitles that identify the corresponding AREA section of work, including the specific Cheetah Sheet questions that their work is responding to. Below these headings, the researcher records the data and below that her questions, thoughts, interpretations, and judgments, often in some other color or font to make the commentary stand out. To download an AREA Journal template filled with digitized Cheetah Sheets, please visit **areamethod.com**.

Below is a sample of Matthew's AREA Journal. He recorded which Cheetah Sheet he was working on and which questions he was answering. Note that Matthew's questions and comments were handwritten in between his data. This is a sample from Matthew's Absolute work, not his complete journal.

Cheetah Sheet 8. Absolute: Target History
Understand the company's business cycle:
are problems new or normal course? Identify
where the company might be vulnerable and
its value drivers.

The business cycle is essentially predicated on two main pressure points: 1) fuel costs; 2) capacity. These two factors will essentially dictate what happens to pricing within the industry. If there's too much capacity, airlines will feel compelled to lower prices and any potential benefits from fuel cost reductions would be passed through to the consumer.

> *How will capacity impact pricing decisions for airlines? How about additional capacity from international carriers?*
>
> *Last summer there was a DoJ investigation/class-action lawsuit alleging price-fixing at the largest airlines. Will this be a continual issue if pricing doesn't rise and fall in tandem w/ fuel costs? (i.e., will airlines have the opportunity to act rationally on pricing even if they want to?)*

Cheetah Sheet 9. Absolute: Leadership
How did the leader arrive in the top spot and what might that say about the leader's strengths and weaknesses?

Delta is in a unique spot because Richard Anderson, the CEO who led the company through bankruptcy, the acquisition of Northwest, and this recent period of unprecedented profitability, will retire in May 2016.

His replacement is Ed Bastian, who is the company's current president and a member of the board. There are some differences between the two: Anderson came from a legal background and had a strong operational background in airlines. Bastian comes more from the analytical, finance, and commercial side of the business.

> *Bastian doesn't appear to have any form of operational background in airlines. Is he the right person for this bigger picture role? Is he the right person to make the strategic decisions for the Company?*

Cheetah Sheet 9: What is the CEO's track record?
How effective has the CEO been at creating value for customers? For shareholders? How consistent has the strategy been and has the CEO been able to follow through on it?

According to Delta, Bastian played a pivotal role in finalizing Delta's acquisition of Northwest Airlines in 2008 and managing the airline's successful integration.

Bastian has also overseen Delta's continued transformation through strategies to make the business less vulnerable to economic cycles. Examples include the purchase of a refinery which is expected to save the airline $300 million annually; reducing Delta's debt to increase its flexibility; and investing in the Delta experience from facilities enhancements at several of Delta's hubs to online and in-flight product improvements, which, combined, are expected to contribute more than $1 billion in annual benefits to Delta.

Bastian also served as chief restructuring officer between 2005 and 2007, playing a critical role in the company's Chapter 11 reorganization.

Share price appreciation as of specific dates
Since Chapter 11 reorganization (April 2007): 88.6%
Since announcement of Delta-Northwest merger (April 2008): 310.2%
5-year return: 261.3%
1-year return: –3.4%

Cheetah Sheet 9: What incentives does the CEO have to perform and over what period of time? How is compensation structured? Are her equity and voting rights aligned? Can you gauge how much of the leader's net worth is tied to company performance?

If we assume that Bastian will have a compensation structure similar to Anderson's 2014 compensation structure, it appears to be very much a "pay for performance" construct, with a substantial portion of total compensation at risk. A few highlights:

- 95% of Anderson's target compensation opportunity was at risk
- 85% of total compensation is concentrated in equity-based opportunities
- 85% of compensation is based on long-term incentives
- Cash-based compensation is below the 25th percentile of Delta's custom peer group
- Long-term incentive plans have a vesting schedule of three years

2014 compensation mix:
Management incentive plan (this is an annual incentive program) is based on Delta's performance in the following areas:

Long-term incentive plans are earned based on achievement of objective, preestablished performance measures, including average annual operating income margin, customer service, and return on invested capital over a three-year performance period **payable to executive officers in stock.**

As of the 2015 proxy, Bastian owned 1.4mm shares of Delta which at its current price of $42.99 equates to approximately $58mm

Critical Concepts

1. What will happen in a sustained low fuel input environment? Will Delta and its competitors act rationally and maintain most of the cost or will it be passed on to consumers?
   Although typically I would expect a low fuel input environment to be a significant tailwind, there is a possibility that Delta and its competitors will essentially compete away the entire amount of the margin expansion by offering lower prices to consumers. The primary question is whether airlines can be the type of business that 1) exceeds required rates of return in good markets (i.e., when fuel costs are low) by holding prices fairly steady and meets acceptable rates of return in bad markets by passing costs on to consumers; or 2) Passes on cost savings to consumers such that companies do not end up earning a return above their cost of capital in either scenario.

2. What is the size/scope of Delta's market opportunity internationally? How will this affect things like passenger load factors (they are lower internationally), operating expenses, and overall passenger mile yields?
   The "other revenue" line item has been increasing substantially over the past few years primarily due to loyalty programs w/Amex. How does this program scale? What are the economics of the loyalty program?

3 What is a reasonable ceiling for Delta's passenger load factor?
   Given things like domestic vs. international, regional (which are likely higher load factors) losing prominence, and the opportunity to potentially take market share from domestic competitors.

4 Competition?
   What is the barrier to entry for low cost competitors to enter Delta routes? More international carriers seem to be coming to major US hubs, too—what does that mean to Delta?

Matthew's final Absolute thesis statement read:

Revenue passenger-miles are increasing steadily both domestically and abroad. Given Delta's strong performance with corporate travelers, a sophisticated customer segmentation strategy that drives higher revenues, and entrenched partnerships with international airlines, the company stands to benefit from this macro trend. This may ultimately narrow the valuation discount that Delta currently has versus high quality peers.

2. Relative: Patricia's Sprint Industry Map

Note: Typically, industry maps are visual displays of an industry, but Patricia developed a map in narrative form.

Wireless Industry: The US wireless industry provides communications services to 292.8 million subscribers, comprising 93% of the US population. The industry generates $155.8 B in revenues across 2.26 trillion minutes of use. The industry is mature from a saturation perspective but the increasing popularity of smart phones is driving game-changing trends on the data side. Whereas an early generation 2G phone would use 25 Mb per month, a 4G smartphone uses 7,000 Mb per month and new wireless products like tablets or laptop cards comprise new sources of data consumption. Furthermore, with 24.5% of US households wireless only today, compared to just 7.7% 5 years ago, people are increasingly looking to the wireless industry for more than just phone calls and texts.

Key Players

Regulators

FCC—Controls spectrum licenses and mandates for carriers (i.e., network capital investments, need to take emergency calls, etc.).

Determines what technologies are legal. Spectrum is critical in
that it determines the data capacity for a given network.
IEEE—Determines standards for wireless technologies (i.e., 2G,
3G, etc.). Dictates what phones must be capable of doing.

Wireless Carriers

Operate networks that allow users to communicate via handsets.
Networks are dealing with increasing data usage across fixed
bandwidth and are strained. They compete for customers on
1) phone selection on network; 2) coverage; 3) plans. High cost
to build networks makes entry difficult, allows competitive
advantages where a carrier is dominant.

Postpaid
Sprint—industry #3, losing subs over past several years
Verizon—industry leader, adding iPhone
AT & T—industry #2, gained market share from iPhone exclusivity,
also became network with heaviest data usage straining capacity,
imposing plan that caps data usage for normal plans and charges
more for unlimited
T-Mobile—industry #4
Clearwire (54% Sprint, 4G network)—developing network, 4G and
Wi-Max technology is superior to existing technologies

Prepaid
Postpaid carriers, Metro PCS, Leap, Tracfone

Landline Networks

Operate networks that allow users to communicate via wireline
technologies. Lease access to wireless carriers and other wireline
carriers in exchange for network and interchange fees.

National / Long Distance
Postpaid carriers, Level 3 Communications, Qwest

Local
ILEC's, CLEC's, Cable companies

Retailers

Sell phones / network subscription plans
Postpaid carriers, Apple, Radioshack, Best Buy

Handset Manufacturers

Smart phone development allows for increased functionality
of phones (i.e., watching videos instead of just calling).
Hypercompetitive space with high market-share turnover. Google
Android technology enabling carriers like Samsung, Motorola,
and HTC to compete with Apple iPhone. RIMM, Samsung, and
Apple are also developing Tablets.
Motorola, RIMM, LG, Sanyo, Samsung, HTC, Apple, Nokia

Tower Companies

Own structures that carriers lease space on to provide coverage.
Demand for tower sites surging in response to growing data usage.
AMT, CCI, SBAC

Technology Designers

Design technologies that enable industry. Technologies focus on
improving ability of phones to communicate more data across
fixed bandwidth.
Qualcomm (CDMA technology: peak rates of 4-8 Mbps)
Nokia, Ericsson, Motorola (TDMA technology: peak rates of 2 Mbps)
Intel, Apple, Google, Microsoft (Wi-Fi / Wi-Max: peak rates of 268
Mbps, but not currently viable for cell phones. Operates in unlicensed
frequencies that could make cell phone networks unnecessary)

Equipment and Systems Providers

Provide bay stations, communication equipment, etc. to landline
and wireless carriers.

Motorola, Ericsson, Alcatel-Lucent, Nokia-Siemens, Huawei
(Chinese company, has competitively used access to government
financing), Qualcomm, IBM, Cisco

3. Exploration: Interview Personas

*I introduced interview personas in chapter 8, on Exploration. There are
three: the Scientist, the Consultant, and the Interrogator. If you need to
refresh your memory about each, please see chapter 8.*

To figure out which interview persona you want to use, decide what
kind of information you need. This is akin to understanding your edges
and pitfalls before you begin researching. The goal with edges and pitfalls
is to think through and challenge your own expectations and assumptions
about how you think about your research process. Similarly, the idea of
choosing a persona is a framing exercise to get at, and to control for, your
assumptions and judgments about how your interview will go. How do
you think you will be able to get the information you need from your
interviewee?

The different interview styles are mutually beneficial. By that I mean
that one or two of these approaches together may better enable you to
use the third approach. For example, while it is logical to follow them
in order, so that using the Scientist and then Consultant may better
enable you to probe as the Interrogator, it also works to use the Scientist
and then the Interrogator to make it easier to be the Consultant, which
necessitates collaboration and a true sharing of information with your
interviewee.

All three interview personas are attractive in their own way, and each
necessitates a different tone, different word choices, and thoughtful sentence structure. For example, the Scientist style emphasizes truth, so questions should be framed objectively, while the Consultant style emphasizes
utility, so questions should be framed analytically. The Interrogator style
emphasizes justice and perseverance. Questions are often framed as probing and may express both fact and opinion. The Interrogator approach

should be used sparingly, only after careful consideration and always with sensitivity to the interviewee.

There are two primary ways that I've found the Interrogator style useful and effective. The first is to "back into" the real question that you want to ask. Small revelations make big ones easier, so begin by asking a series of questions that gets the interviewee to discuss and confirm small facts that don't seem very controversial. By the time you're ready to ask your main question, the interviewee is, as one might say in a poker game, "pot committed"—she's already discussed and divulged information around the main topic so it's not a leap to move into the real issue that you'd like addressed.

The second way to effectively use the Interrogator style is to simply start in the middle of a conversation. In this style of questioning, you insert facts into your questions that show that you have enough of the material already confirmed that it makes sense for the interviewee to continue the thread of the conversation. For example, in a story I wrote for the Council on Foreign Relations about US counterterrorism policies in Africa, I had a government document that criticized parts of the US approach. I knew the subject would be touchy but I wanted a defense official to address the issues. I used the Interrogator style to present him with my evidence and it enabled us to have a frank conversation about some of the drawbacks related to our country's counterterrorism approach.

4. Exploitation: Heuer's Competing Alternative Hypotheses (CAH) Detailed Instructions

1. *Identify the possible hypotheses that merit detailed examination. Use a group of analysts with different perspectives to brainstorm the possibilities. There is no "correct" number of hypotheses.*

Heuer cautions that in screening out your impossible hypotheses, you need to make sure to distinguish between hypotheses that appear to be *disproved* from those that are simply *unproven*. An unproven hypothesis has no evidence demonstrating that it is correct and should be kept alive until disproved. Result: be careful in deleting hypotheses that you are not falling prey to the very biases that you are trying to control by doing this exercise. Part of the point of the exercise is to consider hypotheses, so if you cross them off in a biased way, you've defeated the whole point.

>   2. *Make a list of significant evidence and arguments for and against*
>   *each hypothesis.*

For each hypothesis ask yourself this question: if this hypothesis is true, what should I expect to be seeing or not seeing? Then create broad lists of what you would expect to see. Include factors that have an impact on your judgments about the hypotheses. Include assumptions or logical deductions about other companies' or groups' goals, intentions, or standard procedure. These assumptions may make one or more hypotheses seem likely so include them in the list of "evidence." Heuer reminds us that like the Sherlock Holmes case in which the vital clue was that the dog did *not* bark, it is important to note the absence as well as the presence of evidence.

>   3. *Prepare a matrix with hypotheses across the top and evidence*
>   *down the side. Analyze the "diagnosticity" of the evidence and*
>   *arguments—that is, identify which items are most helpful in*
>   *judging the relative likelihood of the hypotheses.*

This is perhaps the most important element and the step that most differs from the natural, intuitive approach to analysis. Here you create an overview of all of the significant components of your analytic problems, or your investment target's CCs. Put them into a matrix with the hypotheses from step 1 and the evidence and arguments from step 2 so that you may analyze them and weigh the diagnosticity, or value, of each item of evidence relative to the other items. To understand diagnosticity, think of a patient with a fever. The fever may tell the doctor that something is wrong, but not what is wrong with the patient. Having a fever is consistent with so many possible hypotheses about a patient's illness that the data point has limited diagnostic value to a doctor. Evidence is diagnostic when it influences your judgment on the relative likelihood of the various hypotheses identified in step 1. Thus if an evidence item is consistent with all hypotheses, it may have no diagnostic value. When you identify items that are highly diagnostic, use them to drive your judgment, but also recheck them for accuracy or alternative interpretations.

How does each hypothesis fare? How does each piece of evidence relate to each hypothesis? Take one item of evidence at a time and consider how consistent it is with each hypothesis. Work across the matrix. (Later, in step 5, you will work down the columns of the matrix to examine one hypothesis at a time to see how consistent it is with all of the evidence.)

Make notations in the appropriate cell under each hypothesis in the matrix using notations that you are comfortable with, such as pluses/minuses, question marks, C/I for consistent or inconsistent, NA for not applicable, or a textual notation to record a shorthand representation of the complex reasoning that went on as you thought about how well the evidence relates to each hypothesis.

4. *Refine the matrix. Reconsider the hypotheses and delete evidence and arguments that have no diagnostic value.*

Here consider the exact wording of your hypotheses; they are critical to the conclusions that can be drawn from the analysis. Reword hypotheses that seem problematic. Add or alter hypotheses that need to be made to consider significant alternatives. Consider combining hypotheses that seem to have little or no evidence to distinguish between them.

Reconsider your evidence here too. Add or delete evidence or assumptions that now seem important or unimportant. Save these items as a separate list in your AREA journal as a record of information that was considered.

5. *Draw tentative conclusions about the relative likelihood of each hypothesis. Proceed by trying to disprove the hypotheses rather than prove them.*

In step 3, you worked across, focusing on a single item of evidence or argument and examining how it related to your hypothesis. Now work down the matrix. Assess each hypothesis as a whole. Start by looking for ways to disprove or reject hypotheses or to determine that they are unlikely. Only accept those hypotheses that cannot be refuted.

Recognize that no matter how much information is consistent with a given hypothesis, one cannot prove that a hypothesis is true if the same information may also be consistent with one or more other hypotheses. On the other hand, a single item of evidence that is inconsistent with a hypothesis may be sufficient grounds for rejecting that hypothesis. Thus this exercise requires doing the *opposite* of what comes naturally, which would be to concentrate on confirming hypotheses that you already believe to be true.

Heuer recommends that, in examining the matrix, look at the minuses or whatever other notation you used to indicate evidence that may be inconsistent with a hypothesis. The hypothesis with the fewest minuses is probably the most likely one. The hypothesis with the most minuses is probably the least likely one. It does not follow that the hypothesis with the most pluses is the most likely one, because a long list of evidence that is consistent with almost any reasonable hypothesis can be easily made. What is difficult to find, and is most significant when found, is hard evidence that is clearly inconsistent with a reasonable hypothesis.

Keep in mind though: all evidence is not equal. Some evidence is obviously more important than other evidence. By reconsidering the exact nature of the relationship between the evidence and the hypotheses, you will be able to judge how much weight to give it.

When the matrix shows that a given hypothesis is probable or unlikely, you may disagree. If so, check that you have not omitted other factors from the matrix that have an important influence on your thinking. Go back and put them in if need be so that the analysis reflects your best judgment.

> 6. *Analyze how sensitive your conclusion is to a few critical items*
>   *of evidence. Consider the consequences for your analysis if*
>   *that evidence were wrong, misleading, or subject to a different*
>   *interpretation.*

At this point, go back and question the few linchpin assumptions or pieces of evidence that really drive the outcome of your analysis. Are there questionable assumptions or alternative explanations or interpretations? Is any evidence incomplete and therefore misleading? Look at the sources of key evidence too. Is there any reason to suspect deception? Could the information have been manipulated?

Consider that when analysis turns out to be wrong, it is often because key assumptions went unchallenged and were later proven untrue. Yet we know that it is difficult to determine which assumptions merit questioning. One advantage of the CAH exercise is that it tells you what needs to be rechecked. In writing up the results of your matrix, identify critical assumptions that went into your interpretation and note when your conclusion is dependent upon the validity of your assumptions.

7. *Report conclusions. Discuss the relative likelihood of all the hypotheses, not just the most likely one.*

Analytic judgments are never certain. In your reading of your matrix, note the likelihood of all alternative possibilities so that you may make decisions on the basis of a full set of alternative possibilities, not just the single most likely alternative. That way you may also think through what decisions might need to be considered if one of the less likely alternatives turns out to be true.

Quantify your answers: if you say that a certain hypothesis is probably true, that could mean anywhere from a 55-percent to an 85-percent chance that future events will prove it correct. That leaves anywhere from a 15-percent to 45-percent possibility that a decision based on your judgment will be based on faulty assumptions and will turn out to be wrong. Can you be more specific about how confident you are in your judgment? If you're working with other people, they might interpret a subjective measurement like "probably" differently than you intended.

8. *Identify milestones for future observation that may indicate events are taking a different course than expected.*

Outline a list of things that you want to remain alert for, or that if observed would suggest a change to the possibilities. That way, as you follow your target's progress, you already know what might change your mind and are less likely to rationalize such developments or have thesis creep.

5. Exploitation: Patricia's Visual Map of Sprint

The chart on the next page visually displays the possible scenarios for Patricia's Critical Concepts relating to Sprint and the corresponding investment outcomes. It shows the impact of the first CC—the level of needed capital expenditures per year—on the company's valuation and ability to handle its debt load. The chart then displays the impact of the second CC—the

Critical Concept #1–Normalized Cap Ex

Sprint spends $2B in Cap Ex (non-upgrade) and CLWR spends $4.6B (4G upgrade) versus roughly $8B at Verizon and AT&T. If you accept what I've heard from people at Verizon, 50% of their Cap Ex is related to subscriber growth and something in the $3.5B to $4.5B cap Ex range is reasonable as a MCX number for Sprint, but whether it is $3.5B or $4.5B makes a big difference to Sprint's current valuation and ability to cover their interest.

Sprint	
$3.30	Per Share
$10	B Market Cap
$21	B EV*
$5.5	

$4.7	Normal Cap Ex
$0.8	EBITDA-MCX
0.6x	Interest Coverage
28.4x	EBITDA-MCX*

$3.6	Normal Cap Ex
$2.0	EBITDA-MCX
1.6x	Interest Coverage
10.8x	EBITDA-MCX*

Critical Concept #2–Cost of Network Vision

Sprint has announced a plan to consolidate their networks with targeted savings of $2.5B to $3B annually, which I believe are reasonable. However, I am skeptical of Sprint's estimated cost of $4–5B and believe it may even cost $10B, or more. While Sprint's 2016 EBITDA-MCX implies a reasonable valuation in either scenario (unattractive upside in the low CX scenario, moderate upside in the high CX scenario), a higher cost could threaten Sprint's solvency in the high CX scenario.

Cost of NV	$5B	10B
2016 EV	$26	$31
2016 EBITDA-MCX	$5.20	$5.20
2016 EV/EBITDA-MCX	5.1x	6.0x

Cost of NV	$5B	10B
2016 EV	$26	$31
2016 EBITDA-MCX	$3.80	$3.80
2016 EV/EBITDA-MCX	7.0x	8.3x

These CCs make the difference between a low-risk long, with high upside and an attractive short, with a high likelihood of bankruptcy.

Low-Risk, High Upside Long		IRR
2011 Value at 11x EBITDA-MCX	$3.42	$31
2016 Value at 11x EBITDA-MCX (5B cost)	$13.55	33%
2016 Value at 11x EBITDA-MCX (10B cost)	$11.88	29%

Attractive Short, with High Likelihood of Bankruptcy	
2011 Value at 11x EBITDA-MCX	($1.07)
2016 Net Debt at 10B Cost	$41
2016 Net Debt EBITDA-MCX	11.0x

Figure 12.1. Patricia's visual map for Sprint

cost of the network integration plan on Sprint's valuation. The chart concludes with a summary of what each CC means for Sprint as an investment proposition. If the CCs are favorably concluded, Sprint is a low risk bet with high upside; if they are unfavorably concluded, Sprint is a low upside bet with bankruptcy risk.

By visually organizing the information, Patricia was able to clearly see the varied outcomes that corresponded with her CCs. In organizing the information visually, rather than verbally or in writing, the exercise activated different parts of Patricia's brain, helping her better organize and understand the investment proposition before her.

Patricia's thesis statement read as follows:

The visual map shows that Sprint's investment proposition varies widely depending on what the real level of needed cap ex is. It highlights the importance of this factor and also Sprint's sensitivity to it.

6. Exploitation: Matthew's Scenario Analysis

Upside Case

Route expansion is limited for Delta's competition both through lobbying from the Big 3 and unavailable gates/slots. Big 3 continue to "play nice," given that airlines typically have regional monopolies on cities/airports. After a moderate decline in revenue per available seat mile in 2016, yields increase at historical levels of ~3% per year through 2018. Delta's labor negotiations go well. Salaries and wages per available seat mile increase at 5% per year. Fuel prices remain low with supply exceeding demand. Passenger load factors increase to 86% by 2018 (currently 84.9%) amid a steady economic environment.

Base Case

Although low cost carriers expand, the expansion is small enough to be essentially ignored. Revenue per available seat mile declines 3.5% in 2016, and then remains flat in 2017 and 2018. Passenger load factors remain static at 85% through 2018. While oil prices increase, it is modest. Labor costs increase as unions drive meaningful concessions on wages, but not as much as in the downside scenario: salaries and wages per available seat mile increase at 10% per year. The economy chugs along.

Downside Case

Low cost competitors expand rapidly forcing Delta and counterparts to discount prices accordingly. Revenue per available seat mile declines 3.5% in 2016, and then remains flat in 2017 and 2018 (despite increases in fuel price). Labor costs increase significantly as unions drive meaningful concessions on wages, increasing salaries and wages per available seat mile at 15% per year. Passenger load factors decrease to 84% (currently 84.9%). Oil prices increase significantly and the economy goes into recession.

Matthew's base case scenario had the most evidence. For example, his review of the low-cost carriers' order books for new airplanes supported the idea that while these carriers would continue to expand capacity, the increase would not be material relative to the industry as a whole. The downside scenario seemed too draconian and could not be supported with data, and underwriting any investment on the upside scenario would be irresponsible because so many factors would need to go right in order for that scenario to come to fruition. Doing the scenario analysis crystallized for Matthew that danger lurked in both conventional and totally unexpected ways. In addition to the factors he identified he realized that he also needed to consider geopolitical risk, economic recessions, and other exogenous shocks to the domestic and/or world economy that could disrupt the airline industry.

He also noted that in order for Delta to profit it not only had to act rationally, its competitors *also* needed to act rationally. Given the history of this industry and what appeared to be significant capacity increases from competitors, whether or not this would happen was very much "up in the air."

Matthew's thesis from his scenario analysis read:

Delta's likelihood of success is predicated on the Critical Concepts of discount pressures and foreign competition, fuel prices, and broader economic factors. The scenario analysis leads me to believe that even as airline capacity grows, passenger growth will likely level off and competitive pressures will hit prices even as expenses are likely to rise.

7. Exploitation: Fraud Case Studies

Below is a complete list of warning signs from my case study, "Spotting Signs of Fraud and Deception," discussed in abbreviated form in chapter 9, on Exploitation. Following each warning sign is the evidence from each of three famous frauds: Bre-X, Bernard L. Madoff Investment Securities and Enron.

1. **Controlled access to evidence**
   a. Bre-X controlled which gold samples could be evaluated.
      i. Placer Dome and Barrick, two major miners, were not allowed to do their own drilling.
      ii. A mysterious fire destroyed Bre-X's records.
      iii. The independent observer was hired by the company and under heavy influence from them, using data from Bre-X.
      iv. Bre-X provided crushed gold samples, preventing easy source analysis.
      v. Bre-X's exploration manager committed suicide.
   b. Madoff
      i. His firm was never audited by a recognized auditor.
      ii. Madoff was a figure of authority in his industry's regulatory organizations, including the NASDAQ, and the Securities Industry Association.
   c. Enron
      i. Enron's auditor Arthur Andersen shredded documents.
      ii. Enron kept specifics on how they made money secret for "competitive reasons."
      iii. Enron paid big fees to Arthur Andersen.
      iv. Enron paid big fees to Wall Street.
2. **Results were subject to management estimation**
   a. Mines output was based on Bre-X estimations.
   b. Returns were based on Madoff's estimations.

    c. Revenue Recognition was based on Enron's management models of Net Present Values and Special Purpose Entity structures.

3. **Authority bias: someone smart signed on.** In all three cases an outsider with credibility and influence gave credence to management's stories.

    a. Bre-X

       i. Blue chip backing from Lehman Brothers, Barrick Gold, Freeport McMoRan, and J. P. Morgan.

       ii. Bre-X was able to get credible people to invest even after bigger miners (such as the government of Indonesia) passed.

    b. Madoff

       i. Madoff was chairman of the NASDAQ and more.

    c. Enron

       i. Regularly rated the most innovative company by *Fortune* magazine.

       ii. Had a top-end audit committee (including a former head of the CFTC).

       iii. Had ties to former President George W. Bush and former Secretary of the Treasury Robert Rubin.

4. **Inconsistencies in evidence.** In all three cases results were too complicated to easily explain and discrete pieces of data conflicted with one another.

    a. Bre-X

       i. Larger companies had looked at the same mine and could not validate Bre-X's estimations.

       ii. Bre-X claimed gold was visible but outside expert Michael de Guzman's technical report called gold submicroscopic.

       iii. Assayer showed gold consistent with river-panned dust, inconsistent with other samples.

       iv. Key geologist and exploration manager committed suicide

    b. Madoff

       i. No one knew how the investment firm generated returns. Whistleblower Harry Markopolos wrote to the Securities and Exchange Commission three times arguing that Madoff's results were mathematically impossible, as Madoff was trading more than the entire market.

     ii. High returns despite a recession without explanation.

     iii. Only one accountant handled all Madoff accounts.

  c. Enron

     i. Enron's financials were extremely complicated and the company did not explain them.

     ii. Enron's return on equity was not consistent with its shift to a capital-light business.

5. **Focus on the stock market.** In all three cases the company managements told Wall Street what their companies were worth.

  a. Bre-X

     i. Bre-X's website had a program where users could generate their own Bre-X stock chart.

     ii. When the Indonesian government demanded that Bre-X give the country 45% of its mine, Bre-X suddenly adjusted the amount of gold that it claimed to have found so that its value would remain consistent.

  b. Madoff's investment firm was a private company, but its smooth returns were based off a volatile stock market.

  c. Enron told analysts what it thought it was worth.

6. **Results were too good to be true.**

  a. Bre-X's stock went up 1000% in two years

  b. Madoff's investment firm never lost money

  c. Enron was a top company in the unclear new market that it created in trading energy contracts.

7. **How the company is valued.** Although Bre-X and Enron were publicly traded companies, they were not valued on profitability or cash flow.

  a. At Bre-X focus was on future earnings from its gold mine.

  b. At Enron focus was on sales growth.

8. **Management egotism.** All three companies had domineering, brazen chief executives with little boundary between their own interests and their companies.

9. **Nay-sayers were threatened.**

  a. Bre-X threatened legal action.

  b. Madoff did not tolerate questions.

  c. Enron cut off analysts who questioned the company. People who raised questions were called "rock throwers."

10. **Attacking people instead of addressing issues.** When problems arose, the companies blamed others for any weaknesses. All three blamed short sellers, the web, and critics in general.
11. **Put off explanations.** All three made repeated statements that any lack of clarity would soon be resolved.
12. **Shady history.**
    a. Bre-X once was run by a bankrupt broker and stock promoter
    b. Madoff's firm was heavily peopled by family
    c. Enron had a revolving door with Arthur Anderson, its auditor, often hiring Arthur Anderson's executives.
13. **Management failed to follow procedures.** All three had unusual disclosure or other rules.
14. **Internal dissent not tolerated.** Management eliminated internal resistance through firings and use of family personnel.

The bottom line when assessing a company overall is to ask yourself to consider:

1. What pressures for performance may potentially affect the reporting of financial results? Pressure may manifest itself as a tone coming down from the top of a company, or the explicit, or implicit, messages that executives send to employees. Where is emphasis placed? How frequently is the emphasis mentioned and in what ways is it reinforced? A tone that places a heavy emphasis on the stock price and/or financial results may unwittingly send a message that seems to encourage cutting corners.
2. What about the way the company operates causes concern or stress? And where might those stressors manifest themselves? How may concerns be hidden?

8. Analysis: Matthew's AREA Method Thesis Statements

Below are selected thesis statements from Matthew's AREA Method research on Delta Airlines.

Absolute: Just the Numbers Thesis Statement

For Delta, whose operating expenses are relatively fixed, incremental passenger growth is critical, but the macro trends appear to be good for now: revenue passenger miles are increasing, as are available seat miles, passenger mile yield, and load factor. Fuel prices are 35% of Delta's operating expenses, and prices are currently low, but the number of gallons consumed is increasing. Future fuel trends for both usage and cost will be critical to Delta's profitability.

Final Absolute Thesis Statement

Revenue passenger-miles are increasing steadily both domestically and abroad. Given Delta's strong performance with corporate travelers, a sophisticated customer segmentation strategy that drives higher revenues, and entrenched partnerships with international airlines, the company stands to benefit from this macro trend. This may ultimately narrow the valuation discount that Delta currently has versus high quality peers.

Relative Literature Review Thesis Statement

Delta operates in a highly competitive environment and is subject to all sorts of regulations, but doesn't get any upside from the government the way foreign state-owned airlines do. Delta can't control the weather and it isn't operating in a true free market. I am less confident of Delta's investment prospects after having done the literature review.

Relative Earnings Calls Thesis Statement

Despite the unpredictable and uncontrollable forces buffeting the airline, Delta's management projects an air of professionalism and confidence in their operational capabilities.

Relative Final Thesis Statement

To a certain extent, the institutional-heavy ownership structure limits Delta's upside. Since there are so many investment professionals

*covering the name, most of the information that could move
the stock price meaningfully has already been written about,
discussed, and analyzed ad nauseum. More importantly, given
Delta's sheer size, the opportunity for significant upside is more
muted. It's much more difficult for a company to double in value
when it's so large.*

Exploration Thesis Statement

*My interviews revealed that competition is stiff and discounters are
making headway. Fuel prices are a concern for all airlines, and the
consensus is that they will rise. Discounters believe that air travel
is being commoditized and they can win on price—when they can
compete fairly. But the playing field isn't level: Delta controls many
airport slots in major hubs. Can Delta's size and attractive airport
slots keep discounters at bay?*

Exploitation Competing Alternative Hypotheses (CAH) Thesis Statement

*Low cost carriers are increasing capacity significantly, and although
they are a small portion of the overall market, these new routes will
likely be in markets where the Big 4 are earning outsized returns,
which may well pressure Delta's ticket prices. It is unclear whether
Delta's operational excellence is strong enough to withstand these
competitive pressures, especially in the face of increased labor and
fuel costs.*

Exploitation Visual Map Thesis Statement

*In order for Delta to flourish in this industry, airline services
cannot become a commoditized product. Business travelers will
always be restricted by location, however, in choosing an airline
partner. Delta's operational advantage at this point is unclear and*

the visual map suggests that Delta's market opportunity might be saturated.

Exploitation Scenario Analysis Thesis Statement

Delta's likelihood of success is predicated on the Critical Concepts of discount pressures and foreign competition, fuel prices, and broader economic factors. The scenario analysis leads me to believe that even as airline capacity grows, passenger growth will likely level off and competitive pressures will hit prices even as expenses are likely to rise.

Final AREA Method Thesis Statement

Delta is operating at peak earnings in a cyclical industry, with results that have been aided by historically low fuel costs, favorable labor agreements, and industry consolidation. However, the competitive dynamic is shifting due to significant capacity coming on board from discount airlines that will lead to increased competition on many of Delta's most profitable routes and labor expenses, which are increasing sharply, and will further highlight that Delta operates at a structural cost disadvantage relative to its peers. Even in a muted fuel environment, this will result in lower ticket prices, higher operating expenses and weaker profitability.

9. The AREA Hunt Condensed

While I was making final edits on this book, I gave a copy of the manuscript to a forensic accountant friend to get his feedback. He's been using AREA ever since and developed his own "Cheetah Sheets" that truncate AREA to fit his research needs. Many of my students have asked for a template of what an abbreviated version of AREA might look like. What follows are the Cheetah Sheets my accountant friend developed. This is one example of a condensed AREA research hunt.

Idea	Step	Why It Matters
Absolute	Getting to Know Your Target(s)	Gathering basic information about a target is the necessary initial step in every research
	Just the Numbers	Financial research is ultimately about numbers; thus, review of numerical data is a necessary step
	Your Target's Business Model	Understanding target's business model helps put numerical data in perspective
	Reconciling the Data and the Narrative	Comparison of numerical data to qualitative information provides insights into consistency (or lack thereof) of the target's story
	Target History	Target's history often reveals trends and tendencies that can provide valuable insights into the target's present
	Leadership	Leaders set the tone in an organization; therefore, understanding the target's leadership is an important aspect of the research

Idea	Step	Why It Matters
Relative	Industry Mapping	The research target does not exist in isolation—understanding its operating environment will provide additional insights and perspectives to numerical data
	Earnings Calls	Earnings calls represent management's side of the story and provide a researcher an opportunity to evaluate that story in the context of gathered numerical and qualitative data
	Earnings Call Q&A	Earnings call Q&A sessions can provide a researcher additional insights into management's (a) ability and willingness to answer specific questions about numerical data and the target's business; and (b) transparency
	Analyst Research Reports	Analyst reports could serve as good aids to a researcher to understand the target, provided the researcher properly considers analysts' potential biases, conflicts of interests, and breadth of target's analyst coverage

Figure 12.2. The AREA hunt condensed

Idea	Step	Why It Matters
Exploration	Finding Good Prospects	"Good prospects" are experts and other knowledgeable individuals who could provide a researcher with valuable insights about a target, its operating environment, and other relevant issues. Cheetah Sheet 27 provides a great list of potential venues for finding good prospects that the researcher may consider. However, at a minimum, the researcher should consider trade associations and industry conferences, which are generally open to outsiders.
	Great Questions Roadmap	There are four types of great questions: behavior, opinion, feeling, and knowledge questions.
	Types of Great Questions	Getting the right information starts with asking the great questions; thus, every researcher should develop a skill of crafting the great questions
	Taking Great Notes	Asking great questions is not going to accomplish much if the information is subsequently lost because the researcher was unable to capture it during an interview

Idea	Step	Why It Matters
Exploitation	Pro/Con Analysis	The Pro/Con analysis helps a researcher to test the main hypothesis about the target by understanding arguments both in favor of and against it
	Developing a Scenario Analysis	A researcher will likely never have a crystal ball into a target because most of the data and assumptions underlying the research are subject to uncertainty and variability. Scenario and sensitivity analyses are helpful tools in evaluating the likely impact on the target or the researcher's conclusions from key business decisions or changes in the assumptions underlying the research
	Plots and Ploys	Companies can play with reported numbers (legally or otherwise). While a researcher is not expected to be a forensic accountant trained on spotting and untangling corporate fraud, the researcher should be broadly familiar with general signs of financial misrepresentation

Idea	Step	Why It Matters
Analysis	Getting the Data Right	Correct data (i.e., free of computational and bias errors) is a foundation of reliability of the analysis and credibility of the research conclusions
	Appraising Your Thesis Statement	In the end, a researcher should ask a simple question—does the research conclusion make sense in light of all the evidence considered in the analysis?

Figure 12.2. (Continued)

Notes

Chapter Two. Research Like a Cheetah

1. Katie Hiler, "Cheetahs' Secret Weapon: A Tight Turning Radius," *New York Times*, June 12, 2013, https://www.nytimes.com/2013/06/13/science/agility-not-speed-is-cheetahs-meal-ticket-study-says.html.

Chapter Four. Cognitive Biases and the AREA Method

1. Charlie Munger's Harvard speech can be viewed online on the Investor's Podcast, accessed June 4, 2018, https://www.theinvestorspodcast.com/blog/charlie-mungers-famous-speech-harvard-psychology-human-misjudgement/; Cialdini, *Influence: The Psychology of Persuasion*, revised ed. (New York: Harper Collins, 2007).

Chapter Five. AREA at Work and Critical Concepts

1. Austen Hufford, "Netflix Again Tops Forecasts for Subscriber Growth," *Wall Street Journal*, October 16, 2017, https://www.wsj.com/articles/netflix-again-surpasses-subscriber-growth-estimates-1508186507?tesla=y.

Chapter Six. A: Absolute

1. Joanna Klein, "Cleaning a Dirty Sponge Only Helps Its Worst Bacteria, Study Says," *New York Times*, August 4, 2017, https://www.nytimes.com/2017/08/04/science/sponges-bacteria-microwaving-cleaning.html; Judy Stone, "Germs On Your Kitchen Sponge? Get a Grip!" *Forbes*, August 6, 2017, https://www.forbes.com/sites/judystone/2017/08/06/germs-on-your-kitchen-sponge-get-a-grip/#5b02aa91746en the sterilized sponges.

2. Paul Hodgson, "The 5 Most Overrated CEOs," *Fortune*, May 5, 2015, http://fortune.com/2015/05/05/overrated-ceos/.

3. ManpowerGroup Solutions, "Work, for *Me*: Understanding Candidate Demand for Flexibility," 2017, https://www.manpowergroup.co.nz/documents/white-papers/2017_ManpowerGroup_Solutions_Work_for_Me.pdf.

4. "Restoring Open Skies: The Need to Address Subsidized Competition from State-Owned Airlines in Qatar and the UAE," January 28, 2015, http://www.openandfairskies.com/wp-content/themes/custom/media/White.Paper.pdf.

5. Source for figs. 6.2–6.3: Salesforce.com, 2013 10-K, http://s1.q4cdn.com/454432842/files/doc_financials/2013/fy13_annual_report.pdf, pp. 43 and 47.

6. Salesforce.com, 2013 10-K, p. 43.

7. Salesforce.com, 2013 10-K, p. 68.

Chapter Seven.   R: Relative

1. "Bond Insurer FGIC Plans to Split Into Two Companies," *CNBC.com*, February 15, 2008, https://www.cnbc.com/id/23182192.

2. Department of Justice, "Justice Department Files Antitrust Lawsuit to Block United's Monopolization of Takeoff and Landing Slots and Newark Airport," press release no. 15-1384, November 10, 2015, https://www.justice.gov/opa/pr/justice-department-files-antitrust-lawsuit-block-uniteds-monopolization-takeoff-and-landing; Department of Justice, "United Airlines Abandons Attempt to Enhance Its Monopoly at Newark Liberty International Airport," press release no. 16-414, April 6, 2016, https://www.justice.gov/opa/pr/united-airlines-abandons-attempt-enhance-its-monopoly-newark-liberty-international-airport.

3. "Twice-Diverted Delta Flight Finally Lands at JFK after 30 Travel Hours," *CBS New York*, February 17, 2016, http://newyork.cbslocal.com/2016/02/17/delta-flight-diverted-twice-jfk-nyc/.

4. NIRI Analytics, *NIRI Earnings Process Practices Research Report* (Alexandria, VA: National Investors Relationship Institute, 2016), https://www.niri.org/NIRI/media/Protected-Documents_ExcludeGlobalSubs/Analytics%20Reports/Analytics_Guidance/NIRI-Earnings-Process-Practices-Report-2016.pdf.

5. Salesforce CRM Q3 2013 conference call transcript, p. 11.

6. Jie He and Xiun Tian, "The Dark Side of Analyst Coverage: The Case of Innovation," *Journal of Financial Economics* 109, no. 3. Available online at: https://www.researchgate.net/publication/228197747_The_Dark_Side_of_Analyst_Coverage_The_Case_of_Innovation

7. "The Pros and Cons of Tracking Hedge Funds via 13F Filings," *Market Folly* (blog), October 8, 2012, http://www.marketfolly.com/2012/10/hedge-fund-13f-filing-pros-and-cons.html#ixzz4t3Qp7cJG.

8. Cadie Thompson, "Dan Loeb Sends Another Scathing Letter to Yahoo CEO," *CNBC*, March 28, 2012, https://www.cnbc.com/id/46882463.

9. Letter from William A. Ackman to the Board of ADP, September 7, 2017, Securities and Exchange Commission Archives, Exhibit 99.8, https://www.sec.gov/Archives/edgar/data/8670/000119312517278771/d443483dex998.htm (accessed March 25, 2018).

10. Trian Partners, "Revitalize P&G Together: Vote the White Proxy Card," September 6, 2017, https://www.revitalizepg.com.

11. "Baron Funds Q2 Notes Impressive Performance Run; Elon [sic] Compares Musk to John Glenn," *ValueWalk*, September 13, 2017, https://www.valuewalk.com/2017/09/baron-funds-2q17-commentary/.

Chapter Eight. E: Exploration

1. International Finance Corporation, "IFC Annual Portfolio Review, FY11: Development Results," accessed June 7, 2018, https://www.ifc.org/wps/wcm/connect/100e28804a9567c8ace3fe9e0dc67fc6/web_APR2011.pdf?MOD=AJPERES, p. 14.

2. Tom Searcy, "7 Ways to Ensure Your Emails Get Read," *Inc.*, February 20, 2013, https://www.inc.com/tom-searcy/7-ways-to-ensure-your-emails-get-read.html; Jacqueline Whitmore, "Top 10 Ways to Get People to Read and Respond to Your Emails," *Entrepreneur*, June 10, 2014, https://www.entrepreneur.com/article/234561#; John Jantsch, "The Abusive Math of Cold Calling" (blog post), Duct Tape Marketing website, accessed March 28, 2018, https://www.ducttapemarketing.com/the-abusive-math-of-cold-calling/; Andrew Gazdecki, "Sales Statistics: 20 Sales Stats That Will Change Your Approach" (blog post), LeadFuze website, accessed March 28, 2018, https://www.leadfuze.com/sales-statistics/.

Chapter Nine. E: Exploitation

1. Heuer, *Psychology of Intelligence Analysis* (Washington, DC: Center for the Study of Intelligence, 2010), chap. 6.

2. See, for instance, Munger's Harvard speed, available via the Investor's Podcast, accessed June 8, 2018, https://www.theinvestorspodcast.com/blog/charlie-mungers-famous-speech-harvard-psychology-human-misjudgement/.

3. The Coca-Cola infographic identified is © 2018 The Coca-Cola Company and is being shown herein with approval from The Coca-Cola Company.

4. The color version can be viewed at https://www.coca-colacompany.com/content/dam/journey/us/en/private/fileassets/pdf/2018/Coca-Cola-At-A-Glance-2018.pdf.

5. William C. Bradford, "Reaching the Visual Learner: Teaching Property through Art," *The Law Teacher* 11 (2004), https://ssrn.com/abstract=587201.

6. NeoMam Studios, "Thirteen Reasons Why Your Brain Craves Infographics," accessed June 8, 2018, https://neomam.com/interactive/13reasons/.

7. D. R. Vogel, O. W. Dickson, and J. A. Lehman, "Persuasion and the Role of Visual Presentation Support: The UM/3M Study," ThinkTwice Inc., *Working Paper Series*, June 1986, accessed June 8, 2018, http://www.thinktwicelegal.com/olio/articles/persuasion_article.pdf.

8. Some researchers view EBITDA—MCX as a superior valuation metric to EBITDA because it acknowledges the capital needs of the business. The idea behind using Maintenance Cap Ex (MCX) instead of just Cap Ex is that the business's regular Cap Ex needs are more relevant to its ongoing earnings power than the most recent Cap Ex figure, which can fluctuate dramatically with Cap Ex cycles and growth investment for the business.

9. Liberty Interactive Corporation, "Memorandum from Liberty Interactive Corporation to Employees of its Subsidiaris, dated July 14, 2012, available on Seeking Alpha website, accessed June 8, 2018, https://seekingalpha.com/filing/864534.

10. The debt was issued near the peak of the late-twentieth-century tech bubble and was convertible into shares of stock in companies like Sprint, CenturyLink, and Motorola at prices well above market. The debt carried very low cash interest rates, but had higher interest rates for tax purposes. Through a tracking stock structure, Liberty Interactive would use the excess of tax interest rates over cash interest rates to reduce their taxes and pay Liberty Ventures the amount by which they reduced their taxes in cash. When the debt matured, almost twenty years down the road, Liberty Ventures would have to repay the tax deductions Liberty Interactive had taken, but in the meantime they could invest the cash, with no obligation to pay interest on the tax deductions they wouldn't have to repay for almost twenty years.

11. Geoff Gannon, "How Warren Buffett Made His First $100,000" (blog post), *GuruFocus.com*, accessed March 31, 2018, https://www.gurufocus.com/news/169950/how-warren-buffett-made-his-first-100000.

12. "Autonomy Ex-executive Found Guilty of Fraud," *BBC News*, May 1, 2018, http://www.bbc.com/news/business-43959468.

13. Security and Exchange Commission v. WorldCom Inc., Civ No. 02-CV-463 (JSR), United States District Court, Southern District of New York, November 5, 2002, https://www.sec.gov/litigation/complaints/comp17829.htm.

Chapter Ten.   A: Analysis

1. Michael Rapoport, "GE's Numbers Game: Pick from Four Earnings Figures," *Wall Street Journal*, October 30, 2017, https://www.wsj.com/articles/ges-numbers-game-pick-from-four-earnings-figures-1509364801.
2. Kahneman, *Thinking, Fast and Slow* (New York: Farrar, Straus and Giroux, 2011), 218.
3. Delta Airlines, Q1 2018 Earnings Call, April 12, 2018, https://www.nasdaq.com/aspx/call-transcript.aspx?StoryId=4162701&Title=delta-s-dal-ceo-ed-bastian-on-q1-2018-earnings-call-transcript; Leslie Josephs, "Delta Earnings Better Than Expected, despite Rising Costs," *CNBC*, April 12, 2018, https://www.cnbc.com/2018/04/12/delta-earnings-q1-2018-earnings.html.

Index

Page numbers followed by letters *f* and *t* refer to figures and tables, respectively.

10-K filings, 35; disclosures in, 35, 44
10-Q filings, disclosures in, 44
13D filings, 88
13F filings, 88, 89; investor letters attached to, 90–91
13G filings, 88
14-A filings, 53

Absolute, in AREA method, xviii, 7, 34; business model and, 40–42; Cheetah Sheet on, 36; first steps in, 35–36; governance structure and, 54–55; journal entries on, 189–93; leadership and, 51–54; management narrative and, 46, 61–63; numerical data and, 36–40, 61–63; press releases and, 57; and Relative research, disconnect between, 71; Relative sources used to vet, 65; research reports and, 55–56; SEC filings and, 35–36, 42–45; share price performance and, 58–59; thesis statements based on, 38–39, 47, 60–61, 65, 179–80, 193, 208–9; website and, 47–50
academic journals, use in research, 74
accountants, as interview prospects, 102
accounting: hidden value in, 155–59; padded value in, 159–61
Accurint.com, 74
Ackman, Bill, 91
activist investor communications, 90–93; Cheetah Sheet on, 93; letters, 90–91, 93; white papers, 92
Adderley, Terence, 52–53
ADP (company), 91
Advanced Investment Research class, 3, 14, 17, 27, 71, 107, 112, 176, 184

advocacy-adversary model, 176
airline industry: mapping of, 68, 69*f*. *See also* Delta Airlines
Alice in Wonderland (Carroll), 64
Amazon, acquisition of Whole Foods, 52
analysis: conventional, CAH distinguished from, 140; failure of, 131; of interview notes, 125
Analysis, in AREA method, xviii, 7, 166, 168–69; advocacy-adversary model of, 176; checklists in, 176–78; mistakes in data collection and, 171–73; pre-mortem, 173–75; solvability and, 169–71; thesis statement based on, 181
analyst coverage, 84–87; Cheetah Sheet on, 85; influences on, 87
analytical edge/pitfall, 28
Anderson, Richard, 190, 191
Aquamarine Fund, 177
AREA Method, xiii–xiv, 2, 6, 187; abbreviated version of, 211, 212*f*–213*f*; advantages of, 4, 7, 13*f*; cheetah pauses in, 10–11, 13–14; components of, xviii, 7, 8*f*, 16; goals of, 5, 31, 32; idea for, 8–9; as muscle/skill, 4, 33; origins of, 6–7; perspectives in, 7–8, 8*f*, 9; as process, 3, 4, 7; response to, 184–86; steps in, 33; unique characteristics of, 7, 8; visual maps of, xviii, 8*f*, 14*f*, 146
Arthur Andersen, and Enron, 165, 205, 208
assumptions. *See* bias(es); cognitive shortcuts
Assured Guaranty, 71–72; industry map for, 72
AT&T, 70
audit trail, thesis statements as, 20, 183

authority bias, 25*t*, 40; AREA Method remedies for, 25*t*; and fraud, 166, 206
auto industry, pension plans in, 45
AutoNation, 28
Autonomy (company), 161
Avon, 53

background check websites, use in research, 74
bankruptcy process, and hidden value, 158
Barnes and Noble, Nook division of, 157
Baron, Ron, 93
Baron Capital, 93
Barrick Gold Corp, 165, 166, 205, 206
Barron's magazine, 8–9
base rates, tendency to ignore, 172
Bastian, Ed, 183, 190–91, 192
BDCs (business development corporations), 171
Beanie Babies, 68
Bear Stearns, collapse of, xv
behavioral edge/pitfall, 27
behavior questions, in interview, 105
Benioff, Marc, 83
Berkshire Hathaway, 113, 133
Best Buy, price cuts at, 14
Better Business Bureau, 74
Bezos, Jeff, 52
bias(es): common types of, 22*t*–26*t*; counteracting, xiii, 4, 9, 11–12, 13*f*, 21, 22*t*–26*t*, 35, 131–33, 140, 166; and flawed data, 40; hindsight, 20; and limits to quality research, 21; literature on, 22; vs. numerical data, 23*t*, 24*t*, 26*t*, 37; vs. perspective-taking, 11–12, 22*t*
BIAS (edges and pitfalls), 26
Blair, Tony, xiii–xiv
blaming, as warning sign, 165, 208
Blockbuster, 14–15
Bloomberg News: bias created by, 35; investor letters and, 93
board of directors: assessment of, 54–55; shareholders' efforts to influence, 90–91
Bre-X, 22, 163–65, 166, 205–8
Brookfield Asset Management, 112–13
Buffet, Warren, 112–13, 133, 157, 177, 184
Bush, George H. W., 166, 206
business development corporations (BDCs), 171
business libraries, 74

business model, of research target, 40–42; Cheetah Sheet on, 41

CAH exercise. *See* Competing Alternative Hypotheses exercise
call pitch, 120–22; assurance at end of, 122–23; developing, 98; and follow-up call, 122; practicing, 104
Camden, Carl, 52
"Can You Fight Poverty with a Five-Star Hotel?" (Einhorn), 97–99
capital expenditures, vs. depreciation and amortization, 162
CapitalIQ, 88
capitalized operating expenses, 162
capital structure: and industry mapping, 66; red flags in, 43
CARE, 13*f*
Carradine, David, 6
cash flows, vs. net income, 162
cash taxes, 162
CCs. *See* Critical Concepts
Charity Navigator, 36, 53
checklist(s): fundamental investment, 177; to reduce bias, 23*t*. *See also* Cheetah Sheet(s)
cheetah: analogy with, xiii, 10, 11, 13–14, 18; secret to hunting success of, 10
cheetah pauses, in AREA Method, 10–11, 13–14; advantages of, 10, 13*f*, 18; behavioral edge and, 27; CAH exercise compared to, 139; after industry mapping, 70; reducing narrative bias with, 24*t*
Cheetah Sheet(s), 17, 19; on absolute information, 36; on activist investor communications, 93; on analyst coverage, 85; on AREA Method, xviii; on business model, 41; on CAH exercise, 141; on data analysis, avoiding mistakes in, 172–73; downloadable, 17, 33, 189; on earnings calls, 80, 82–83; on Exploration, planning ahead for, 66; on fraud, warning signs of, 162, 164–65; fundamental investment checklist, 177; on governance structure, 55; on hidden value, 156–57; on history of research target, 51; on industry mapping, 67; on interview questions, 105, 106, 108, 109, 110, 114, 116; on interviews, help with, 104; on interviews, staying on track in, 109; on leadership of research target, 54; on literature review, 73–74, 75, 76,

77; on management narrative, 46, 63; on note-taking, during interviews, 126; on numerical data, 37; on padded value, 160; on pre-mortem analysis, 174; on press releases, 57; on pro/con analysis, 134; recording in AREA journal, 189, 190; on research reports, 56; on scenario analysis, 152, 153; on shareholder base, 89; on share price performance, 58; on thesis statements, 19, 179; using as quick reference, 33; using to counteract biases, 22t; on visual mapping, 148; on website of research target, 48

Chesapeake Energy, 43
Chipotle, 27–28, 99
Christopher, John, 28–29, 32–33
Cialdini, Robert, 22
clarification questions, in interview, 108
Clinton, Hillary, 140
Coca-Cola Company, 146; product portfolio of, visual map of, 146, 147f; website homepage of, 49
cognitive shortcuts: AREA method controlling for, 13f; examples of, 129–30; and limits to quality research, 21; managing, 2, 8, 10, 130. See also bias(es)
colleges, interview prospects at, 101
Columbia Business School, courses at, 3–4, 17, 21
Columbia University Graduate School of Journalism, courses at, xv, 3–4
company capsules, 101
compensation structure, evaluation of, 52–54; journal entry on, 191–92
Competing Alternative Hypotheses (CAH) exercise, 137, 139–45; Cheetah Sheet on, 141; examples of, 142–45, 143f, 145f; reducing bias with, 22t, 23t, 24t, 25t; step-by-step instructions for, 197–201; thesis statements based on, 144, 145, 180–81, 210
competitive advantage, 68
competitive landscape, research target's, 65, 66–72
competitor companies, employees at, as interview prospects, 102
conclusion: in thesis statement, 19, 211; working backwards from, 133
conference call transcripts, 65
confidential information, avoiding in interviews, 122–23

confirmation bias, 22t–23t, 140
Consultant, interviewer as, 112, 115, 196
context, use in research, 4, 40–42
contractors, as interview prospects, 102
contracts, and hidden value, 157
correlation, example of, 39, 39f
court filings, interview prospects in, 101
credit situation, red flags in, 43
Critical Concepts (CCs), 12–13, 13f, 30; in AREA journal, 16, 192–93; CAH exercise and, 141, 144; defining accurately, xiii; edges/pitfalls and, 29; focus on outcome in, 31, 32; and informational edge, developing, 31; interview questions focused on, 106, 115; multiple narratives for, 24t; pro/con analysis and, 136; revising and refining, 13, 14, 18, 128; scenario analysis and, 153, 155; solvability of, 169–71; thesis statements and, 18; time horizons and, 31–32; visual mapping and, 150, 201–3, 202f
Crocs shoes, 68
Crown Castle, 159
customers, as interview prospects, 102

data. See numerical data
databases, use in research, 36, 73
data fishing, avoiding, 172–73
D&B Hoovers, 36
decision-making: AREA Method and, xiii–xiv, 2, 5, 187; landmines in, 11; research and, 2, 7
Def 14-A filings, 53
deferred revenue, and hidden value, 157
Delta Airlines: analysis of performance of, 170–71; AREA journal on, 189–93; CAH exercise for, 142–44, 143f, 154; compensation structure at, 53–54, 191–92; conclusion regarding, 211; Critical Concepts for, 192–93; current performance of, 182–83; earnings calls of, 81, 83; history of, 189–90; industry map for, 68, 69f; interviews on, 111, 114–16; leadership of, 190–91; literature review on, 75, 77–78; numerical data on, 38; performance compared with peers, visual map of, 149, 150–51, 150f, 155; pro/con analysis of, 137–39, 138f, 154; recommendation regarding, 182; as research target, 17; scenario analysis for, 153, 155, 203–5; shareholder base

Delta Airlines (*cont.*)
  of, 89–90; thesis statements regarding,
    38–39, 60–61, 208–11; white paper
    used in assessment of, 56–57
depreciation, excess, 159
Development Outcome Tracking System
    (DOTS), 97
Dexter Shoes, 177
disconfirmation, 132–33; in CAH exercise,
    140, 141, 142
DISH, 157
dissonance, looking for, 61–63
DOTS (Development Outcome Tracking
    System), 97
Dual Coding Theory, 146
Dun & Bradstreet, 101

earnings calls, 78–84; archived transcripts
    of, 79; Cheetah Sheets on, 80, 82–83;
    question-and-answer part of, 82–83; thesis
    statements based on, 81, 84, 180, 209
edges and pitfalls: categories of, 26–29;
    Critical Concepts and, 31; and interview
    persona, choice of, 196; recognizing,
    26, 29
Einstein, Albert, 1, 18, 168
email, interview via, 116
email pitch, 120; likelihood of receiving
    response to, 121, 122; timing of, 122
Embarq, 52
empathy, building, 4, 8
employees, in support positions, as
    interview prospects, 102
employees' unions, finding interview
    prospects through, 101
Enron, 22, 163, 165–66, 205–8;
    disclosures on financial notes of, 45;
    relationship with Wall Street, 86
Equifax, 112
equity stakes, and hidden value, 156
evaluation, vs. interpretation, 131
evidence: controlled access to, 163–65,
    205; inconsistencies in, 164, 206
Exide, 9
Expedia, 156
Exploitation, in AREA method, xviii,
    7, 95, 96, 130, 166; and insight, 131;
    thesis statements based on, 137, 144,
    145, 151, 180–81, 210–11; tools and
    techniques of, 131
Exploration, in AREA method, xviii, 7,
    95–96, 185; in absence of Absolute or

Relative data, 27–28, 99; components
    of, 96; importance of, 127–28; planning
    ahead for, 65, 66, 74, 98; return to, 144;
    thesis statements based on, 128, 180,
    210. See also interview(s)

Facebook, data privacy scandal involving,
    140
FactSet, 88; bias created by, 35
false consensus bias, 23*t*
feeling questions, in interview, 105
financial analytics firms, bias created
    by, 35
financial crisis of 2008, xv
financial decisions, xiii, xiv, 6
financial research, guidebook for, 6
financial statements: interview prospects
    found in, 101; misrepresentations
    in, 155–62. See also Securities and
    Exchange Commission (SEC) filings
footnote(s), gleaning information from, 97
footnote disclosures, 44–45, 61, 62
foreign language, help with, 104
Franklin, Benjamin, 133
fraud, warning signs of, 21–22, 161–66,
    205–8
Freedom of Information Act Filing (FOIA),
    74
freelance reporters, help with interviews,
    104
Freeport-McMoRan, 166, 206

GAAP, 159, 160
GameStop, 14–15
Gartner Group, 67
General Electric, earnings calculations by,
    173
General Growth Properties (GGP), 158
General Motors, restructuring of, visual
    map of, 149, 149*f*
Glass Door, 103
Glenn, John, 93
Good Prospects (interview), 96, 99;
    Cheetah Sheets on, 101–2; identifying,
    100–103
Google: purchase of Motorola, 157; search
    on, disadvantages of, 73
Google Scholar, 73
governance structure: evaluation of,
    54–55; shareholders' efforts to influence,
    90–91. See also leadership
government entities, researching, 36

government officials, as interview prospects, 102

Great Questions (interview), 96, 99; Cheetah Sheets on, 105, 106, 108, 109, 110, 114, 116; crafting, 104–11; types of, 105

groupthink, 172

GuideStar, 36, 53

headhunters, as interview prospects, 102

headset, use during phone interviews, 125

Hesse, Dan, 52, 60; as capital allocator, 70; compensation of, 53

Heuer, Richards, 131, 132, 139, 141; on CAH exercise, 139, 197–201

Hewlett Packard (HP), 161

hidden value, 155–59; examples of, 155–56, 158, 159; potential sources of, 156–58, 159

high-tech industry, pension plans in, 45

hindsight, prospective, 174

hindsight bias, avoiding, 20

history, of research target, 50–51; Cheetah Sheet on, 51; journal entry on, 189–90; shady, 165, 208

Hologic, 178–79

Holt, Adam, 83

Hoover's, 101

Howard Hughes Corporation (HHC), 158

Hurston, Zora Neale, 16

Hussain, Sushovan, 161

hypotheses: CAH exercise testing, 140–41, 197–201; disconfirmation of, 132–33, 140, 141; disproved vs. unproven, 197; vs. facts, 132; most probable, 140; standardized approach to testing, 132

IBIS World, 67

ideas: good, botched by poor process, 2–3; research and, 2

Indeed.com, 103

industry conferences, developing sources at, 100, 101

industry groups, researching, 67, 73

industry journals, identifying sources from, 101

industry mapping, 66–72; Cheetah Sheet on, 67; examples of, 68–72, 69f, 72f, 193–96; and potential sources, 98

information: multiple ways of reading, 131; primary-source, 34

informational edge/pitfall, 27–28, 31

insider-trading issues, avoiding in interviews, 122–23

insight: Exploitation research and, 131; Exploration research (interviews) and, 113

Institutional Investor Magazine, 87

insurance representatives, as interview prospects, 102

International Finance Corporation (IFC), 97–99

Internet search, disadvantages of, 73

Interoil, 57

interpretation(s): vs. evaluation, 131; in thesis statement, 19

Interrogator, interviewer as, 112, 115, 117, 196–97

interview(s): additional, 144; "after-interview" process, 124, 126–27; background research prior to, 117; call pitch prior to, 98, 104, 120–23; conducting, 123–25; effective, 114; face-to-face, 125; feedback during, 108, 109; formula for, 99–100; help in, 104; insights from, 113; listening during, importance of, 124; maintaining control of, 109; material nonpublic information in, avoiding, 122–23; note-taking during, 125–26; recording, 125; rehearsing, 116; and relationship building, 124; script for, 111; sharing research in, 116–17; styles of, 111–12; thesis statements based on, 128, 180, 210; timing of, 113–14; via email, 116. See also interview questions; interview sources

interview guide: benefits of, 111, 120; creating, 98, 114–16; example of, 117–19

interview personas, 112, 115, 117, 196–97

interview questions: broad, 106; Cheetah Sheets on, 105, 106, 108, 109, 110, 114, 116; clarification, 108; closing, 110, 116; collaborating on, 120; crafting, 96, 99, 104–11; direct, 106; examples of, 107, 115, 118–19; focus on Critical Concepts in, 106, 115; leading, avoiding, 110–11; logical progression of, 114–15, 116; neutral, 110; open-ended, 110; opening, 117; simulation, 109; standardized, 111; theoretical, 106; two sets of, 119–20; types of, 105, 106; vetting of, 113–14; wording of, 108, 110. See also Great Questions interview sources: developing, 65, 96, 98, 100–103; low-level, starting with, 98, 104. *See also* Good Prospects

inventory, and hidden value, 157

investigative journalism: AREA method and, 6; author's experience with, 8–9; impact of, 9; techniques of, 96

investment analysis: AREA method and, xiv, 6; fundamental investment checklist, 177

investment analytics tools, bias created by, 35

investors: efforts to shape public opinion, 90–93; letters by, 90–91, 93; white papers by, 92

Iraq, U.S. invasion of, 132

Iridium, 172

Jacobi, Carl Gustav, 133

J. C. Penney, value padding by, 159–60

J. D. Power (company), 84

Johnson, Ron, 159

journal, AREA, 16; components of, 189; Critical Concepts in, 16, 192–93; downloadable template for, 17, 33, 189; list of potential sources in, 65, 104; pre-mortem analysis in, 174–75; questions in, 36, 47; sample, 189–93; thesis statements in, 17–20, 193; thesis statements in, reconciling, 178; using templates in, 14; visual maps in, 149

journalism. *See* investigative journalism

Journalismjobs.com, 104

Journal of Financial Economics, 85

J. P. Morgan, 166, 206

judgments: in thesis statement, 19. *See also* bias(es); cognitive shortcuts

Kahneman, Daniel, 177

Kelly Services, 52–53

knowledge questions, in interview, 105

Ladders.com, 103

Lafley, A. G., 80–81

Lawrence, Peter, 3

lawsuits: and hidden value, 157; and prospective sources, 101

lawyers, as interview prospects, 102

leadership, evaluation of, 51–54; actions in stock market and, 53; Cheetah Sheet on, 54; compensation structure and, 52–54; egotism of, as warning sign, 164, 207;

journal entry on, 190–91. *See also* board of directors; management narrative

legal search databases, 73

Lehman Brothers: and Bre-X fraud, 166, 206; collapse of, xv

LexisNexis, 73

Liberty Interactive, 155–56

librarians, help with interviews, 104

libraries, business, 74

licenses, and hidden value, 157

LIFO (last-in-first-out) inventory accounting, 157

liking bias, 25t

LinkedIn, prospective sources in, 101

listening, during interviews: importance of, 124; and note-taking, 125

literature review, 65, 72–78, 185; analysis in, 75; bibliography in, 76; looking for sources in, 98; sources and search techniques for, 73–74; synthesizing, 76, 77; thesis statements based on, 78, 209

Loeb, Dan, 90–91

Lollapalooza effect, 22

loss aversion, 24t

Madoff, Bernie, 22, 163, 165, 166, 205–8

Magritte, Henri, 1, 4, 5; *The Palace of Curtains,* 1, 2f

Mail Chimp, 122

mailing lists, and hidden value, 157

management narrative: Cheetah Sheets on, 46, 63; in earnings calls, 78–84; and numerical data, dissonance between, 61–63; and numerical data, reconciling, 46. *See also* leadership

mapping. *See* industry mapping; visual mapping

Markopolos, Harry, 206

material nonpublic information, avoiding in interviews, 122–23

McClendon, Aubrey, 43

McCoy, Sheri, 53

McIlroy, Rory, 25t

McKee, Robert, 10

McLean, Bethany, 86

MediaBistro.com, 104

media coverage, of research target: 13F filings, 90; review of, 65, 72–78

medical research, 133

mental shortcuts. *See* bias(es); cognitive shortcuts

mergers and acquisitions: goodwill or distorted value from, 162; hidden value prior to, 157

Merrill Lynch, 86

Midrash, 168

mirroring effect, perspective-taking and, 11

mistakes, avoiding, 186–87; checklists for, 176–78; in data collection/analysis, 171–73; and reducing bias, 24t

Monster.com, 103

Morningstar, 79

mosaic theory of research, 123

Moses, 168

Motorola, 157, 158

multitasking, during interview, 123–24

Munger, Charlie, 22, 133

Musk, Elon, 93

MVC Capital, 171

narrative bias, 24t; remedies for, 24t, 37

narrative essays, in pro/con analysis, 134, 135–36

National Investor Relations Institute (NIRI), 79

Netflix, 14; as investment opportunity, research on, 31–32

net income, vs. free cash flow, 162

net operating loss (NOL) carry-forwards, 156

Newton, Isaac, 96

Nextel, merger with Sprint, 17, 51, 52, 69–70

Nike, and authority bias, 25t

nonprofits: disclosure forms of, 53; researching, 36, 53

nonverbal communication, during face-to-face interviews, 125

note-taking, during interviews, 125–26

numerical data: Cheetah Sheet on, 37; countering bias with, 23t, 24t, 26t, 37; flawed, 39–40; limiting initial focus to, 36–40; and management narrative, reconciling, 46, 61–63; misrepresentation of, 155–62; mistakes in, avoiding, 171–73; multiple hypotheses supported by, 140, multiple narratives for, 63; putting in context, 40–42; questioning, 132–33; use in research, 4, 36–40

Oda Foundation, 28–29, 32–33

opinion questions, in interview, 105

optical illusion, 129, 131

optimism bias, 23t

outcome, focus on, Critical Concepts and, 31, 32

Pabrai, Mohnish, 177–78

Pabrai Investment Funds, 177

Pacer (database), 73

padded value, 159–61

The Palace of Curtains (Magritte), 1, 2f

Palo Alto Research Center (PARC), 2–3

Pandora (company), 30–31

Partnership for Open and Fair Skies, 56

patents, and hidden value, 157, 158

pauses: in interviews, 125; in research, 10. See also cheetah pauses

payables: stretching out, 160. See also compensation structure

Peltz, Nelson, 92

Penn National Gaming, 158

PepsiCo, website of, 49–50

Pershing Square, 91

perspective(s), in AREA Method, 7–8, 8f, 9; absolute, 34; advantages of, 13f; evaluating one's own, 130; relative, 65

perspective-taking: to counter bias, 11–12, 22t, 23t, 25t, 26; mirroring effect of, 11; to recognize edges and pitfalls, 26

phone companies, help in interviews, 104

phone interviews, 125; call pitch for, 98, 104, 120–23. See also interview(s)

Piktochart, 148

Placer Dome, 163, 205

planning fallacy, 22t

poker, research compared to, 32

policy reports, research target's, 55

PolyMedica, 9

preinvestment checklist, 177

pre-mortem analysis, 173–75; reducing bias with, 22t, 23t, 24t, 25t; thesis statements based on, 175, 181

presidential election of 2016, 140

press releases: and share price performance, 59; use in research, 57

Priestly, Joseph, 133

primary-source information, 34; vs. investment analytics, 35

privately held company, researching, 36

Problem Solved (Einhorn), xiii, 6–7, 184

process, decision-making: AREA Method and, xiii–xiv, 3, 4, 7; flexibility in, 33; importance of, 2, 3, 4; poor, example of, 2–3 pro/con analysis, 133–39, 176; Cheetah Sheet on, 134; examples of, 134–39, 138*f*; reducing bias with, 22*t*, 23*t*, 24*t*, 25*t*; scenario analysis compared to, 151; thesis statements based on, 137, 180

Proctor & Gamble: activist investors and, 92; earnings call of, 80–81

profits, multiple ways to compute, 173

projection bias, 23*t*

prospective hindsight, 174

proxy (Def 14-A) filings, 53

Psychology of Intelligence Analysis (Heuer), 131, 139

public companies: earnings calls of, 78–84; financial filings of, 35–36; management bios and compensation disclosures by, 53; Regulation Fair Disclosure (Reg FD) and, 102; Relative research on, 65; share price performance of, 58–59

Qatar Airways, 56

questions: importance of, 95, 96; numerical data and formulation of, 37; objective, to reduce bias, 22*t*, 23*t*; pro/con analysis and, 137, 139; during research process, 17, 20; thoughtful and strategic, 97; writing in AREA journal, 36, 47. *See also* interview questions

QVC, 155

real estate, and hidden value, 158

real estate brokers, as interview prospects, 102

real estate investment trust (REIT), 158

recommendations, in thesis statements, 19, 211

Redbox, 14

Regulation Fair Disclosure (Reg FD), 102

Relative, in AREA method, xviii, 7; and Absolute research, disconnect between, 71; activist investor communications and, 90–93; analyst coverage and, 84–87; earnings calls and, 78–84; elements of, 65; industry mapping and, 66–72; literature review and, 65, 72–78, 185; potential sources identified in, 98; shareholder base and, 88–94; thesis statements from perspective of, 70–71, 78, 81, 84, 87, 90, 180, 209–10

relativity bias, 25*t*

research: beyond traditional materials, 95; chance in, 21; (cheetah) pauses in,

10, 13–14; context in, 4, 40–42; data in, 4, 36–40; and decision-making, 2, 7; edges and pitfalls in, recognizing, 26; first steps in, 35–36, 45–46; focusing, Critical Concepts (CCs) and, 12–13; and ideas, 2; landmines in, 11; multiple approaches to, 33; open-ended, 12; organizing, 16; poker compared to, 32; questions arising in, 17, 20; solid, characteristics of, 14; Szent-Gyorgyi on, 30; time management in, 22*t*, 64; value-added, 32. *See also* target(s), research

research and development costs, capitalizing, 160

research reports, target's, 55–56

revenue: deferred, and hidden value, 157; net income vs. cash flows, 162

Ripoff Report, 74

Rockwood Chocolate, 157

Rubin, Robert, 166, 206

Rule of Three, 172; reducing bias with, 22*t*

S-1 prospectus, potential interview sources in, 101

Sagan, Carl, 34

Salesforce.com, 61–62; analyst coverage of, 87; earnings call of, 83–84; revenue growth of, 62*f*

salience bias, 24*t*

satisficing, 140–41

scarcity bias, 26*t*

scenario analysis, 151–55; examples of, 153–54, 155, 203–5; reducing bias with, 23*t*, 24*t*, 25*t*; thesis statements based on, 181, 204–5, 211

scientific method, 132

scientific studies, understanding design and conduct of, 39–40

Scientist, interviewer as, 112, 196

search engines: biased results of, 35, 73; use in research, 73

Securities and Exchange Commission (SEC) filings, 35–36, 42–45; 10-K, 35, 44; 10-Q, 44; 13 series, 88, 89; Def 14-A, 53; disclosures in, 44; footnotes in, 44–45; red flags in, 43; risk factors in, 42; thesis statement based on, 179–80; unusual transactions in, 43; vague categories in, 43; write-offs in, 44

Seeking Alpha, 79

self-awareness, increasing, 4

Selye, Hans, 21

shareholder(s), as interview prospects, 102

shareholder base review, 88–94; Cheetah Sheet on, 89; thesis statements from, 90, 94, 180

share price performance, 58–59; Cheetah Sheet on, 58; press release and, 59

shorthand, use during note-taking, 125

simulation questions, 109

Smartest Guys in the Room (McLean), 86

social proof, 23*t*

solvability, 169–71

sources of information: essential, identifying, 11; external (relative), 65; Rule of Three for, 172. *See also* interview sources

Spier, Guy, 177

Sprint, 45–47; Absolute thesis statements regarding, 47, 60, 179–80; board of directors of, 60; CAH exercise for, 144–45, 145*f*; Clearwire strike and, 170; compensation structure at, 53; Critical Concepts (CCs) regarding, 128; earnings calls of, review of, 84; Exploration research of, 100–102, 128; industry map for, 69–70, 193–96; leadership of, 52; liquidity issues of, 175; merger with Nextel, 17, 51, 52, 69–70; pre-mortem analysis of, 175; pro/con analysis written for, 134–37; recommendation regarding, 181–82; Relative thesis statement regarding, 70–71; as research target, 17; scenario analysis for, 153–54; SEC filings of, 45; shareholder base of, 94; thesis statements regarding, 47, 60, 70–71, 179–82; visual map of, 201–3, 202*f*

Stein, Ken Shubin, 3

stock market, focus on, as warning sign, 164, 207

strategy consultants, as interview prospects, 102

structural edge/pitfall, 28–29

SumZero, 74

suppliers, employees at, as interview prospects, 102

Sushi Status, 148

Sway, 148

Szent-Gyorgyi, Albert, 30

target(s), research: analyst coverage of, 84–87; business model of, 40–42; competitive landscape of, 65, 66–72;

governance structure of, 54–55; history of, 50–51; identifying, 36; leadership of, 51–54; management narrative of, reconciling with numerical data, 46, 61–63; media coverage of, 65, 72–78; multiple, 35; numerical data provided by, 36–40; press releases by, 57; product/ service provided by, personal experience of, 59; research reports by, 55–56; share price performance of, 58–59; website of, 35, 36, 47–50

taxes: and hidden value, 156–57, 158; and warning signals, 162

technology, unpredictable trajectory of, 170

Tejon Ranch, 127

Tesla, 93

thesis creep, preventing, 16

thesis statement(s), 167; from Absolute perspective, 38–39, 47, 60–61, 65, 179–80, 193, 208–9; from analyst coverage, 87; in AREA journal, 17–20, 193; as audit trail, 20, 183; brevity and clarity of, 18, 19; from CAH exercise, 144, 145, 180–81, 210; Cheetah Sheets on, 19, 179; counteracting bias with, 22*t*, 24*t*; from earnings calls, 81, 84, 180, 209; elements of, 19, 178; examples of, 18–19, 38–39; from Exploitation research, 137, 144, 145, 151, 180–81, 210–11; from Exploration research (interviews), 128, 180, 210; final, 211; after industry mapping, 70; judgment call in, 19; as learning and teaching tools, 178; from literature review analysis, 78, 209; from pre-mortem analysis, 175, 181; from pro/ con analysis, 137, 180; reconciling, 169, 178–83; from Relative perspective, 70–71, 78, 81, 84, 87, 90, 180, 209–10; from scenario analysis, 181, 204–5, 211; from shareholder base review, 90, 94, 180; summative, 60–61; from visual mapping, 151, 181, 203, 210–11

Third Point, 90

Thompson, Scott, 90

threats, use of, as warning sign, 165, 207

time management, in research, 22*t*, 64

TipRanks, 87

Tivo, 157

trade shows, developing sources at, 100, 101

translation, help with, 104
Trian Partners, 92
TripAdvisor: Exploration research of, 100; ownership of, 156
Trump, Donald, 140
Twain, Mark, 129
Twitter, 68; investment version of, 90; prospective sources on, 101

Ulta Beauty, 185
uncertainty: embracing, 131; scenario analysis and management of, 151
Unclue, 74
United Airlines, antitrust case against, 75
universities, interview sources at, 101, 103
use rights, and hidden value, 157

valuation allowance, 156–57
value-added research, 32
Value Investor's Club, 74
Value Walk, 93
Vault, 103
Verizon, 70, 144
vision of success: in AREA journal, 16; AREA process and, 12
visual mapping, 146–51; Cheetah Sheet on, 148; Critical Concepts and, 150, 201–3, 202f; examples of, 149–51, 149f, 150f, 201–3, 202f; reducing bias with, 24t; thesis statements based on, 151, 181, 203, 210–11
voicemail messages: likelihood of receiving response to, 121; optimal length of, 122; tone of, 122
Voltaire, 95, 96, 141

Wall Street: analysts on, coverage of research target by, 84–87; research target's relationship with, 86
Walmart, price cuts by, 14
website(s): of activist investors, 92; author's, xvi, 17, 33, 99, 119, 189; useful, 73–74, 88; and visual mapping, 148
website(s), research target's: Cheetah Sheet on, 48; earnings calls information on, 79, 81; historical look at, 48; studying, 35, 36, 47–50
Westlaw, 73
white papers: company/industry, 56–57, 92; investor, 92
Whole Foods, acquisition by Amazon, 52
Wilson, Alan M., 10
Wilson, Harry, 90
wireless industry: mapping of, 69–70, 193–96. See also Sprint
Wolf, Michael, 90
World Bank, 97
WorldCom, 162

Xerox, Palo Alto Research Center (PARC) of, 2–3

Yahoo, 13F investor letter to, 90–91
Yahoo!Finance, 88
Yang, Gene Luen, 64

Zacks Investment Research, 87
Zeno, 124
Zero Hedge, 93
Zucker, Jeff, 90

Lightning Source UK Ltd.
Milton Keynes UK
UKHW030335261019
352349UK00010B/665/P

9 781501 730948